KU-338-226

BENNION ON STATUTORY INTERPRETATION

BENNION ON STATUTORY INTERPRETATION

A Code

Supplement to Fifth Edition
including Replacement Index

Oliver Jones, LLB (Hons) BA (Int'l Studies)
(UTS); BCL (Oxon)

Assistant Professor, Faculty of Law,
University of Hong Kong

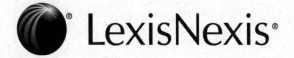 LexisNexis®

Members of the LexisNexis Group worldwide

United Kingdom	LexisNexis Butterworths, a Division of Reed Elsevier (UK) Ltd, Halsbury House, 35 Chancery Lane, London, WC2A 1EL, and RSH, 1–3 Baxter's Place, Leith Walk Edinburgh EH1 3AF
Argentina	LexisNexis Argentina, BUENOS AIRES
Australia	LexisNexis Butterworths, CHATSWOOD, New South Wales
Austria	LexisNexis Verlag ARD Orac GmbH & Co KG, VIENNA
Canada	LexisNexis Butterworths, MARKHAM, Ontario
Chile	LexisNexis Chile Ltda, SANTIAGO DE CHILE
Czech Republic	Nakladatelství Orac sro, PRAGUE
France	Editions du Juris-Classeur SA, PARIS
Germany	LexisNexis Deutschland GmbH, FRANKFURT and MUNSTER
Hong Kong	LexisNexis Butterworths, HONG KONG
Hungary	HVG-Orac, BUDAPEST
India	LexisNexis Butterworths, NEW DELHI
Italy	Giuffrè Editore, MILAN
Malaysia	Malayan Law Journal Sdn Bhd, KUALA LUMPUR
New Zealand	LexisNexis Butterworths, WELLINGTON
Poland	Wydawnictwo Prawnicze LexisNexis, WARSAW
Singapore	LexisNexis Butterworths, SINGAPORE
South Africa	LexisNexis Butterworths, Durban
Switzerland	Stämpfli Verlag AG, BERNE
USA	LexisNexis, DAYTON, Ohio

First edition of main work 1984; supplement to first edition 1989; second edition of main work 1992; first supplement to second edition 1993; second supplement to second edition (cumulative) 1995; third edition of main work 1997; supplement to third edition 1999; fourth edition of main work 2002; supplement to fourth edition 2005; fifth edition of main work 2004.

© Reed Elsevier (UK) Ltd 2010
Published by LexisNexis Butterworths

All rights reserved. No part of this publication may be reproduced in any material form (including photocopying or storing it in any medium by electronic means and whether or not transiently or incidentally to some other use of this publication) without the written permission of the copyright owner except in accordance with the provisions of the Copyright, Designs and Patents Act 1988 or under the terms of a licence issued by the Copyright Licensing Agency Ltd, 90 Tottenham Court Road, London, England W1T 4LP. Applications for the copyright owner's written permission to reproduce any part of this publication should be addressed to the publisher.
Warning: The doing of an unauthorised act in relation to a copyright work may result in both a civil claim for damages and criminal prosecution.
Crown copyright material is reproduced with the permission of the Controller of HMSO and the Queen's Printer for Scotland. Parliamentary copyright material is reproduced with the permission of the Controller of Her Majesty's Stationery Office on behalf of Parliament. Any European material in this work which has been reproduced from EUR-lex, the official European Communities legislation website, is European Communities copyright.
A CIP Catalogue record for this book is available from the British Library.

ISBN 0 406 96648 6

Typeset by Letterpart Ltd, Reigate, England
Printed and bound in Great Britain by William Clowes Limited, Beccles, Suffolk
Visit LexisNexis Butterworths at www.lexisnexis.co.uk

Prefatory Note

General

In general this Supplement to the fifth edition of Bennion's Statutory Interpretation, which was published in 2008, aims to present the law as at 1 July 2010.

The Supplement begins with the updating of Parts I to XXIX of the Code by means of textual amendments to the affected pages in the main work.

*The Supplement goes on to include updated versions of **Appendix C** (text of Interpretation Act 1978).*

The Supplement ends with a complete updated and corrected version of the Index to the work.

Page numbering

To avoid confusion with the main work, the page numbers in the Supplement have the prefix S.

This means that in all cases a page reference in the revised Index should be checked with this Supplement. Either (if it has an S prefix) it will refer to a page contained in the Supplement or (if it does not have an S prefix) it will refer to a page in the original volume which may be modified by the Supplement.

Contents

Table of Cases

A

A v B (Investigatory Powers Tribunal: jurisdiction) [2009] UKSC 12,
[2010] 1 All ER 1149, [2010] 2 WLR 1, (2009) Times, 11 December, [2009]
All ER (D) 78 (Dec) S9
A v H (Registrar General for England and Wales intervening) [2009] EWHC 636
(Fam), [2009] 4 All ER 641, [2009] 3 FCR 95, [2009] Fam Law 917, [2009]
All ER (D) 136 (Jun) S53
A v Hoare and other appeals [2008] UKHL 6, [2008] 1 AC 844, [2008] 2 All ER 1,
[2008] 2 WLR 311, [2008] Fam Law 402, 100 BMLR 1, [2008] NLJR 218,
(2008) Times, 31 January, [2008] All ER (D) 251 (Jan) S13
A v Securities and Futures Commission [2008] 1 HKLRD 591 .... S26, S28
AS (Somalia) v Secretary of State for the Home Department [2009] UKHL 32,
[2009] 4 All ER 711, [2009] 1 WLR 1385, (2009) Times, 22 June, 153 Sol Jo
(no 24) 32, [2009] All ER (D) 163 (Jun) S59
Aboriginal Development Commission, Re [1988] FCA 160 .... S16
Ackland v Yonge-Esplanade Enterprises Ltd (1992) 10 OR (3d) 97 .... S44
Action Aid Ltd v Revenue Commissioners [1997] IEHC 196 .... S32
Adorian v Metropolitan Police Comr [2009] EWCA Civ 18, [2009] 4 All ER 227,
[2009] 1 WLR 1859, (2009) Times, 23 February, [2009] All ER (D) 176 (Jan) S5
Ahmed v HM Treasury (No 2) [2010] UKSC 5, [2010] 2 WLR 378, [2010] All ER
(D) 40 (Feb) S41, S42
Algama v Minsiter for Immigration and Mulitcultural Affairs (2001) 115 FCR 253,
261 .... S13
Ali v Birmingham City Council [2009] UKHL 36, [2009] 4 All ER 161,
[2009] 1 WLR 1506, [2009] LGR 749, [2009] PTSR 1270, 153 Sol Jo (no 26)
29, [2009] All ER (D) 19 (Jul) S56
Application by the Local Government Auditor, Re [2003] NIQB 21 .... S25, S26, S38
Aribisala v St James Homes (Grosvenor Dock) Ltd [2007] EWHC 1694 (Ch), [2007]
All ER (D) 101 (Jun) S6
A-G's Reference (No 3 of 1999), Re British Broadcasting Corpn [2009] UKHL 34,
[2010] 1 AC 145, [2010] 1 All ER 235, [2009] 3 WLR 142, (2009) Times,
18 June, 153 Sol Jo (no 24) 31, 27 BHRC 522, [2009] EMLR 421, [2009] All
ER (D) 175 (Jun) S52
A-G's Reference (No 24 of 2008); R v Sanchez [2008] EWCA Crim 2936,
[2009] 3 All ER 839, [2009] 2 Cr App Rep (S) 289, [2008] All ER (D) 62
(Dec) S23
Austereo Ltd v Trade Practices Commission (1993) 41 FCR 1, 37 .... S25
Australasian Correctional Management Ltd v Corrections Association of New
Zealand (Inc) [2002] 3 NZLR 250 .... S51
Australian Securities Commission v Lucas (1992) 36 FCR 165, 170–171 .... S38
Avowal Administrative Attorneys Ltd v District Council at North Shore [2007]
NZHC 714 .... S32

B

B (children) (sexual abuse: standard of proof), Re [2008] UKHL 35, [2009] AC 11,
[2008] 4 All ER 1, [2008] 3 WLR 1, [2008] 2 FCR 339, [2008] 2 FLR 141,
[2008] Fam Law 837, [2008] Fam Law 619, (2008) Times, 12 June, [2008] All
ER (D) 134 (Jun) S22, S23, S52
BCGEU v British Columbia (2007) 283 DLR (4th) 307 .... S38
BUPA Purchasing Ltd v Revenue and Customs Comrs [2007] EWCA Civ 542,
[2008] STC 101, (2007) Times, 5 July, [2007] All ER (D) 84 (Jun) S49

Baker v R [1975] AC 774, [1975] 3 All ER 55, [1975] 3 WLR 113, 119 Sol Jo 491,
PC S12
Barnard v Ford; Carrick v Ford (1869) 4 Ch App 247, 38 LJ Ch 671, 17 WR 478, 20
LT 289 .... S45
Begg v Commissioner of Inland Revenue [2009] 3 NZLR 353 .... S29
Behzadi v Shaftesbury Hotels Ltd [1992] Ch 1, [1991] 2 All ER 477, [1991] 2 WLR
1251, 62 P & CR 163, [1990] NLJR 1385, CA S55
Beoku-Betts v Secretary of State for the Home Department [2008] UKHL 39,
[2009] AC 115, [2008] 4 All ER 1146, [2008] 3 WLR 166, (2008) Times,
8 July, 152 Sol Jo (no 26) 31, 25 BHRC 245, [2008] All ER (D) 335 (Jun) S48
Birmingham City Council v Shafi [2008] EWCA Civ 1186, [2009] 3 All ER 127,
[2009] 1 WLR 1961, [2009] LGR 367, [2009] PTSR 503, [2009] HLR 429, 152
Sol Jo (no 43) 31, [2008] All ER (D) 304 (Oct) S7
Blackpool Council v Howitt [2008] EWHC 3300 (Admin), [2009] 4 All ER 154,
[2009] PTSR 1458, 173 JP 101, [2008] All ER (D) 28 (Dec) S56
Boardwalk Reit LLP v Edmonton (2008) 91 Alta LR (4th) 1 .... S47, S54
Bocardo SA v Star Energy UK Onshore Ltd [2009] EWCA Civ 579, [2010] Ch 100,
[2010] 1 All ER 26, [2009] 3 WLR 1010, [2009] 2 P & CR 419, [2010] RVR
127, [2009] 25 EG 136 (CS), [2009] All ER (D) 132 (Jun); affd [2010] UKSC
35, [2010] 3 All ER 975, [2010] 3 WLR 654, [2010] NLJR 1114, [2010] 31 EG
63 (CS), (2010) Times, 29 July, [2010] All ER (D) 333 (Jul) S21, S23
Boswell v Secretary, Department of Foreign Affairs and Trade (1993) 46 FCR 434,
441 .... S55
Bournemouth University Higher Education Corpn v Buckland [2009] ICR 1042,
[2009] IRLR 606, [2009] All ER (D) 160 (Aug), EAT; revsd sub nom Buckland
v Bournemouth University Higher Education Corporation [2010] EWCA Civ
121, [2010] 4 All ER 186, [2010] ICR 908, [2010] IRLR 445, (2010) Times,
3 May, [2010] All ER (D) 299 (Feb) S51
Bovale Ltd v Secretary of State for Communities and Local Government
[2009] EWCA Civ 171, [2009] 3 All ER 340, [2009] 1 WLR 2274,
[2009] 2 P & CR 103, (2009) Times, 23 March, [2009] All ER (D) 115 (Mar) S9
Bowers v Gloucester Corpn [1963] 1 QB 881, [1963] 1 All ER 437, [1963] 2 WLR
386, 61 LGR 209, 127 JP 214, 107 Sol Jo 94, DC S41
Boyle v SCA Packaging Ltd (Equality and Human Rights Commission intervening)
[2009] UKHL 37, [2009] NI 317, [2009] 4 All ER 1181, [2009] ICR 1056,
[2009] IRLR 746, 109 BMLR 53, (2009) Times, 6 July, 153 Sol Jo (no 26) 27,
[2009] All ER (D) 05 (Jul) S35
Braganza v Minister for Immigration and Multicultural Affairs (2001) 109 FCR 364,
376 .... S47
Braymist Ltd v Wise Finance Co Ltd [2002] EWCA Civ 127, [2002] Ch 273,
[2002] 2 All ER 333, [2002] 3 WLR 322, [2002] 1 BCLC 415, [2002] BCC
514, [2002] 13 LS Gaz R 25, (2002) Times, 5 April, 146 Sol Jo LB 60, [2002]
All ER (D) 267 (Feb) S4
Briere v Hailstone [1969] Crim LR 36 .... S53
British Broadcasting Corp v Information Comr [2009] EWHC 2348 (Admin),
[2010] EMLR 121, [2009] All ER (D) 10 (Oct) S35
British Broadcasting Corp v Sugar [2009] UKHL 9, [2009] 4 All ER 111,
[2009] 1 WLR 430, [2009] IP & T 876, (2009) Times, 12 February, 153 Sol Jo
(no 7) 31, [2009] All ER (D) 101 (Feb) S59
BBC Scotland v Souster 2001 SC 458, [2001] IRLR 150, Ct of Sess S32
Brown v Innovatorone plc [2009] EWHC 1376 (Comm), [2010] 2 All ER (Comm)
80, 153 Sol Jo (no 25) 27, [2009] All ER (D) 211 (Jun) S38
Buckland v Bournemouth University Higher Education Corporation. See
Bournemouth University Higher Education Corpn v Buckland
Byrne v Australian Airlines Ltd (1995) 185 CLR 410, 459–4640 .... S46
Byrne v Transport Accident Commission [2008] VSC 92 .... S49

C

C & E Pty Ltd v CMC Brisbane Pty Ltd (Administrators Appointed) [2004] QCA
60 .... S31
Caltex Oil (Aust) Pty Ltd v Best (1990) 170 CLR 516, 522 .... S6

Campbell v Tow Truck Directorate of Victoria (1995/34314) [2000] VICCAT 3 .... S5
Carroll v DPP [2009] EWHC 554 (Admin), 173 JP 285, [2009] All ER (D) 35
(Mar) S22
Cassell & Co Ltd v Broome [1972] AC 1027, [1972] 1 All ER 801, [1972] 2 WLR
645, 116 Sol Jo 199, HL S12, S13
Chan Ching Kit v Lam Sik Shi [2002] HKCFI 132 .... S31
China Field Ltd v Appeal Tribunal (Buildings) (No 2) [2009] 5 HKLRD 662 .... S39
Christian v R [2006] UKPC 47, [2007] 2 AC 400, [2007] 2 WLR 120, (2006) Times,
15 November, 150 Sol Jo LB 1464, [2007] 1 LRC 726, [2006] All ER (D) 358
(Oct) S15
Coke-Wallis v Institute of Chartered Accountants in England and Wales
[2009] EWCA Civ 730, [2009] All ER (D) 147 (Jul) S51
Commissioner of Inland Revenue v Common Empire Ltd [2006] 1 HKLRD 942 .... S46
Commissioner of Inland Revenue v Loganathan [2000] 1 HKLRD 914 .... S47
Commissioner of Inland Revenue v N Evans [2008] NZHC 1017 .... S32
Commissioner of Taxation v Citibank Ltd (1989) 20 FCR 403, 432–433 .... S40
Commissioner of Taxation v Lamesa Holdings BV (1997) 77 FCR 597, 603–605 .... S34
Comptroller and Auditor General v Ireland [1997] 1 IR 248 .... S37
Corporate Officer of the House of Commons v Information Comr [2008] EWHC
1084 (Admin), [2009] 3 All ER 403, [2008] NLJR 751, (2008) Times, 22 May,
[2008] All ER (D) 217 (May) S60, S61
Courage Ltd v Crehan [1999] Eu LR 834, [1999] 25 LS Gaz R 29, [1999] EGCS 85,
[1999] All ER (D) 551, CA; refd sub nom Courage Ltd v Crehan: C-453/99
[2002] QB 507, [2001] ECR I-6297, [2001] All ER (EC) 886, [2001] 3 WLR
1646, [2001] 5 CMLR 1058, [2002] ICR 457, [2001] All ER (D) 55 (Sep),
ECJ S12
Craftrule Ltd v 41–60 Albert Palace Mansions (Freehold) Ltd [2010] EWHC 1230
(Ch), [2010] 3 All ER 952, [2010] 31 EG 64, [2010] NLJR 806, (2010) Times,
20 July, [2010] All ER (D) 267 (May), sub nom 41–60 Albert Palace Mansions
(Freehold) Ltd v Craftrule Ltd [2010] 1 WLR 2046 .... S17
Cropp v A Judicial Committee [2008] 3 NZLR 774 .... S41, S42

D

DS (Afghanistan) v Secretary of State for the Home Department [2009] EWCA Civ
226, [2009] 3 All ER 564, [2009] All ER (D) 234 (Mar) S35
Dairy Farmers of Britain Ltd, Re [2009] EWHC 1389 (Ch), [2010] Ch 63,
[2009] 4 All ER 241, [2010] 2 WLR 311, [2010] 1 BCLC 637, [2009] All ER
(D) 205 (Jun) S29
Dale Farm Dairy Group Ltd v Akram [1998] ICR 349, CA S25
Davidson v M [2009] CSIH 70, [2010] IRLR 439, 2010 SC 100, 2009 SLT 1009 .... S56
Davidson v Scottish Ministers [2005] UKHL 74, (2005) Times, 19 December, 2006
SLT 110, 2006 SCLR 249 .... S20, S33
Department of Land Affairs v Goedgelegen Tropical Fruits [2007] ZACC 12 .... S27
Deputy Public Prosecutor in Creteil, France v Moulai [2009] UKHL 2,
[2009] 3 All ER 1035, [2009] 1 WLR 276, (2009) Times, 27 January, 153 Sol
Jo (no 4) 28, [2009] All ER (D) 135 (Jan) S28
Deutsche Morgan Grenfell Group plc v IRC [2006] UKHL 49, [2007] 1 AC 558,
[2007] 1 All ER 449, [2006] 3 WLR 781, [2007] 1 CMLR 429, [2007] STC 1,
78 TC 120, 9 ITLR 201, (2006) Times, 26 October, 150 Sol Jo LB 1430, [2006]
All ER (D) 298 (Oct) S4
DPP v Wright [2009] EWHC 105 (Admin), [2010] QB 224, [2009] 3 All ER 726,
169 JP 173, (2009) Times, 17 February, [2009] All ER (D) 30 (Feb) S52
Distribution Group v Commissioner of Taxation (2000) 45 ATR 494, 500–502 .... S57
Dolphin Quays Developments Ltd v Mills [2008] EWCA Civ 385, [2008] 4 All ER
58, [2008] 1 WLR 1829, [2008] Bus LR 1520, [2008] 2 BCLC 774, [2008] All
ER (D) 257 (Apr), sub nom Mills v Birchall [2008] BCC 471, [2008] 4 Costs
LR 599, [2008] BPIR 607 .... S26

E

ETI Euro Telecom International NV v Republic of Bolivia [2008] EWCA Civ 880,
[2009] 2 All ER (Comm) 37, [2009] 1 WLR 665, [2009] Bus LR 310,
[2008] 2 Lloyd's Rep 421, [2008] All ER (D) 358 (Jul) S38
East Devon District Council v Electoral Commission (The Boundary Committee for
England) [2009] EWHC 4 (Admin) S31
Eastman v Commissioner of Superannuation (1987) 15 FCR 139, 148 .... S59
Elders New Zealand Ltd v PGG Wrightson Ltd [2009] 1 NZLR 577 .... S40
Electrical Supply Assoc of Australia Ltd v ACCC (2001) 113 FCR 250, 258 .... S25
Enfield v R (2008) 51 MVR 200 .... S24
Equuscorp Pty Ltd v Belperio [2006] VSC 14 .... S49

F

FA (Iraq) v Secretary of State for the Home Department [2010] EWCA Civ 696,
[2010] 1 WLR 2545, [2010] All ER (D) 161 (Jun) S34
Fairfax v Ireton [2009] 1 NZLR 540 .... S56
Farah Constructions Pty Ltd v Say-Dee Pty Ltd [2007] HCA 22, 230 CLR 89, 10
ITELR 136, [2007] 3 LRC 374, Aus HC S12
Farnell Electronic Components Pty Ltd v Collector of Customs (1996) 72 FCR 125 .... S53
Fletcher (Executrix of the estate of Carl Fletcher (deceased)) v A Train & Sons Ltd
[2008] EWCA Civ 413, [2008] 4 All ER 699, [2008] All ER (D) 333 (Apr) S11
Fong Yau Hei v Gammon Construction Ltd [2008] 3 HKLRD 604 .... S44
41–60 Albert Palace Mansions (Freehold) Ltd v Craftrule Ltd. See Craftrule Ltd v
41–60 Albert Palace Mansions (Freehold) Ltd
Freeman v Higher Park Farm [2008] EWCA Civ 1185, [2009] PIQR P103, 152 Sol
Jo (no 43) 32, [2008] All ER (D) 310 (Oct) S55
Frucor Beverages Ltd v Rio Beverages Ltd [2001] 2 NZLR 604 .... S25, S47
Futures Commission v Stock Exchange of Hong Kong Ltd [1992] 1 HKLR 135,
144 .... S27

G

Generics (UK) Ltd v H Lundbeck A/S [2008] EWCA Civ 311, [2008] RPC 437, 101
BMLR 52, [2008] All ER (D) 152 (Apr); affd [2009] UKHL 12,
[2009] 2 All ER 955, [2009] Bus LR 828, [2009] RPC 407, [2009] IP & T 496,
107 BMLR 121, 153 Sol Jo (no 8) 30, [2009] All ER (D) 258 (Feb) S34
George Wimpey UK Ltd v Tewkesbury Borough Council (MA Holdings Ltd
intervening) [2008] EWCA Civ 12, [2008] 3 All ER 859, [2008] 1 WLR 1649,
127 ConLR 17, (2008) Times, 25 February, [2008] All ER (D) 177 (Jan) S44
Gibson v Government of United States of America [2007] UKPC 52, [2007] 1 WLR
2367, (2007) Times, 3 August, 70 WIR 34, [2008] 3 LRC 30, [2007] All ER
(D) 358 (Jul) S46
Giles v Rhind [2009] Ch 191, [2008] 3 All ER 697, [2008] 3 WLR 1233, [2008] Bus
LR 1103, [2008] 2 BCLC 1, [2008] EWCA Civ 118, [2008] BPIR 342, [2008]
All ER (D) 410 (Feb), CA S24, S39
Glasgow City Council v AD [2005] Scot SC 35 .... S6
Goshawk Dedicated (No 2) Ltd v Governor and Co of Bank of Scotland
[2005] EWHC 2906 (Ch), [2006] 2 All ER 610, [2005] All ER (D) 205 (Dec) S5
Government of Canada v Aronson [1990] 1 AC 579, [1989] 2 All ER 1025,
[1989] 3 WLR 436, 90 Cr App Rep 199, HL S16
Grays Timber Products Ltd v Revenue and Customs Comrs [2010] UKSC 4,
[2010] 2 All ER 1, [2010] 1 WLR 497, [2010] STC 782, (2010) Times,
4 February, 2010 SC (UKSC) 1, 154 Sol Jo (no 5) 30, [2010] All ER (D) 31
(Feb) S3, S13, S35
Gregory v Turner [2003] EWCA Civ 183, [2003] 2 All ER 1114, [2003] 1 WLR
1149, [2003] 3 EGLR 129, (2003) Times, 21 February, [2003] All ER (D) 267
(Feb) S10
Guelph (City) v Wyndham Street Investments Inc (2003) 63 OR (2d) 481 .... S55
Gumbs v A-G of Anguilla [2009] UKPC 27, [2010] 2 LRC 221, [2009] All ER (D)
92 (Nov) S47

H

HKSAR v Cheun Kwun Yin (November 2008, unreported) S34
HKSAR v Lam Kwong Wai [2006] 3 HKLRD 808 .... S60
HKSAR v Tang Hoi On [2003] 3 HKC 123 .... S42
HKSAR v Tin's Label Factory Ltd (2008) 11 HKCFAR 637 .... S10, S50
Hampstead Heath Winter Swimming Club v Corpn of London [2005] EWHC 713
    (Admin), [2005] LGR 481, [2005] NLJ 827, (2005) Times, 19 May, [2005] All
    ER (D) 353 (Apr), sub nom R (on the application of Hampstead Heath Winter
    Swimming Club) v Corpn of London [2005] 1 WLR 2930 .... S39
Hanchett-Stamford v A-G [2008] EWHC 330 (Ch), [2009] Ch 173, [2008] 4 All ER
    323, [2009] 2 WLR 405, [2008] 2 P & CR 102, [2009] PTSR 1, [2008] NLJR
    371, [2008] All ER (D) 391 (Feb) S11, S61
Hanna v Migration Agents Registration Authority (1999) 94 FCR 358, 363 .... S16, S17
Hatzl v XL Insurance Co Ltd [2009] EWCA Civ 223, [2009] 3 All ER 617, [2009] 2
    All ER (Comm) 699, [2010] 1 WLR 470, [2009] RTR 326, [2009] 1 Lloyd's
    Rep 555, (2009) Times, 16 April, [2009] All ER (D) 212 (Mar) S34
Health Service Commissioners for Valuation [2008] IEHC 178 .... S29
Henry Boot Construction (UK) Ltd v Malmaison Hotel (Manchester) Ltd [2001] QB
    388, [2001] 1 All ER 257, [2000] 2 All ER (Comm) 960, [2000] 3 WLR 1824,
    [2000] 2 Lloyd's Rep 625, 72 ConLR 1, [2000] NLJR 867, [2000] BLR
    509, CA S56
Hertfordshire County Council v Veolia Water Central Ltd (formerly Three Valleys
    Water plc) [2010] EWHC 278 (QB), [2010] PTSR 871, [2010] All ER (D) 273
    (Feb); revsd sub nom Hertfordshire County Council v Veolia Water Central Ltd
    [2010] EWCA Civ 887, (2010) Times, 4 October, [2010] All ER (D) 282
    (Jul) S17
Hilali, Re [2008] UKHL 3, [2008] 1 AC 805, [2008] 2 All ER 207, [2008] 2 WLR
    299, (2008) Times, 1 February, [2008] All ER (D) 245 (Jan) S43
Hillingdon London Borough Council v ARC Ltd [1999] Ch 139, [1998] 3 WLR 754,
    [1999] LGR 282, 75 P & CR 346, [1998] 15 LS Gaz R 34,
    [1998] 20 LS Gaz R 34, [1998] RVR 242, [1998] 39 EG 202, 142 Sol Jo LB
    149, CA S22
Hin Lin Yee v HKSAR [2010] 2 HKLRD 826 .... S51
Honeygan-Green v Islington London Borough Council [2008] UKHL 70, [2009] AC
    636, [2009] 2 All ER 829, [2009] 2 WLR 78, [2009] 1 P & CR 519, [2009]
    PTSR 281, [2008] 50 EG 73 (CS), (2008) Times, 15 December, 153 Sol Jo (no
    1) 32, [2008] All ER (D) 115 (Dec) S44
Horton v Sadler [2006] UKHL 27, [2007] 1 AC 307, [2006] 3 All ER 1177,
    [2006] 2 WLR 1346, [2006] RTR 330, 91 BMLR 60, [2006] NLJR 1024,
    (2006) Times, 19 June, 150 Sol Jo LB 808, [2007] 3 LRC 146, [2006] All ER
    (D) 130 (Jun) S13
Housden v Conservators of Wimbledon and Putney Commons [2008] EWCA Civ
    200, [2008] 3 All ER 1038, [2008] 1 WLR 1172, [2008] 12 EG 97 (CS), [2008]
    All ER (D) 266 (Mar) S12
Hrushka v Canada (Minister of Foreign Affairs) [2009] FCA 69 .... S29
Hyde Park Residence Ltd v Secretary of State for the Environment, Transport and the
    Regions (2000) 80 P & CR 419, [2000] 1 PLR 85, [2000] NPC 7, [2000] EGCS
    14, [2000] JPL 936, [2000] All ER (D) 64, CA S23

I

Ianroid Eireann v Social Welfare Tribunal [2007] IEHC 406 .... S52
Ignatious v Minister for Immigration & Multicultural & Indigenous Affairs
    (2004) 139 FCR 254, 268 .... S17
Independent Committee for the Supervision of Standards of Telephone Information
    Services v Hornan [2007] EWHC 2307 (Admin), [2007] All ER (D) 114
    (Sep) S43
Inglis v Loh Lai Kuen Eda [2005] 3 HKC 115, 127 .... S13
Insurance and Superannuation Commisioner v Hiscock (1995) 59 FCR 1, 3 .... S40
Interchase Corp Ltd (in liq) (No 2), Re (1993) 47 FCR 253, 260–261 .... S29
International AG v Perfect Recovery Ltd [2009] 3 HKLRD 13 .... S44

Isle of Anglesey County Council v Welsh Ministers [2009] EWCA Civ 94,
    [2010] QB 163, [2009] 3 All ER 1110, [2009] 3 WLR 813, 153 Sol Jo (no 8)
    27, [2009] All ER (D) 237 (Feb) S33

J

JF v Minister for Health and Children [2008] IESC 16 .... S37
J P Garrett Electrical Ltd v Cotton [2005] 4 All ER 1346, [2005] ICR 1702,
    [2005] IRLR 782, [2005] All ER (D) 64 (Aug), EAT; revsd sub nom Woodward
    v Abbey National plc [2006] EWCA Civ 822, [2006] 4 All ER 1209,
    [2006] ICR 1436, [2006] IRLR 677, (2006) Times, 11 July, 150 Sol Jo LB 857,
    [2006] All ER (D) 253 (Jun) S4
JT (Cameroon) v Secretary of State for the Home Department [2008] EWCA Civ
    878, [2009] 2 All ER 1213, [2009] 1 WLR 1411, [2008] All ER (D) 348 (Jul) ... S27, S42
Jade City International Ltd v Director of Lands [2002] 3 HKLRD 33, 47 .... S40
James, Re [2005] NIQB 38 .... S56
Jayasinghe v Minister for Immigration & Ethnic Affairs (1997) 76 FCR 301, 315 .... S25
Jeffrey v Sawyer (1993) 16 OR (3d) 75, 78 .... S44
Joseph's Estate, Re (1993) 14 OR (3d) 628 .... S40

K

KJM Superbikes Ltd v Hinton [2008] EWCA Civ 1280, [2009] 3 All ER 76,
    [2009] 1 WLR 2406, [2008] NLJR 1683, [2008] All ER (D) 200 (Nov) S8
Kalway v Secretary, Department of Social Security (1992) 38 FCR 295, 299 .... S36
Kao Lee & Yip (a firm) v Lau Wang (2008) 11 HKCFAR 576 .... S37
Kay v Metropolitan Police Comr [2008] UKHL 69, [2009] 2 All ER 935,
    [2008] 1 WLR 2723, [2009] RTR 176, (2008) Times, 27 November, 152 Sol Jo
    (no 46) 31, [2008] All ER (D) 255 (Nov) S23, S58
Kennet District Council v Young [1999] RTR 235, 163 JP 622, 163 JP 854 .... S21
King v Director of Serious Fraud Office [2009] UKHL 17, [2009] 2 All ER 223,
    [2009] 1 WLR 718, [2009] 2 Cr App Rep 43, (2009) Times, 19 March, 153 Sol
    Jo (no 11) 27, [2009] All ER (D) 189 (Mar) S21
King's Application for Judicial Review, Re [2002] NICA 48, [2003] NI 43, NI CA S50
Kirk v Walton [2008] EWHC 1780 (QB), [2009] 1 All ER 257, [2008] All ER (D)
    323 (Jul) S8
Knowsley Housing Trust v White [2008] UKHL 70, [2009] AC 636, [2009] 2 All ER
    829, [2009] 2 WLR 78, [2009] 1 P & CR 519, [2009] PTSR 281, [2008] 50 EG
    73 (CS), (2008) Times, 15 December, 153 Sol Jo (no 1) 32, [2008] All ER (D)
    115 (Dec) S44
Kok Cheng Weng v Wiener (2007) 2 SLR 709, 731–732 .... S23

L

Ladele v London Borough of Islington [2009] EWCA Civ 1357, [2010] 1 WLR 955,
    [2010] LGR 690, [2010] ICR 532, [2010] IRLR 211, [2010] PTSR 982, (2010)
    Times, 1 January, [2009] All ER (D) 148 (Dec) S61
Lai v Chamberlains [2007] 2 NZLR 7 .... S39
Landlord's Association for Northern Ireland, Re [2005] NIQB 22 .... S43
Lau Suk Ching Peggy v Ma Hing Lam [2010] HKCFA 20 .... S55
Law Society v Sephton & Co [2006] UKHL 22, [2006] 2 AC 543, [2006] 3 All ER
    401, [2006] 2 WLR 1091, [2006] NLJR 844, (2006) Times, 11 May, 150 Sol Jo
    LB 669, [2006] All ER (D) 123 (May) S22
Law Society of Upper Canada v Ontario (Attorney-General) (1995) 21 OR (3d)
    666 .... S17
Lawson v Serco Ltd [2004] EWCA Civ 12, [2004] 2 All ER 200, [2004] ICR 204,
    [2004] IRLR 206, (2004) Times, 30 January, 148 Sol Jo LB 148, [2004] All ER
    (D) 217 (Jan); revsd [2006] UKHL 3, [2006] 1 All ER 823, [2006] IRLR 289,
    [2006] 06 LS Gaz R 36, [2006] NLJR 184, 150 Sol Jo LB 131, [2006] All ER
    (D) 184 (Jan) S21
Lee Chez Kee v Public Prosecutor [2008] SGCA 20 .... S40

Lee Yiu Kee v Chinese University of Hong Kong [2010] HKCA 218 .... S31, S32
Legal Services Commission v Rasool [2008] EWCA Civ 154, [2008] 3 All ER 381,
    [2008] 1 WLR 2711, [2008] NLJR 414, (2008) Times, 21 April, [2008] 4 Costs
    LR 529, [2008] All ER (D) 43 (Mar) S22
Lewisham London Borough Council v Malcolm [2008] UKHL 43, [2008] 1 AC
    1399, [2008] 4 All ER 525, [2008] 3 WLR 194, [2008] LGR 549,
    [2008] 2 P & CR 358, [2008] IRLR 700, 102 BMLR 170, (2008) Times,
    26 June, 152 Sol Jo (no 26) 29, [2008] All ER (D) 342 (Jun) S33
Li Wang Pong v Medical Council of Hong Kong [2009] HKCFI 2 .... S39
Liu Pik Han v Hong Kong Federation of Insurers Appeals Tribunal [2005] 3 HKC
    242 .... S25
Luckins, ex p Columbia Pictures Industries Inc, Re (1996) 67 FCR 549, 556–557 .... S21

M

M v Secretary of State for Education [2001] EWCA Civ 332, [2002] LGR 584,
    [2002] ICR 15, [2001] 2 FCR 11, [2001] ELR 773, [2001] 19 LS Gaz R 36,
    [2001] All ER (D) 119 (Mar) S50
M v Watson [2009] HJC 3 .... S60
MH (Syria) v Secretary of State for the Home Department [2009] EWCA Civ 226,
    [2009] 3 All ER 564, [2009] All ER (D) 234 (Mar) S35
McCombie v Cadotte (2001) 53 OR (3d) 704 .... S7
Macmillan & Co v Dent [1907] 1 Ch 107, 76 LJ Ch 136, 51 Sol Jo 46, 95 LT 730,
    23 TLR 45, CA S18
Maguire v Director of Public Prosecutions [2004] 3 IR 241 .... S44
Majeau Carrying Co Pty Ltd v Coastal Rutile Ltd (1973) 129 CLR 48, 1 ALR 1, Aus
    HC S19
Majorstake Ltd v Curtis [2008] UKHL 10, [2008] 1 AC 787, [2008] 2 All ER 303,
    [2008] 2 WLR 338, [2008] 1 P & CR D65, [2008] 2 P & CR 20, [2008] 14 EG
    102, [2008] NLJR 262, [2008] 06 EG 131 (CS), (2008) Times, 12 February,
    [2008] All ER (D) 70 (Feb) S56
Manchester City Council v Moran [2009] UKHL 36, [2009] 4 All ER 161,
    [2009] 1 WLR 1506, [2009] LGR 749, [2009] PTSR 1270, 153 Sol Jo (no 26)
    29, [2009] All ER (D) 19 (Jul) S56
Manly Council v Malouf (2004) 61 NSWLR 394 .... S28
Manor Electronics Ltd v Dickson (1990) Times, 8 February S13
Mason v Boscawen [2008] EWHC 3100 (Ch), [2009] 1 All ER 1006,
    [2009] 1 P & CR 499, [2009] STC 624, [2009] 02 EG 80 (CS), [2008] All ER
    (D) 228 (Dec) S46, S48
Masri v Consolidated Contractors International Co SAL [2009] UKHL 43,
    [2010] 1 AC 90, [2009] 4 All ER 847, [2010] 1 All ER (Comm) 220,
    [2009] 3 WLR 385, [2009] Bus LR 1269, [2009] 2 Lloyd's Rep 473,
    [2009] 2 BCLC 382, [2009] NLJR 1250, (2009) Times, 13 August, [2009] All
    ER (D) 340 (Jul) S21
Mastercigars Direct Ltd v Withers LLP [2007] EWHC 2733 (Ch), [2008] 3 All ER
    417, [2009] 1 WLR 881, [2008] IP & T 946, [2007] NLJR 1731, [2008] 1
    Costs LR 72, [2007] All ER (D) 385 (Nov) S22
Medcalf v Mardell [2002] UKHL 27, [2003] 1 AC 120, [2002] 3 All ER 721,
    [2002] 3 WLR 172, [2002] 31 LS Gaz R 34, [2002] NLJR 1032, (2002) Times,
    28 June, [2002] All ER (D) 228 (Jun) S17
Medical Council of Hong Kong v Chow Siu Shek (2000) 3 HKCFAR 144, [2000] 2
    HKLRD 674 .... S1, S27, S40
Metronet Rail BCV Ltd (in PPP administration), Re; Metronet Rail SSL Ltd (in PPP
    administration), Re [2007] EWHC 2697 (Ch), [2008] 2 All ER 75, [2008] Bus
    LR 823, [2008] 1 BCLC 760, [2007] All ER (D) 370 (Nov) S11
Midland Bank Trust Co Ltd v Hett, Stubbs & Kemp (a firm) [1979] Ch 384,
    [1978] 3 All ER 571, [1978] 3 WLR 167, 121 Sol Jo 830 .... S13
Midlands Co-operative Society Ltd v Revenue and Customs Comrs [2008] EWCA
    Civ 305, [2008] Bus LR 1187, [2008] STC 1803, (2008) Times, 22 April,
    [2008] SWTI 1199, [2008] All ER (D) 121 (Apr) S54

Miliangos v George Frank (Textiles) Ltd [1976] AC 443, [1975] 3 All ER 801,
    [1975] 3 WLR 758, [1975] 2 CMLR 585, [1976] 1 Lloyd's Rep 201, 9 LDAB
    408, 119 Sol Jo 774, HL S12, S13
Mills v Birchall. See Dolphin Quays Developments Ltd v Mills
Minster for Immigration and Multicultural Affairs v Hu (1997) 79 FCR 309 .... S28
Morris v London Iron and Steel Co Ltd [1988] QB 493, [1987] 2 All ER 496,
    [1987] 3 WLR 836, [1987] ICR 855, [1987] IRLR 182, 131 Sol Jo 1040,
    [1987] LS Gaz R 2274, CA S3
Mount Lawley Pty Ltd v Western Australi Planning Commission [2004] WASCA
    149; (2004) 136 LGERA 16 .... S42
Moweno Pty Ltd v Stratis Promotions Pty Ltd [2003] NSWCA 376 .... S29
Mucelli v Government of Albania [2009] UKHL 2, [2009] 3 All ER 1035,
    [2009] 1 WLR 276, (2009) Times, 27 January, 153 Sol Jo (no 4) 28, [2009] All
    ER (D) 135 (Jan) S28
Mullins v Harnett [1997] IEHC 18, [1998] 4 IR 426 .... S19, S20, S27, S28
Munn v Agus (1997) 6 NTLR 84 .... S29

N

N (a child) (McKenzie friends: rights of audience), Re [2008] EWHC 2042 (Fam),
    [2008] 1 WLR 2743, [2008] 3 FCR 642, [2008] 2 FLR 1899, [2008] Fam Law
    1093, [2008] All ER (D) 116 (Aug) S9, S10, S11
Nangles Nurseries v Commissioners of Valuation [2008] IEHC 73, 41 .... S27
New South Wales Crime Commission v Yu [2009] NSWCA 349 .... S10
New Zealand Customs Service v Wang [2010] NZAR 322 .... S28
Ng Ka Ling v Director of Immigration (1999) 2 HKCFAR 4 .... S27
Nguyen v Minister for Health & Ageing [2002] FCA 1241 .... S26
Niagara-on-the-Lake (Town) v Gross Estate (1993) 12 OR (3d) 1 .... S49
Nolan v Wright [2009] EWHC 305 (Ch), [2009] 2 All ER (Comm) 503,
    [2009] 3 All ER 823, [2009] NLJR 395, [2009] BPIR 854, [2009] All ER (D)
    45 (Mar) S4

O

Oakley Inc v Animal Ltd (Secretary of State for Trade and Industry intervening)
    [2005] EWCA Civ 1191, [2006] Ch 337, [2006] 2 WLR 294, [2006] RPC 301,
    [2006] IP & T 251, (2005) Times, 7 November, [2005] All ER (D) 222 (Oct) S16
Oceania Manufacturing Co Ltd v Pang Kwong-Hon [1979] HKLR 445, 448–449,
    452 .... S19
Odelola v Secretary of State for the Home Department [2009] UKHL 25,
    [2009] 3 All ER 1061, [2009] 1 WLR 1230, (2009) Times, 22 May, [2009] All
    ER (D) 180 (May) S15, S20, S50
Official Bay Heritage Protection Society Incoporated v Auckland City Council [2007]
    NZCA 511 .... S38
Ofulue v Bossert [2009] UKHL 16, [2009] AC 990, [2009] 3 All ER 93,
    [2009] 2 WLR 749, [2010] 1 FLR 475, [2009] Fam Law 1042, [2009] 11 EG
    119 (CS), (2009) Times, 13 March, 153 Sol Jo (no 11) 29, [2009] All ER (D)
    119 (Mar) S53
Omagh District Council, Re, Judicial Review [2007] NIQB 61 .... S56
Osbourne v Chief Executive of Ministry of Social Development [2010] 1 NZLR
    559 .... S44
Oyarce v Cheshire County Council [2008] EWCA Civ 434, [2008] 4 All ER 907,
    [2008] ICR 1179, [2008] IRLR 653, [2008] All ER (D) 24 (May) S16

P

P, Re [2009] EWHC 163 (Ch), [2010] Ch 33, [2009] 2 All ER 1198, [2009] All ER
    (D) 160 (Feb) S40
PNPF Trust Co Ltd v Taylor [2010] EWHC 1573 (Ch), [2010] All ER (D) 251
    (Jun) S17

Palm Developments Ltd v Secretary of State for Communities and Local Government
 [2009] EWHC 220 (Admin), [2009] 2 P & CR 262, [2009] NLJR 308, [2009]
 All ER (D) 132 (Feb) S57
Pang Yiu Hung v Commissioner of Police [2003] 2 HKLRD 125, 161 .... S47
Paulin v Paulin [2009] EWCA Civ 221, [2009] 3 All ER 88n, [2010] 1 WLR 1057,
 [2009] 2 FCR 477, [2009] 2 FLR 354, [2009] Fam Law 567, [2009] NLJR 475,
 [2009] BPIR 572, [2009] All ER (D) 187 (Mar) S10
Penny's Bay Investment Co Ltd v Director of Lands [2010] HKCFA 12 .... S29
Pepper v Attorney-General (No 2) [2008] QCA 207 .... S58
Pepper (Inspector of Taxes) v Hart [1990] 1 WLR 204, [1990] STC 6, 65 TC 421;
 affd [1991] Ch 203, [1991] 2 All ER 824, [1991] 2 WLR 483, [1990] STC 786,
 65 TC 421, [1991] ICR 681, [1991] IRLR 125, 134 Sol Jo 1479, CA; revsd
 [1993] AC 593, [1993] 1 All ER 42, [1992] 3 WLR 1032, [1992] STC 898, 65
 TC 421, [1993] ICR 291, [1993] IRLR 33, [1993] NLJR 17, [1993] RVR
 127, HL S33
Perpetual Trusteee Company Ltd v Albert and Rose Khoshaba [2006] NSWCA 41 .... S10
Perrin v Northampton Borough Council [2007] EWCA Civ 1353, [2008] 4 All ER
 673, [2008] 1 WLR 1307, [2008] LGR 379, [2008] 1 P & CR 454, [2008] BLR
 137, [2008] 02 EG 146 (CS), (2008) Times, 21 January, 152 Sol Jo (no 2) 34,
 [2007] All ER (D) 286 (Dec) S27
Pilling v Reynolds [2008] EWHC 316 (QB), [2009] 1 All ER 163, [2008] All ER (D)
 54 (Mar) S56
Poets Chase Freehold Co Ltd v Sinclair Gardens Investments (Kensington) Ltd. See
 Sinclair Gardens Investments (Kensington) Ltd v Poets Chase Freehold Co Ltd
Porter v Shepherds Bush Housing Association [2008] UKHL 70, [2009] AC 636,
 [2009] 2 All ER 829, [2009] 2 WLR 78, [2009] 1 P & CR 519, [2009] PTSR
 281, [2008] 50 EG 73 (CS), (2008) Times, 15 December, 153 Sol Jo (no 1) 32,
 [2008] All ER (D) 115 (Dec) S44
Practice Note (Family Courts: McKenzie Friends) (No 2) [2008] 1 WLR 2757 .... S9
Prem Singh v Director of Immigration [2003] 1 HKLRD 550, 575 .... S53
Premier Foods (Holdings) Ltd v Revenue and Customs Comrs [2007] EWHC 3134
 (Ch), [2008] STC 176, [2007] SWTI 2462, [2007] All ER (D) 363 (Oct) S29
Project Blue Sky v Australian Broadcasting Authority (1998) 194 CLR 355, 384 .... S3, S23
Purba v Ryan (2006) 61 Alta LR (4th) 112 .... S24

Q

QBE Worker's Compensation (Vic) Ltd v Freisleben [1999] 3 VR 401 .... S47
Quinlivan v Governer of Portlaoise Prison [1997] IEHC 181, [1998] 2 IR 113 .... S19, S20, S28

R

R v A [2008] EWCA Crim 2908, [2009] 2 All ER 898, [2009] 1 Cr App Rep 347,
 [2009] Crim LR 739, [2008] All ER (D) 03 (Dec), sub nom R v Andrews
 [2009] 1 WLR 1947 .... S52, S53
R (W) v Alberta (2006) 62 Alta LR (4th) 6 .... S48
R v Athwal [2009] EWCA Crim 789, [2009] 1 WLR 2430, [2009] 2 Cr App Rep
 204, [2009] Crim LR 726, (2009) Times, 14 July, [2009] All ER (D) 61
 (May) S52
R (on the application of Jackson) v A-G [2005] UKHL 56, [2006] 1 AC 262,
 [2005] 4 All ER 1253, [2005] 3 WLR 733, [2005] NLJR 1600, (2005) Times,
 14 October, [2006] 2 LRC 499, [2005] All ER (D) 136 (Oct) S8
R v B [2000] EWCA Crim 42 .... S5
R v Barker [2010] EWCA Crim 4, (2010) Times, 5 February, [2010] All ER (D) 126
 (Jan) S10, S52
R (on the application of Boyejo) v Barnet London Borough Council; R (on the
 application of Smith) v Portsmouth City Council [2009] EWHC 3261 (Admin),
 (2010) Times, 22 January, [2009] All ER (D) 169 (Dec) S16
R (on the application of Newcastle City Council) v Berwick-upon-Tweed Borough
 Council [2008] EWHC 2369 (Admin), [2009] LGR 195, [2009] RTR 413,
 [2008] All ER (D) 33 (Nov) S7

R (on the application of C) v Birmingham City Council [2008] EWHC 3036
(Admin), [2009] 1 All ER 1039, [2009] 1 FCR 657, [2009] 1 FLR 838,
[2009] Fam Law 200, [2008] All ER (D) 171 (Nov); affd on other grounds sub
nom R (on the application Clue) v Birmingham City Council [2010] EWCA
Civ 460, [2010] 4 All ER 423, [2010] LGR 485, [2010] 2 FLR 1011,
[2010] Fam Law 802, (2010) Times, 7 May, 154 Sol Jo (no 18) 29, [2010] All
ER (D) 27 (May) S11
R (on the application of Okandeji) v Bow Street Magistrates Court [2005] EWHC
2925 (Admin), [2006] 1 WLR 674, [2005] All ER (D) 166 (Nov) S9
R (on the application of Risk Management Partners Ltd) v Brent London Borough
Council; Risk Management Partners Ltd v Brent London Borough Council
[2008] EWHC 692 (Admin), [2008] LGR 331, [2008] All ER (D) 302 (Apr);
affd sub nom Risk Management Partners Ltd v Brent London Borough Council
[2008] EWHC 1094 (Admin), [2008] LGR 429, [2008] All ER (D) 226 (May);
affd [2009] EWCA Civ 490, [2009] LGR 99, [2010] PTSR 349, [2009] All ER
(D) 109 (Jun) S26, S35, S36
R v Bristol [2007] EWCA Crim 3214, 172 JP 161, 172 JPN 421, [2007] All ER (D)
47 (Dec) S6
R v Bygrave [2008] EWCA Crim 1323, [2008] 4 All ER 890, [2009] 1 Cr App Rep
(S) 333, [2008] Crim LR 805, [2008] All ER (D) 274 (Jun) S48
R v C [2007] EWCA Crim 2581, [2008] 1 WLR 966, [2008] 1 Cr App Rep 311,
[2007] All ER (D) 102 (Nov), sub nom R v Cartwright (2007) Times,
6 December S19
R (on the application of G) v Chief Constable of West Yorkshire Police
[2008] EWCA Civ 28, [2008] 4 All ER 594, [2008] 1 WLR 550, [2008] 2 Cr
App Rep 53, [2008] Crim LR 558, (2008) Times, 21 February, [2008] All ER
(D) 46 (Feb) S42
R (on the application of Hilali) v City of Westminster Magistrates' Court
[2008] EWHC 2892 (Admin), [2009] 1 All ER 834, [2010] 1 WLR 241, [2008]
All ER (D) 241 (Nov) S15
R v Clark (application under s 58 of the Criminal Justice Act 2003) [2007] EWCA
Crim 2532, (2007) Times, 29 October, [2007] All ER (D) 120 (Oct), sub nom
R v Clarke (application under s 58 of the Criminal Justice Act 2003)
[2008] 1 Cr App Rep 403 .... S10
R v Cockburn [2008] EWCA Crim 316, [2008] QB 882, [2008] 2 All ER 1153,
[2008] 2 WLR 1274, [2008] 2 Cr App Rep 47, [2008] Crim LR 802, [2008] All
ER (D) 401 (Feb) S45
R (on the application of Hampstead Heath Winter Swimming Club) v Corpn of
London. See Hampstead Heath Winter Swimming Club v Corpn of London
R (on the application of A) v Croydon London Borough Council; R (on the
application of M) v Lambeth London Borough Council [2009] UKSC 8,
[2010] 1 All ER 469, [2009] 1 WLR 2557, [2010] LGR 183, [2010] PTSR 106,
[2009] 3 FCR 607, [2010] 1 FLR 959, [2010] Fam Law 137, [2009] NLJR
1701, (2009) Times, 30 November, 153 Sol Jo (no 46) 34, [2009] All ER (D)
288 (Nov) S61
R (on the application of Guest) v DPP [2009] EWHC 594 (Admin), [2009] 2 Cr
App Rep 426, 173 JP 511, [2009] Crim LR 730, [2009] All ER (D) 53 (Mar) S8
R (on the application of Corner House Research) v Director of the Serious Fraud
Office (BAE Systems plc, interested party) [2008] UKHL 60, [2009] AC 756,
[2008] 4 All ER 927, [2009] Crim LR 47, [2008] NLJR 1149, (2008) Times,
31 July, 152 Sol Jo (no 32) 29, [2009] 1 LRC 343, [2008] All ER (D) 399
(Jul) S8
R (Breckland) v Electoral Commission Boundary Committee for England [2009]
PTSR 1611 .... S31
R (on the application of Thomas) v Greenwich Magistrates' Court [2009] EWHC
1180 (Admin), 173 JP 345, [2009] Crim LR 800, [2009] All ER (D) 85
(May) S54
R (on the application of Charlson) v Guildford Magistrates Court [2006] EWHC
2318 (Admin), [2007] 3 All ER 163, [2006] 1 WLR 3494, 170 JP 739, 171 JPN
193, (2006) Times, 29 September, [2006] All ER (D) 41 (Sep) S4
R (on the application of Warden and Fellows of Winchester College) v Hampshire
County Council [2008] EWCA Civ 431, [2008] 3 All ER 717, [2009] 1 WLR
138, [2008] RTR 301, [2008] 18 EG 127 (CS), (2008) Times, 8 May, [2008] All

R (on the application of Warden and Fellows of Winchester College) v Hampshire County
Council [2008] EWCA Civ 431, [2008] 3 All ER 717, [2009] 1 WLR 138, [2008] RTR
301, [2008] 18 EG 127 (CS), (2008) Times, 8 May, [2008] All – *contd*
ER (D) 396 (Apr) S54
R v Hape [2007] 2 SCR 292 .... S41
R (on the application of Attwood) v Health Service Commissioner [2008] EWHC
2315 (Admin), [2009] 1 All ER 415, [2009] PTSR 1330, [2008] All ER (D) 40
(Oct) S7
R v Henry [2005] 3 SCR 609 .... S12
R (on the application of Kaupthing Bank hf) v HM Treasury [2009] EWHC 2542
(Admin), [2009] All ER (D) 220 (Oct) S59
R v Horncastle [2010] 2 All ER 359, [2010] 2 WLR 47, [2010] 1 Cr App Rep 194,
[2010] Crim LR 496, (2009) Times, 10 December, [2009] UKSC 14, 153 Sol Jo
(no 48) 32, [2009] All ER (D) 88 (Dec), SC S52, S59
R v Hughes (2000) 202 CLR 535, 563 .... S24
R v Ikram [2008] EWCA Crim 586, [2008] 4 All ER 253, [2009] 1 WLR 1419,
[2008] 2 Cr App Rep 347, [2008] 2 Cr App Rep (S) 648, [2008] Crim LR 912,
[2008] All ER (D) 305 (Mar) S22
R (on the application of the Secretary of State for the Home Department) v
Immigration Appeal Tribunal [2001] EWHC Admin 261, [2001] QB 1224,
[2001] 4 All ER 430, [2001] 3 WLR 164, [2001] All ER (D) 85 (Apr) S58
R (on the application of Bhatt Murphy (a firm) v Independent Assessor
[2008] EWCA Civ 755, (2008) Times, 21 July, 152 Sol Jo (no 29) 29, [2008]
All ER (D) 127 (Jul) S50
R (on the application of British Broadcasting Corp) v Information Tribunal
2009] UKHL 9, [2009] 4 All ER 111, [2009] 1 WLR 430, [2009] IP & T 876,
(2009) Times, 12 February, 153 Sol Jo (no 7) 31, [2009] All ER (D) 101
(Feb) S59
R v Kelly [2008] EWCA Crim 137, [2008] 2 All ER 840, [2009] 1 WLR 701,
[2008] 2 Cr App Rep 133, 172 JP 231, 172 JPN 474, [2008] All ER (D) 122
(Feb) S53
R v Knights [2002] EWCA Crim 2954, [2003] 3 All ER 508, [2003] 1 WLR 1655,
[2003] 1 Cr App Rep 575, [2003] 2 Cr App Rep (S) 207, [2003] Crim LR 642,
[2003] 08 LS Gaz R 29, (2002) Times, 27 December, 147 Sol Jo LB 148,
[2002] All ER (D) 233 (Dec); affd sub nom R v Knights [2005] UKHL 50,
[2006] 1 AC 368, [2005] 4 All ER 347, [2005] 3 WLR 330, [2006] 1 Cr App
Rep (S) 460, [2006] Crim LR 171, [2005] NLJR 1316, (2005) Times, 27 July,
[2005] All ER (D) 307 (Jul) S6
R v L [2009] 1 Cr App R 16 .... S3
R (on the application of D) v Life Sentence Review Comrs (Northern Ireland)
[2008] UKHL 33, [2008] NI 292, [2008] 4 All ER 992, [2008] 1 WLR 1499,
[2009] 1 FLR 700, [2009] Fam Law 192, (2008) Times, 24 June, 152 Sol Jo (no
25) 32, [2008] All ER (D) 119 (Jun) S52
R (on the application of Gilboy) v Liverpool City Council [2008] EWCA Civ 751,
[2009] QB 699, [2008] 4 All ER 127, [2009] 3 WLR 300, [2008] LGR 521,
[2008] 2 P & CR 544, [2009] PTSR 987, (2008) Times, 20 August, 152 Sol Jo
(no 27) 30, [2008] All ER (D) 13 (Jul) S11
R v McFaul [2002] EWCA Crim 2954, [2003] 3 All ER 508, [2003] 1 WLR 1655,
[2003] 1 Cr App Rep 575, [2003] 2 Cr App Rep (S) 207, [2003] Crim LR 642,
[2003] 08 LS Gaz R 29, (2002) Times, 27 December, 147 Sol Jo LB 148,
[2002] All ER (D) 233 (Dec); affd sub nom R v Knights [2005] UKHL 50,
[2006] 1 AC 368, [2005] 4 All ER 347, [2005] 3 WLR 330, [2006] 1 Cr App
Rep (S) 460, [2006] Crim LR 171, [2005] NLJR 1316, (2005) Times, 27 July,
[2005] All ER (D) 307 (Jul) S6
R v Marquis [2010] 2 All ER 359, [2010] 2 WLR 47, [2010] 1 Cr App Rep 194,
[2010] Crim LR 496, (2009) Times, 10 December, [2009] UKSC 14, 153 Sol Jo
(no 48) 32, [2009] All ER (D) 88 (Dec), SC S52, S59
R (on the application of L) v Metropolitan Police Comr [2009] UKSC 3,
[2010] 1 AC 410, [2010] 1 All ER 113, [2009] 3 WLR 1056, [2010] PTSR 245,
[2010] 2 FCR 25, [2010] 1 FLR 643, [2010] Fam Law 21, [2009] NLJR 1549,
153 Sol Jo (no 42) 30, [2009] All ER (D) 296 (Oct) S61

R (on the application Public and Commercial Services Union) v Minister for the
    Civil Service [2010] EWHC 1027 (Admin), [2010] ICR 1198, (2010) Times,
    24 May, [2010] All ER (D) 70 (May) S33, S37
R v Mohammed [2008] EWCA Crim 1465, [2008] 4 All ER 661, [2009] 1 Cr App
    Rep (S) 402, [2008] Crim LR 906, (2008) Times, 15 July, 152 Sol Jo (no 29)
    32, [2008] All ER (D) 104 (Jul) S4
R v Morgan [2008] EWCA Crim 1323, [2008] 4 All ER 890, [2009] 1 Cr App Rep
    (S) 333, [2008] Crim LR 805, [2008] All ER (D) 274 (Jun) S48
R v North and East Devon Health Authority, ex p Coughlan (Secretary of State for
    Health and another intervening) [2001] QB 213, [2000] 3 All ER 850,
    [2000] 2 WLR 622, 97 LGR 703, [1999] Lloyd's Rep Med 306, 51 BMLR 1,
    [1999] 31 LS Gaz R 39, 2 CCL Rep 285, 143 Sol Jo LB 213, [1999] All ER
    (D) 801, CA S16
R (on the application of Morris) v North Somerset Council [2003] EWCA Civ 183,
    [2003] 2 All ER 1114, [2003] 1 WLR 1149, [2003] 3 EGLR 129, (2003) Times,
    21 February, [2003] All ER (D) 267 (Feb) S10
R v Omarjee (1995) 79 A Crim R 355 .... S18
R (on the application of Langley) v Preston Crown Court [2008] EWHC 2623
    (Admin), [2009] 3 All ER 1026, [2009] 1 WLR 1612, 172 JP 605, 172 JPN
    845, [2008] All ER (D) 300 (Oct) S7, S61
R (on the application of Gentle) v Prime Minister [2006] EWCA Civ 1689,
    [2007] QB 689, [2007] 2 WLR 195, (2007) Times, 1 January, [2006] All ER
    (D) 147 (Dec); affd [2008] UKHL 20, [2008] 1 AC 1356, [2008] 3 All ER 1,
    (2008) Times, 10 April, 27 BHRC 1, [2008] All ER (D) 111 (Apr) S15
R v Rahman [2008] EWCA Crim 1465, [2008] 4 All ER 661, [2009] 1 Cr App Rep
    (S) 402, [2008] Crim LR 906, (2008) Times, 15 July, 152 Sol Jo (no 29) 32,
    [2008] All ER (D) 104 (Jul) S4
R v Raza [2009] EWCA Crim 1413, [2009] Crim LR 820 .... S26
R (on the application of Heffernan) v Rent Service [2008] UKHL 58,
    [2009] 1 All ER 173, [2009] LGR 87, [2008] HLR 738, (2008) Times,
    20 August, [2008] All ER (D) 404 (Jul) S28
R v S [2009] EWCA Crim 85, [2009] 2 Cr App Rep 171, [2009] Crim LR 723,
    [2009] All ER (D) 84 (Feb) S54
R v St Lawrence Cement Inc (2002) 60 OR (3d) 712 .... S38
R (on the application of Shrewsbury and Atcham Borough Council) v Secretary of
    State for Communities and Local Government [2008] EWCA Civ 148,
    [2008] 3 All ER 548, (2008) Times, 12 March, [2008] All ER (D) 25 (Mar) S14, S15,
                                                                                        S33
R (on the application of Animal Defenders International) v Secretary of State for
    Culture, Media and Sport [2008] UKHL 15, [2008] 1 AC 1312, [2008] 3 All ER
    193, [2008] 2 WLR 781, [2008] IP & T 902, 24 BHRC 217, [2008] EMLR 299,
    [2008] 5 LRC 687, [2008] All ER (D) 155 (Mar) S60
R (on the application of Friends of the Earth and others) v Secretary of State for
    Energy and Climate Change [2009] EWCA Civ 810, [2010] HLR 313, (2009)
    Times, 13 October, [2009] All ER (D) 331 (Jul) S32
R v Secretary of State for the Environment, Transport and the Regions, ex p O'Byrne
    [2001] EWCA Civ 499, [2002] HLR 567, [2001] 16 LS Gaz R 36,
    [2001] EGCS 52, [2001] All ER (D) 47 (Apr); affd [2002] UKHL 45,
    [2003] 1 All ER 15, [2002] 1 WLR 3250, [2003] LGR 1, [2003] HLR 398,
    [2002] 46 LS Gaz R 35, [2002] 48 EGCS 138, (2002) Times, 18 November,
    146 Sol Jo LB 262, [2002] All ER (D) 197 (Nov) S18
R v Secretary of State for the Environment, Transport and the Regions, ex p Spath
    Holme Ltd [2001] 2 AC 349, [2001] 1 All ER 195, [2001] 2 WLR 15, 33 HLR
    301, [2000] NLJR 1855, 150 NLJ 1855, 145 Sol Jo LB 39, HL S17
R (on the application of Bancoult) v Secretary of State for Foreign and
    Commonwealth Affairs [2008] UKHL 61, [2009] AC 453, [2008] 4 All ER
    1055, [2008] 3 WLR 955, [2008] NLJR 1530, (2008) Times, 23 October, 152
    Sol Jo (no 41) 29, [2008] 5 LRC 769, [2008] All ER (D) 219 (Oct) ... S15, S21, S50, S62
R v Secretary of State for Health, ex p Hammersmith and Fulham London Borough
    Council (1997) 96 LGR 277, 30 HLR 525; affd [1998] EWCA Civ 1300,
    (1998) 31 HLR 475, 49 BMLR 201, CA S46

R (on the application of Wright) v Secretary of State for Health [2009] UKHL 3,
[2009] AC 739, [2009] 2 All ER 129, [2009] 2 WLR 267, [2009] PTSR 401,
106 BMLR 71, (2009) Times, 23 January, 153 Sol Jo (no 4) 30, 26 BHRC 269,
[2009] All ER (D) 150 (Jan) S60
R (on the application of Black) v Secretary of State for Justice [2009] UKHL 1,
[2009] AC 949, [2009] 4 All ER 1, [2009] 2 WLR 282, (2009) Times,
30 January, 153 Sol Jo (no 4) 27, 26 BHRC 664, [2009] All ER (D) 138 (Jan) S61
R (on the application of Shields) v Secretary of State for Justice [2008] EWHC 3102
(Admin), [2010] QB 150, [2009] 3 All ER 265, [2009] 3 WLR 765, (2009)
Times, 14 January, [2008] All ER (D) 182 (Dec) S14
R (on the application of Bromley) v Secretary of State for Justice [2010] EWHC 112
(Admin), [2010] All ER (D) 23 (Feb) S5
R (on the application of Kelly) v Secretary of State for Justice, Re Gibson
[2008] EWCA Civ 177, [2009] QB 204, [2008] 3 All ER 844, [2008] 3 WLR
1044, [2008] All ER (D) 172 (Mar) S44
R (on the application of BAPIO Action Ltd) v Secretary of State for the Home
Department [2008] UKHL 27, [2008] 1 AC 1003, [2009] 1 All ER 93,
[2008] 2 WLR 1073, [2008] ICR 659, (2008) Times, 1 May, [2008] All ER (D)
410 (Apr) S7, S14, S35
R (on the application of Staff Side of the Police Negotiating Board) v Secretary of
State for the Home Department [2008] EWHC 1173 (Admin), [2008] All ER
(D) 101 (Jun) S33
R (on the application of Niazi) v Secretary of State for the Home Department
[2008] EWCA Civ 755, (2008) Times, 21 July, 152 Sol Jo (no 29) 29, [2008]
All ER (D) 127 (Jul) S50
R (on the application of BA (Nigeria)) v Secretary of State for the Home Department
[2009] UKSC 7, [2010] 1 AC 444, [2010] 2 All ER 95, [2009] 3 WLR 1253,
(2009) Times, 1 December, 153 Sol Jo (no 46) 33, [2009] All ER (D) 285
(Nov) S31
R (on the application of Daly) v Secretary of State for the Home Department
[2001] UKHL 26, [2001] 2 AC 532, [2001] 3 All ER 433, [2001] 2 WLR 1622,
[2001] 26 LS Gaz R 43, 145 Sol Jo LB 156, [2001] 4 LRC 345, [2001] All ER
(D) 280 (May) S32
R (on the application of Baiai) v Secretary of State for the Home Department; R (on
the application of Bigoku) v same; R (on the application of Tilki) v same
[2008] UKHL 53, [2009] AC 287, [2008] 3 All ER 1094, [2008] 1 FCR 1,
[2008] 2 FLR 1462, [2008] Fam Law 994, [2008] Fam Law 955, [2008] NLJR
1225, (2008) Times, 13 August, 152 Sol Jo (no 31) 29, 26 BHRC 429, [2008]
All ER (D) 411 (Jul) S26
R v Secretary of State for Social Security, ex p Sarwar [1997] 3 CMLR 648 .... S16
R (on the application of Irving) v Secretary of State for Transport [2008] EWHC
1200 (Admin), 172 JP 425, 172 JPN 594, [2008] All ER (D) 124 (May) S59
R (on the application of Bradley) v Secretary of State for Work and Pensions
[2008] EWCA Civ 36, [2009] QB 114, [2008] 3 All ER 1116, [2008] 3 WLR
1059, (2008) Times, 25 February, [2008] All ER (D) 98 (Feb) S8
R (on the application of DM) v Secretary of State for Work and Pensions; R (on the
application of EM) v same [2010] EWCA Civ 18, [2010] 1 WLR 1782, 112
BMLR 140, (2010) Times, 1 February, [2010] All ER (D) 172 (Jan) S27
R v Sekhon [2002] EWCA Crim 2954, [2003] 3 All ER 508, [2003] 1 WLR 1655,
[2003] 1 Cr App Rep 575, [2003] 2 Cr App Rep (S) 207, [2003] Crim LR 642,
[2003] 08 LS Gaz R 29, (2002) Times, 27 December, 147 Sol Jo LB 148,
[2002] All ER (D) 233 (Dec); affd sub nom R v Knights [2005] UKHL 50,
[2006] 1 AC 368, [2005] 4 All ER 347, [2005] 3 WLR 330, [2006] 1 Cr App
Rep (S) 460, [2006] Crim LR 171, [2005] NLJR 1316, (2005) Times, 27 July,
[2005] All ER (D) 307 (Jul) S6
R (on the application of M) v Slough Borough Council [2008] UKHL 52,
[2008] 4 All ER 831, [2008] 1 WLR 1808, [2008] LGR 871, [2008] HLR 763,
(2008) Times, 5 September, 152 Sol Jo (no 32) 30, [2008] All ER (D) 412
(Jul) S56
R v Smith [2003] NSWCCA 381 .... S10
R (on the application of Morgan Grenfell & Co Ltd) v Special Comr of Income Tax
[2002] UKHL 21, [2003] 1 AC 563, [2002] 3 All ER 1, [2002] 2 WLR 1299,
[2002] STC 786, 74 TC 511, 4 ITLR 809, [2002] 25 LS Gaz R 35, (2002)

R (on the application of Morgan Grenfell & Co Ltd) v Special Comr of Income Tax
[2002] UKHL 21, [2003] 1 AC 563, [2002] 3 All ER 1, [2002] 2 WLR 1299, [2002] STC
786, 74 TC 511, 4 ITLR 809, [2002] 25 LS Gaz R 35, (2002) – *contd*
Times, 20 May, 146 Sol Jo LB 126, [2002] All ER (D) 239 (May) S41
R (on the application of Green & Green Scaffolding Co) v Staines Magistrates' Court
[2008] EWHC 1443 (Admin), 172 JP 353, [2008] All ER (D) 211 (May), sub
nom R (on the application of Green 172 JPN 525 .... S52
R v T [2009] 1 Ac 1310 .... S51
R v T [2010] 1 WLR 630 .... S43
R (on the application of Scott and others) v Taunton Dean Magistrates' Court
[2009] EWHC 105 (Admin), [2010] QB 224, [2009] 3 All ER 726, 169 JP 173,
(2009) Times, 17 February, [2009] All ER (D) 30 (Feb) S52
R v Tran Viet Tran [1992] 2 HKLR 184, 188–189 .... S20
R (on the application of Cart) v Upper Tribunal [2009] EWHC 3052 (Admin),
[2010] 1 All ER 908, [2010] 2 WLR 1012, [2010] STC 493, [2010] PTSR 824,
[2010] 2 FCR 309, [2009] SWTI 3167, [2009] All ER (D) 22 (Dec); affd on
other grounds sub nom R (on the application of Cart) v Upper Tribunal
[2010] EWCA Civ 859, [2010] NLJR 1115, (2010) Times, 4 October, [2010]
SWTI 2272, [2010] All ER (D) 246 (Jul) S8
R (on the application of Sivasubramaniam) v Wandsworth County Court; R (on the
application of Sivasubramaniam) v Kingston upon Thames County Court
[2002] EWCA Civ 1738, [2003] 2 All ER 160, [2003] 1 WLR 475,
[2003] 03 LS Gaz R 34, (2002) Times, 30 November, [2002] All ER (D) 431
(Nov) S8
R v Wonderland Gifts Ltd (1996) 140 Nfld & PEIR 219 .... S3
R v Zafar [2008] EWCA Crim 184, [2008] QB 810, [2008] 4 All ER 46,
[2008] 2 WLR 1013, [2008] 2 Cr App Rep 84, [2008] NLJR 298, (2008) Times,
15 February, [2008] All ER (D) 189 (Feb) S34
Radin v Vekic [1997] NCWSC 234 .... S19
Registrar of Liquor Licences v Iliadis (1988) 19 FCR 311, 315–316 .... S43
Repatriation Commission v Morris (1997) 79 FCR 455, 461 .... S49
Revenue and Customs v Stringer (sub nom Ainsworth v IRC) [2009] UKHL 31,
[2009] 4 All ER 1205, [2009] ICR 985, [2009] IRLR 677, (2009) Times,
15 June, [2009] All ER (D) 168 (Jun) S18
Revenue and Customs Comrs v Dunwood Travel Ltd [2008] EWCA Civ 174,
[2008] STC 959, [2008] SWTI 434, [2008] All ER (D) 104 (Mar) S16
Revenue and Customs Comrs v Halcyon Films LLP [2010] EWCA Civ 261,
[2010] STC 1125, [2010] SWTI 1285, [2010] All ER (D) 197 (Mar) S36
Risk Management Partners Ltd v Brent London Borough Council. See R (on the
application of Risk Management Partners Ltd) v Brent London Borough
Council; Risk Management Partners Ltd v Brent London Borough Council
Roberts v Secretary of State for Social Security [2001] EWCA Civ 910 .... S53
Runa Begum v Tower Hamlets London Borough Council [2003] UKHL 5,
[2003] 2 AC 430, [2003] 1 All ER 731, [2003] 2 WLR 388, [2003] LGR 205,
[2003] HLR 448, [2003] 13 LS Gaz R 28, (2003) Times, 17 February, 147 Sol
Jo LB 232, 14 BHRC 400, [2003] All ER (D) 191 (Feb) S61
Ruttle Plant Ltd v Secretary of State for the Environment, Food and Rural Affairs
[2008] EWHC 238 (TCC), [2009] 1 All ER 448, [2008] BPIR 1395, [2008] All
ER (D) 270 (Jun) S39

S

S (L) v P (E) (1999) 67 BCLR (3d) 254 .... S19
Sandvik Australia Pty Ltd v Commonwealth of Australia [1990] FCA 386 .... S54
Schanka v Employment National (Administration) Ltd (2000) 97 FCR 186 .... S57
Scottish & Newcastle plc v Raguz [2008] UKHL 65, [2009] 1 All ER 763, [2009] 2
All ER (Comm) 447, [2008] 1 WLR 2994, [2009] Bus LR 72, [2009] 1 P & CR
127, [2008] NLJR 1567, [2008] 44 EG 114 (CS), (2008) Times, 3 November,
152 Sol Jo (no 42) 30, [2008] All ER (D) 283 (Oct) S36, S47
Seafairers' Retirement Fund Pty Ltd v Oppenhuis (1999) 94 FCR 594, 597–598 .... S13
Secretary of State for Justice v Lau Suk Han [1998] 2 HKLRD 14, 22 .... S56
Secretary of State for Justice v Tang Ben [1999] 3 HKC 647, 652, 658 .... S56

Secretary of State for Work and Pensions v Deane [2010] EWCA Civ 699, [2010] All
    ER (D) 201 (Jun) S16
Sellers v Maritime Safety Inspector [1999] 2 NZLR 44, 61, 62 .... S41
Seray-Wurie v Hackney London Borough Council (No 2) [2002] EWCA Civ 909,
    [2002] 3 All ER 448, [2003] 1 WLR 257, [2002] 33 LS Gaz R 21, (2002)
    Times, 4 July, [2002] All ER (D) 199 (Jun) S10
Serious Fraud Office v Lexi Holdings plc [2008] EWCA Crim 1443, [2009] QB 376,
    [2009] 1 All ER 586, [2009] 2 WLR 905, [2009] Bus LR 647, [2009] 1 Cr
    App Rep 295, (2008) Times, 18 August, [2008] BPIR 1598, [2008] All ER (D)
    149 (Jul) S51
Serious Organised Crime Agency v Perry (proceedings under the Proceeds of Crime
    Act 2002) [2009] EWHC 1960 (Admin), [2010] 1 WLR 910, [2009] All ER (D)
    337 (Jul); affd sub nom Serious Organised Crime Agency v Perry
    [2010] EWCA Civ 907, (2010) Times, 13 October, [2010] All ER (D) 317
    (Jul) S20
Sharratt v London Central Bus Co Ltd [2002] EWHC 9006 (Costs) S35
Sharratt v London Central Bus Co Ltd (The Accident Group Test Cases); Hollins v
    Russell [2003] EWCA Civ 718, [2003] 28 LS Gaz R 30, [2003] 4 All ER 590,
    [2003] 1 WLR 2487, [2003] NLJR 920, (2003) Times, 10 June, 147 Sol Jo LB
    662, [2003] All ER (D) 311 (May) S4
Shields v Chief Commissioner of Police [2008] VSC 2 .... S17
Sinclair Gardens Investments (Kensington) Ltd v Poets Chase Freehold Co Ltd
    [2007] EWHC 1776 (Ch), [2008] 2 All ER 187, [2007] 49 EG 104,
    [2007] NLJR 1427, [2007] 32 EG 89 (CS), [2007] All ER (D) 425 (Jul), sub
    nom Poets Chase Freehold Co Ltd v Sinclair Gardens Investments
    (Kensington) Ltd [2008] 1 WLR 768 .... S44, S50
Sloane v Minister of Immigration, Local Government and Ethnic Affairs
    (1992) 37 FCR 429, 443 .... S24
Smith v Northamptonshire County Council [2009] UKHL 27, [2009] 4 All ER 557,
    [2009] ICR 734, 110 BMLR 15, [2009] PIQR P292, (2009) Times, 21 May, 153
    Sol Jo (no 20) 39, [2009] All ER (D) 170 (May) S24
Society Promoting Environmental Conservation v Canada (Attorney-General) (2002)
    FTR 236 .... S43
Solicitor 24/07 v Law Society of Hong Kong [2008] 2 HKLRD 576 .... S52
Sonea v Mehedinti District Court, Romania [2009] EWHC 89 (Admin),
    [2009] 2 All ER 821, [2009] All ER (D) 167 (Jan) S44
Specialiser Tech Inc v Specialalloy Indsuctries Ltd [1999] 12 WWR 139 .... S56
Spencer v Secretary of Work and Pensions; Moore v Secretary of State for Transport
    [2008] EWCA Civ 750, [2009] QB 358, [2009] 1 All ER 314, [2009] 2 WLR
    593, [2008] 3 CMLR 429, [2009] RTR 39, [2008] ICR 1359, [2008] IRLR 911,
    [2008] PIQR P374, (2008) Times, 24 July, 152 Sol Jo (no 27) 31, [2008] All
    ER (D) 20 (Jul) S59
Spencer-Franks v Kellogg Brown and Root Ltd [2008] UKHL 46, [2009] 1 All ER
    269, [2008] ICR 863, [2008] NLJR 1004, [2008] PIQR P389, (2008) Times,
    3 July, 2008 SLT 675, 2008 SCLR 484, 152 Sol Jo (no 27) 30, [2008] All ER
    (D) 26 (Jul) S59
Spirerose Ltd (in admin) v Transport for London (formerly London
    Underground Ltd) [2009] UKHL 44, [2009] 4 All ER 810, [2009] 1 WLR 1797,
    [2009] PTSR 1371, [2009] RVR 225, (2009) Times, 17 August, [2009] All ER
    (D) 324 (Jul) S23
Syed v DPP [2010] EWHC 81 (Admin), [2010] 1 Cr App Rep 480, 174 JP 97,
    [2010] 04 LS Gaz R 14, (2010) Times, 26 January, [2010] All ER (D) 48
    (Jan) S57
Szombathely City Court v Fenyvesi [2009] EWHC 231 (Admin), [2009] 4 All ER
    324, [2009] All ER (D) 202 (Feb) S12

T

Taylor v Centennial Newstan Pty Ltd [2009] NSWCA 276 .... S44
Taylor v Lawrence [2002] EWCA Civ 90, [2003] QB 528, [2002] 2 All ER 353,
    [2002] 3 WLR 640, [2002] 12 LS Gaz R 35, [2002] NLJR 221, (2002) Times,
    8 February, 146 Sol Jo LB 50, [2002] All ER (D) 28 (Feb) S10

Taylor Woodrow Property Co Ltd v Lonrho Textiles Ltd (1986) 52 P & CR 28,
    [1985] 2 EGLR 120, 275 Estates Gazette 632 .... S13
Transpower New Zealand Ltd v Taupo District Council [2007] NZHC 999 .... S32
Trent Taverns Ltd v Sykes (1999) Eu LR 492, (1999) Times, 5 March, CA S12
Tse Mui Chun v HKSAR (2003) 6 HKCFAR 601 .... S52

U

U v Special Immigration Appeals Commission [2009] EWHC 3052 (Admin),
    [2010] 1 All ER 908, [2010] 2 WLR 1012, [2010] STC 493, [2010] PTSR 824,
    [2010] 2 FCR 309, [2009] SWTI 3167, [2009] All ER (D) 22 (Dec); affd on
    other grounds sub nom R (on the application of Cart) v Upper Tribunal
    [2010] EWCA Civ 859, [2010] NLJR 1115, (2010) Times, 4 October, [2010]
    SWTI 2272, [2010] All ER (D) 246 (Jul) S8
Uganda Co (Holdings) v Government of Uganda [1979] 1 Lloyd's Rep 481, 123 Sol
    Jo 48 .... S13
UK Waste Management, Re [1999] NICA 2 .... S25
United States Securities and Exchange Commission v Manterfield [2009] EWCA Civ
    27, [2009] 2 All ER 1009, [2009] 2 All ER (Comm) 941, [2009] 1 Lloyd's Rep
    399, (2009) Times, 18 March, [2009] All ER (D) 225 (Jan) S15

V

Vector Ltd v Transpower New Zealand Ltd [1999] 3 NZLR 646 .... S13
Victims Compensation Fund Corporation v Brown (2003) 201 ALR 260 .... S11, S57

W

WD, Re [2007] Scot CS CSOH 139 .... S48
Waitakere CC v Bennett [2008] NZCA 428 .... S20
Walker v New South Wales (1994) 182 CLR 45, 49 .... S21
Wang v Minster for Immigration & Multicultural Affairs (1997) 71 FCR 386, 396 ..... S25, S49
Ward v Chief Adjudication Officer [1998] EWCA Civ 1552 .... S32, S36
Ward-Price v Mariners Haven Inc (2001) 57 OR (3d) 410 .... S50
Warren v Random House Group Ltd [2008] EWCA Civ 834, [2009] QB 600,
    [2009] 2 All ER 245, [2009] 2 WLR 314, [2009] EMLR 1, [2008] All ER (D)
    224 (Jul) S51
Wealthcare Financial Planning Pty Ltd v Financial Industry Complaints Service Ltd
    (2009) 69 ACSR 418 .... S28
Webster, Re [2009] EWCA Civ 59, [2009] 2 All ER 1156, [2009] 1 FCR 673,
    [2009] 1 FLR 1378, [2009] Fam Law 381, 153 Sol Jo (no 7) 31, [2009] All ER
    (D) 106 (Feb) S39
Webster v Norfolk County Council [2009] EWCA Civ 59, [2009] 2 All ER 1156,
    [2009] 1 FCR 673, [2009] 1 FLR 1378, [2009] Fam Law 381, 153 Sol Jo (no 7)
    31, [2009] All ER (D) 106 (Feb) S39
Welwyn Hatfield Borough Council v Secretary of State for Communities and Local
    Government [2010] EWCA Civ 26, [2010] 2 P & CR 157, [2010] PTSR 1296,
    [2010] 13 EG 84, [2010] 07 LS Gaz R 19, 154 Sol Jo (no 5) 28, [2010] All ER
    (D) 199 (Jan) S49
Wicken (Litigation Guardian of) v Harssar (2004) 73 OR (3d) 600 .... S47, S48
Woodward v Abbey National plc [2005] 4 All ER 1346, [2005] ICR 1702,
    [2005] IRLR 782, [2005] All ER (D) 64 (Aug), EAT; revsd sub nom Woodward
    v Abbey National plc [2006] EWCA Civ 822, [2006] 4 All ER 1209,
    [2006] ICR 1436, [2006] IRLR 677, (2006) Times, 11 July, 150 Sol Jo LB 857,
    [2006] All ER (D) 253 (Jun) S4

X

XC v Special Immigration Appeals Commission [2009] EWHC 3052 (Admin),
[2010] 1 All ER 908, [2010] 2 WLR 1012, [2010] STC 493, [2010] PTSR 824,
[2010] 2 FCR 309, [2009] SWTI 3167, [2009] All ER (D) 22 (Dec); affd on
other grounds sub nom R (on the application of Cart) v Upper Tribunal
[2010] EWCA Civ 859, [2010] NLJR 1115, (2010) Times, 4 October, [2010]
SWTI 2272, [2010] All ER (D) 246 (Jul) S8

Y

Yarl's Wood Immigration Ltd v Bedfordshire Police Authority [2009] EWCA Civ
1110, [2010] 2 All ER 221, [2010] 2 WLR 1322, [2009] All ER (D) 246
(Oct) S33
Yearworth v North Bristol NHS Trust [2009] EWCA Civ 37, [2010] QB 1,
[2009] 2 All ER 986, [2009] 3 WLR 118, 107 BMLR 47, (2009) Times,
10 February, 153 Sol Jo (no 5) 27, [2009] All ER (D) 33 (Feb) S30
Yemshaw v Hounslow LBC [2009] EWCA Civ 1543 .... S35

Z

Zaoui v Attorney-General (No 2) [2006] 1 NZLR 289 .... S41

Supplementary Table of Statutes

Animals Act 1971
  s 5(2) S55
Anti-terrorism, Crime and Security
    Act 2001
  s 109 .... S21
Care Standards Act 2000
  s 82(4)(b) S60
Companies Act 1985 .... S7
  s 36C(1) S4, S14
  s 356 .... S6
  s 726(1) S49
  s 736, 736A S19
Courts and Legal Services Act 1990
  s 27(2)(c) S9
  s 28 .... S9
Criminal Justice Act 1967
  s 91(1) S22
Criminal Justice Act 2003
  s 44(6) S37
  s 78 .... S52
  s 166(3)(b) S26
  s 269, 270 .... S23
Criminal Justice and Immigration
    Act 2008
  s 79 .... S14
  s 149 .... S14
  s 153(2) S14
  Sch 28 .... S14
Criminal Law Act 1967
  s 14 .... S39
Defamation Act 1996
  s 2–4 .... S51
Extradition Act 2003
  s 34 .... S42
Firearms Act 1968
  s 5(1A) S19
Gaming Act 1968
  s 52(1) S53
Healthcare Identifiers Act 2010
  s 15 .... S55

Human Rights Act 1998 .... S15
  s 3(1) S41, S60
Hunting Act 2004
  s 1 .... S52
Immigration Act 1971
  s 22(2)(a) S57, S58
Immigration, Asylum and Nationality
    Act 2006
  s 54 .... S34
Immigration (Treatment of Claimants,
    Etc) Act 2004
  s 19(3)(b) S26
Income Tax (Earnings and Pensions)
    Act 2003 .... S13
  Pt 7 .... S3
Interpretation Act 1901
  s 13(3) S55
Interpretation Act 1978
  s 6(c) S31
Interpretation Act 2005 .... S30
Limitation Act 1980
  s 2 .... S59
Local Government and Public
    Involvement in Health Act 2007
  s 5(3)(c) S30
  s 7(1)(b) S30
Patents Act 1977
  s 130(7) S34
Police and Criminal Evidence
    Act 1984
  s 17(1)(e) S57
Public Order Act 1986
  s 11 .... S58
Restrictive Trade Practices Act 1976 ..... S24
Sexual Offences Act 2003
  s 72 .... S21
Terrorism Act 2000
  s 1 .... S34

Supplementary Table of Statutory Instruments

Supplementary Table of European Material

Supplementary Table of Foreign Enactments

Introduction

In the preface to the Fifth Edition of his great work, Francis Bennion stated that the writing had comprised:

> "thorough rereading and reconsidering because owing to advancing years (I am 85) this is the last edition I shall prepare myself, and I wish to pass on a work that is in the best condition possible".

True to his word, the Fifth Edition built significantly on its predecessors and the task of updating the Fifth Edition through a Supplement fell to me. However, it would be a mistake to suppose that Francis Bennion had no further involvement with the Supplement. His detailed updating notes have greatly assisted me in performing my role.

Even with this assistance, I found the Supplement a daunting task. Nearly 60 years of age is not all that separates Francis Bennion and myself. I have neither his academic nor practical standing. I am left with the energy that flows from my deep enjoyment of legal research and writing. In addition:

– I am presently teaching an advanced undergraduate elective subject in statutory interpretation. As I have elsewhere indicated, I hope that such a subject will one day become a mandatory part of the legal curriculum across the common law world; and
– my present jurisdiction, Hong Kong, is one of the few that has overtly adopted the essence of Francis Bennion's approach to statutory interpretation, being the basic rule set out in section 193 (*Medical Council of Hong Kong v Chow Siu Shek* (2000) 3 HKCFAR 144). I have submitted an article on this development to the *Hong Kong Law Journal*.
– Francis Bennion has regularly complained that, while a global methodology for all questions of statutory interpretation lies at the heart of his work, it has been ignored by advocates and judges. I am currently producing an analysis of the methodology, which I will submit to an English law journal.

I cannot succeed Francis Bennion and, whatever my additions, *Bennion on Statutory Interpretation* will always be his work. Yet, I hope I can bring something thereto. In particular, given my background, I hope *Bennion on Statutory Interpretation* will one day cover a wide range of common law systems. I have begun this project by adding to the Supplement authorities of various ages from, in particular, Australia, Canada, Hong Kong, New Zealand and South Africa, especially where those authorities have expressly considered *Bennion on Statutory Interpretation*. As to English law, the Supplement covers the period 1 April 2007 to 1 July 2010. In these endeavours, and many more, I am indebted to Sarah Cheng.

Professor Oliver Jones

Parts I to XXIX

Updates

INTRODUCTION

(p 6)
In footnote 3 delete second sentence and insert–

See generally Devolution: Its Effect on the Practice of Legislation at Westminster HK Paper 192, 18 November 2004, including the paper by C Himsworth at App 1. See also, by the same author, 'Devolution and its Jurisdictional Assymetries', (2007) 70 MLR 31–58.

S 1

(p 23)
In footnote 5, at end insert–

Compare the remark by the Hon Murray Gleeson, when Chief Justice of Australia, 'I shall use the words "interpretation" and "construction" interchangeably, as they are in the Acts Interpretation Act 1901 (Cth) in 'The meaning of legislation: context, purpose and respect for fundamental rights" ' (2009) 20 Public Law Review 26, xx.

S 2

(p 25)
After sideheading Subsection (2), insert–

This subsection of the Code has been judicially approved.[5A]

(p 25)
In the new footnote indicator 5A, insert–

See the decision of the Newfoundland Supreme Court, Appeal Division in *R v Wonderland Gifts Ltd* (1996) 140 Nfld & PEIR 219, [20].

(p 25)
In footnote 6, delete citation and insert–

[1988] QB 493.

(p 25)
In footnote 7, at end insert–

See also paper dated April 1997 by Legal Department of Hong Kong available at www. legco. gov. hk/ yr96–97/ english/ panels/ ajls/ papers/ zzz2604z.htm.

(p 25)
In footnote 10, at end insert–

See also the endorsement of the term 'legal meaning' by the High Court of Australia in *Project Blue Sky v Australian Broadcasting Authority* (1998) 194 CLR 355, 384.

S 3

(p 25)   **After heading 'Comment on Code s 3', at end of first sentence, insert footnote indicator 10A, with following text in footnote–**

Use of the term 'real doubt' was effectively endorsed by the UK Supreme Court in *Grays Timber Products Ltd v Revenue and Customs Commissioners* [2010] 1 WLR 497, 509 where Lord Walker JSC said: 'I am left in real doubt as to whether Parliament has, in Part 7 of ITEPA 2003, enacted [a certain scheme].'

S 4

(p 27)   **After reference to 'Companies Act 1985 s 36C(1)', insert–**

(repealed)

(p 27)   **In footnote 4, delete citations and insert–**

[2002] Ch 273.

S 6

(p 32)   **In footnote 3, replace 'Charleson' with–**

Charlson

(p 32)   **Also in footnote 3, add to citation–**

[2007] 3 All ER 163

S 7

(p 36)   **In Example 7.3, after 'Conditional Fee Agreements Regulations 2000', insert–**

(repealed)

(p 36)   **In footnote 4, at end insert–**

See also *Hollins v Russell* [2003] EWCA Civ 718; [2003] 4 All ER 590.

S 8

(p 38)   **In footnote 6, at end insert–**

See also *Woodward v Abbey National Plc (No 2)* [2005] 4 All ER 1346.

(p 39)   **In footnote 7, at end insert–**

; *Nolan v Wright* [2009] 3 All ER 823.

S 9

(p 41)   **At end of fifth paragraph, immediately before subheading 'Mistake as a defence', insert–**

In 2008, the Court of Appeal stated that 'Ignorance of the law is no defence, but it can sometimes amount to mitigation': *R v Rahman (Abdul)* [2008] 4 All ER 661, [43]. The Court proceeded to allow in mitigation the fact that the appellant was aware of the general nature of recently enacted anti-terrorism legislation, but unaware that his conduct had, as a result, become an offence. The Court indicated, though, that such mitigation would be unlikely for that offence in the future, due to anticipated knowledge of the 'successful prosecutions that have now taken place': *Ibid*.

(p 41)   **In footnote 10, delete citations and insert–**

[2007] 1 AC 558.

S 10

(p 45)   **After heading 'Comment on Code s 10', at end of first sentence, before footnote indicator 1, insert–**

and in a 2000 case.

(p 45)   **In footnote 1, at end insert–**

; *R v B* [2000] EWCA Crim 42.

(p 45)   **In second sentence, delete 'in a 2000 case' and insert–**

in another 2000 case.

(p 45)   **In footnote 8, at end insert–**

Note, though, that Lord Steyn remarked that the distinction and 'its many artificial requirements' had 'outlived their usefulness'. Instead, 'the emphasis ought to be on the consequences of non-compliance, and posing the question whether Parliament can fairly be taken to have intended total invalidity': *ibid*, [23]. Lords Cullen and Brown agreed: *ibid*, [52], [70].

(p 46)   **In footnote 5, at end insert–**

See also the decision of the Divisional Court in *R (Bromley) v Secretary of State for Justice* [2010] EWHC 112 (Admin), [43].

(p 46)   **In footnote 7, at end insert–**

; *Adorian v Commissioner of Police* [2009] 4 All ER 227, [42].

(p 47)   **In footnote 3, at end insert–**

In the context of civil procedure, the disobedience may be reflected in costs: *Adorian v Commissioner of Police* [2009] 4 All ER 227.

(p 48)   **In the final paragraph, at the end of the second sentence, immediately before Example 10.4, insert footnote indicator 7A and, in the footnote, insert–**

This passage was considered in *Goshawk Dedicated (No 2) Ltd v Bank of Scotland* [2006] 2 All ER 610, [108].

(p 49)   **At end of sentence beginning 'A duty to do a thing in a certain way', insert footnote indicator 4A and, in the footnote, insert–**

This passage was applied by an Australian tribunal in *Campbell v Tow Truck Directorate of Victoria* (1995/34314) [2000] VICCAT 3.

(p 52)   **At the end of the first sentence, insert footnote indicator 1 and, in the footnote, insert–**

This sentence was applied in *R v B* [2000] EWCA Crim 42.

(p 52)   **Replace footnote indicators 1 to 10 with footnote indicators 2 to 11 respectively.**

(p 52)   **Before subheading 'Interference with property', insert–**

Similarly, procedures required of the police in the context of a search of a person may, if not observed, lead to a conviction arising out of the search being quashed.[7A]

(p 52)   **In the new footnote indicator 7A, insert–**

R v Bristol [2007] EWCA Crim 3214.

(p 56)   **In Example 10.25, after 'Companies Act 1985 s 356' insert–**

(repealed).

(p 56)   **In footnote 2, at end of second sentence, insert–**

This passage was approved in *Glasgow City Council v AD* [2005] Scot SC 35, [22].

(p 56)   **In footnote 2, at end insert–**

Note that Parliament sometimes states expressly that purely technical contraventions are not to vitiate an act: see e g Proceeds of Crime Act 2002 s 14(11) and *Sekhon & Ors v R* [2002] EWCA Crim 2954 at [28].

S 11

(p 60)   **In Example 11.2, at end insert–**

(repealed)

S 12

(p 61)   **In footnote 7, at end insert–**

For an interesting discussion of the construction of a similar provision by
the High Court of Australia, see *Caltex Oil (Aust) Pty Ltd v Best* (1990)
170 CLR 516, 522.

(p 62)   **After paragraph beginning 'The law has taken the view', insert–**

Jurisdiction of courts Similarly, it has been held that, where a statutory
provision confers a jurisdiction on the courts, and the jurisdiction
necessarily involves interference with contractual rights agreed between
the parties, it would be inconsistent 'for the legislature at the same time
to allow for the parties to contract out of that interference'.[8A]

(p 62)   **In the newly created footnote indicator 8A, insert–**

Aribisala v St James Homes (Grosvenor Dock) Ltd [2007] EWHC 1694
(Ch), [36].

S 14

(p 71)   **In footnote 1, at end insert–**

See also, generally, *Morrison Sports Ltd v Scottish Power Plc* [2010]
1 WLR 1934, [29].

(p 74)   **In footnote 9, at end insert–**

As to the use of this provision in place of a relator action see Example
87.3 and *Birmingham City Council v Shafi and another* [2009] 1 WLR
1961; [2009] 3 All ER 127.

(p 74)   **In footnote 10, at end insert–**

See also the decision of the Ontario Court of Appeal in *McCombie v
Cadotte* (2001) 53 OR (3d) 704, [30].

(p 75)   **In footnote 2, at end insert–**

The passage to which this footnote relates was approved by the Ontario
Court of Appeal in *McCombie v Cadotte* (2001) 53 OR (3d) 704, [30].

(p 80)   **In footnote 6, at end insert–**

Note that the ombudsman, in exercising the supervisory duties, may be operating under enabling legislation which has not drawn the clear line necessary between standards of conduct justifying a finding of negligence and those justifying an adverse finding by an Ombudsman: *R (Attwood) v Health Service Commissioner* [2009] 1 All ER 415, [29]–[30], [35].

(p 83)   **In Example 14.20, after s 320, insert–**

(repealed)

S 15

(p 86)   **In footnote 2, at end insert–**

In *R (Bapio Action Ltd) v Secretary of State for the Home Department* [2008] 1 AC 1003 at 1018, Lord Rodger of Earlsferry said that the Interpretation Act 'expresses a principle of constitutional law of considerable practical importance: all Secretaries of State carry on Her Majesty's government and can, when required, exercise any of the powers conferred by statute on the Secretary of State.'

(p 88)   **At top of page, in first quotation, after 'Companies Act 1985' insert–**

(repealed)

(p 90)   **In footnote 1, after 'R v Crown Court at Stafford, ex p Shipley [1998] 2 All ER 465 insert–**

; *R (Newcastle City Council) v Berwick-upon-Tweed BC* [2008] EWHC 2369 (Admin) at [29],

S 17

(p 94)   **In footnote 3, at end insert–**

As to hybridity and appeals see *R (Langley) v Preston Crown Court* [2009] 1 WLR 1612, 1618–1619.

S 18

(p 100)   **In footnote 1, at end insert–**

As to judicial review in relation to cautions see *R (Guest) v DPP* [2009] EWHC 594; [2009] Crim LR 730. See further on judicial review *R (on the application of Corner House and another) v Director of Serious Fraud Office (BAE Systems plc, interested party)* [2009] 1 AC 756.

(p 100)   **In footnote 8, at end insert–**

Akin to the right of private prosecution is the right to bring proceedings
for contempt of court under CPR r. 32.14: see *KJM Superbikes Limited v
Hinton* [2008] EWCA Civ 1280. These are public law civil proceedings
with a criminal standard of proof: *Kirk v Walton* [2008] EWHC 1780
(QB), [2009] 1 All ER 257, at [25[–[27].

S 19

(p 104)   **In footnote 4, at end insert–**

There is, also, a 'separation, in national government, between the powers
of the executive and the powers of Parliament': *R (on the application of
Bradley and Others) v Secretary of State for Work and Pensions* [2009]
QB 114, 167, 169.

(p 108)   **In footnote 4, at end insert–**

See also *R (Sivasubramaniam) v Wandsworth* [2003] 2 All ER 160, [44].
Note the criticism of this approach, and alternative appeal to constitutional law, in *R (C) v Upper Tribunal* [2009] EWHC 3052, [33]. See
further p 109 footnote 8. As to ouster of jurisdiction by contract see
Code s 12, including the authority cited at p 62 footnote 9.

(p 109)   **In footnote 8, at end insert–**

Note that Lord Steyn has suggested that the ouster clause would be
ineffective, not due to the scope of its terms, but possibly as a matter of
constitutional law, representing a limit on the doctrine of parliamentary
sovereignty: *R (Jackson) v Attorney-General* [2006] 1 AC 262, 302–303.
Compare the view that the retention of judicial involvement despite
ouster clauses is referable to the rule of law and, in truth, an affirmation
of parliamentary sovereignty: *R (C) v Upper Tribunal* [2010] 1 All ER
908, [38]–[39].

(p 110)   **At end of first complete quotation, insert new paragraph–**

An *Anisminic* clause has also been contrasted by the Supreme Court of
the United Kingdom with a clause that, instead of purporting to remove
any judicial supervision of a determination by an inferior as to its own
jurisdiction, allocates scrutiny of a certain subject matter to a court or
other judicial body of like standing and authority to that of the High
Court, even if it operates with special procedures apt for the subject
matter and without a right of appeal.[2A] Indeed, it has been said that a
provision restricting appeals does not warrant 'any special rule of
construction'.[2B]

(p 110)   **In newly created footnote indicator 2A, insert–**

A v B [2010] 2 WLR 1, 9–10.

(p 110)   **In newly created footnote indicator 2B, insert–**

Okandeji v Bow Street Magistrates Court [2006] 1 WLR 674, 678–679.

(p 111)   **After subheading 'Inherent jurisdiction', in the first quotation,**
                        replace 'only the Supreme Court' with–

only the Supreme Court [of England and Wales].

(p 112)   **In footnote 2, delete second sentence and insert–**

As to practice directions, rules of court and similar matters see Example
45.2 and *Bovale Ltd v Secretary of State for Communities and Local
Government* [2009] 3 All ER 340.

(p 112)   **In footnote 5, at end insert–**

This is subject to additional step of the *McKenzie* friend being granted
rights of audience under the Courts and Legal Services Act 1990, as
discussed at the end of this page.

(p 112)   **In footnote 6, at end insert–**

For a full update regarding the use of a *McKenzie* friend see *Re: N (A
Child)* [2008] 1 WLR 2743.

(p 112)   **Delete the penultimate paragraph beginning 'The Courts and**
                        Legal Services Act' and insert–

The Courts and Legal Services Act 1990 ss 27 and 28 permit lay
representation in some circumstances. In particular, a *McKenzie* friend
may be granted rights of audience under s 27(2)(c). At least in the
context of the latter step, there is no general principle that exceptional
circumstances are required.[10A]

(p 112)   **In footnote indicator 11, delete text and insert–**

Re: N (A Child) [2008] 1 WLR 2743; Practice Note (Family Courts:
McKenzie Friends) (No 2) [2008] 1 WLR 2757.

(p 113)   **At end of sentence beginning 'A court has an inherent power',**
                                        insert–

Further, a court has power to recall and vary an order before it is
perfected[3A] and, in the case of an appellate court, even after perfection.[3B]

(p 113)   **In newly created footnote indicator 3A, insert–**

Paulin v Paulin [2009] 3 All ER 88n. See also, in Hong Kong, *HKSAR v
Tin's Label Factory Ltd* (unreported, Court of Final Appeal, Li CJ,
Bokhary Chan and Ribeiro PJJ and Lord Woolf of Barnes NPJ, FACC
5/2008, 5 December 2008) and the slip rule discussed on p 110 above.

(p 113)   **In newly created footnote indicator 3B, insert–**

Taylor v Lawrence [2003] QB 528. See also *Seray-Wurie v Hackney LBC*
[2002] 3 All ER 448; *Gregory v Turner* [2003] 2 All ER 1114.

(p 114)   **In footnote 1, at end delete–**

As to a court's power to reopen a judgment.

(p 118)   **After heading 'Open court principle', at end of first paragraph,
                                    insert–**

The principle has recently been described as "transparency" in the
current jargon'.[3A]

(p 118)   **In newly created footnote indicator 3A, insert–**

Re: N (A Child) [2008] 1 WLR 2743, 2748.

                                      S 20

(p 128)   **In footnote 7, at end insert–**

This article, and the distinction between judgment and discretion, has
been approved by the NSW Court of Appeal: *New South Wales Crime
Commission v Yu* [2009] NSWCA 349, [7].

(p 128)   **At end of penultimate paragraph, insert–**

Similarly, the Court of Appeal, including Lord Judge LCJ, recently said:

> '[A]lthough the distinction is a fine one, whenever the competency
> question is addressed, what is required is not the exercise of a
> discretion but the making of a judgment, that is whether the
> witness fulfils the statutory criteria. In short, it is not open to the
> judge to create or impose some additional but non-statutory
> criteria … '[8A]

(p 128)   **In newly created footnote indicator 8A, insert–**

R v Barker [2010] EWCA Crim 4, [39]. See also *R v Clarke* [2007]
EWCA Crim 2532, [29] and, in Australia, see, eg, *R v Smith* [2003]
NSWCCA 381, [95] and *Perpetual Trustee Company Limited v Albert
and Rose Khoshaba* [2006] NSWCA 41, [34].

(p 130)   **In footnote 2, at end insert–**

This may be affected by the extent to which the relevant pronouncement
is considered binding, a matter which will depend upon whether the
court intended to articulate a mere rule of practice, subject to subsequent
variation, or to lay down a rule of law, leaving no room for doubt: *A
Train & Sons Ltd v Fletcher* [2008] 4 All ER 699, at [11], [24]. See also
p 168 footnote 5.

(p 130)   **In footnote 3, at end insert–**

Re: N (A Child) [2008] 1 WLR 2743, 2753 (discretion conferred by Courts and Legal Services Act 1990 s 27(2)(c) to grant rights of audience to a layperson, including a *McKenzie* friend).

(p 131)   **In footnote 3, at end insert–**

See also the remark by Heydon J of the High Court of Australia in *Victims Compensation Fund Corporation v Brown* (2003) 201 ALR 260, at [10]: 'It is, of course, common for seemingly small points of construction to generate such sharp and evenly held differences of opinion …'.

S 21

(p 137)   **In footnote 12, at end insert–**

A similar statement has been made in relation to local authorities and illegal immigrants: *R (Clue) v Birmingham City Council* [2008] EWHC 3036 (Admin), [2].

(p 137)   **In paragraph beginning 'Judicial notice is also taken of the facts of nature', insert after second sentence–**

However, this does not necessarily extend to the perception of nature. Thus, in response to a submission as to a shift in the public perception of animals and their welfare, Lewison J did not consider 'an alleged social transformation of that kind is one of which the court can take judicial notice'.[14A]

(p 137)   **In newly created footnote indicator 14A, insert–**

Hanchett-Stamford v Attorney General [2009] Ch 173, 182.

S 23

(p 143)   **In footnote 8, at end insert–**

An additional reason has been propounded by Patten J, namely that construing statutory provisions in the absence of relevant factual information 'risks giving the words used an over-wide or unrealistic explanation …': *Re Metronet Rail BCV Ltd (In PPP Administration)* [2008] 2 All ER 75, at [21], [22].

(p 144)   **In footnote 3, at end insert–**

For a case similar to Example 23.1 see *R (Gilboy) v Liverpool City Council* [2009] QB 699, 704.

(p 150)   **In footnote 7, at end insert–**

As to the circumstances in which fresh evidence will be admitted on appeal: see *Hungary v Fenyvesi* [2009] 4 All ER 324 at [2].

S 26

(p 168)   **In the second paragraph, at the end of the third sentence insert–**

The *ratio decidendi* is binding. This can, albeit to a diminished extent, be contrasted with *obiter dictum*. The term derives from the Latin for a saying uttered 'by the way', originally two words ob iter. The OED (2nd edn 1992) cites, from the title page of Augustine Birrell's book *Obiter Dicta* (1884): 'An obiter dictum, in the language of the law, is a gratuitous opinion, an individual impertinence [that is something strictly not pertinent] which, whether it be wise or foolish, right or wrong, bindeth none – not even the lips that utter it.'

In 2008 Mummery LJ said: 'There is no point in cluttering up the law reports with *obiter dicta*, which could, in some cases, embarrass a court having to decide the issue later on'. [3A] Nevertheless they are so cluttered up. Indeed, appellate courts in England and the Commonwealth have gone so far as to create a category of *obiter dicta* that are authoritative, ie pronouncements so fully considered by the court as to bind lower courts in the same way as the *ratio decidendi*.[3B]

(p 168)   **In newly created footnote 3A, insert–**

Housden v Conservators of Wimbledon and Putney Commons [2008] 3 All ER 1038, [31].

(p 168)   **In newly created footnote 3B, insert–**

Trent Taverns Ltd v Sykes [1999] Eu LR 492, 497–498; *Crehan v Courage Ltd* [1999] EU LR 834, 895; *R v Henry* [2005] 3 SCR 609, [57]; *Farah Constructions Pty Ltd v Say Dee Pty Ltd* (2007) 230 CLR 89, [134], [158].

(p 174)   **In footnote 5, after 'followed by the Court of Appeal in' insert–**

R v BR [2003] 4 All ER 882 and

(p 174)   **In footnote 5, delete sentence beginning 'This passage of the Code'
              and insert in footnote 4 at the end.**

(p 174)   **Delete sentence beginning 'The doctrine of course' and the
              sentence beginning 'It also applies'. Insert–**

The doctrine applies in the Court of Appeal in relation to previous decisions of that court. However, there is high authority that the rule is not generally available to a court in relation to a decision of a court placed above it in the judicial hierarchy.

(p 174)   **In footnote 5, at beginning insert–**

Broome v Cassell & Co Ltd [1972] AC 1027, 1054, 1113, 1131, 1132; *Baker v R* [1975] AC 774, 788, 795; *Miliangos v George Frank (Textiles) Ltd* [1976] AC 443, 477–480; *Algama v Minister for Immigration and Multicultural Affairs* (2001) 115 FCR 253, 261; *Inglis v Loh Lai*

Kuen Eda [2005] 3 HKC 115, 127. The exception, if it be one, is where a lower court judge is faced with irreconcilable decisions by the same higher court, where the later decision has not expressly considered the earlier: *Broome v Cassell & Co Ltd* [1972] AC 1027, 1107; *Uganda Co (Holdings) Ltd v Government of Uganda* [1979] 1 Lloyds Rep 481, 484; *Midland Bank Trust Co Ltd v Hett, Stubbs and Kemp* [1979] Ch 384, 405; *Taylor Woodrow Property Co Ltd v Lonrho Textiles Ltd* (1986) 52 P&CR 28, 39–40; *Manor Electronics Ltd v Dickson* (The Times, 8 February 1990).

(p 175)   **In footnote 1, delete ' [2006] UKHL 27, [2006] 3 All ER 1777'**
and insert–

[2007] 1 AC 307; *A v Hoare* [2008] 1 AC 844.

S 28

(p 188)   **In footnote 6, at beginning insert–**

This passage was applied by the Federal Court of Australia in *Seafarers' Retirement Fund Pty Ltd v Oppenhuis* (1999) 94 FCR 594, 597–598.

(p 191)   **In second sentence under sideheading 'Tax law rewrite project',**
after 'Income Tax (Earnings and Pensions) Act 2003', insert–

(repealed) (ITEPA 2003)

(p 191)   **In footnote 5, at end insert–**

Note that, on occasions, the fruits of the project have been undermined. In *Grays Timber Products Ltd v Revenue and Customs (Scotland)* [2010] 1 WLR 497, Lord Walker JSC said, on behalf of the United Kingdom Supreme Court, (at 501): 'It is regrettable that ITEPA 2003, which came into force on 6 April 2003 and was intended to rewrite income tax law (as affecting employment and pensions) in plain English, was almost at once overtaken by massive amendments which are in anything but plain English'. Lord Hope JPSC spoke, also with the agreement of the Court, to similar effect: *Ibid*, 515.

S 32

(p 198)   **Under sideheading 'Rug analogy', at sentence ending 'the Act is**
repealed', create footnote indicator 3A.

(p 198)   **In newly created footnote 3A insert–**

The foregoing sentences of the rug analogy were described by a majority of the New Zealand Court of Appeal as 'graphically put': *Vector Ltd v Transpower New Zealand Ltd* [1999] 3 NZLR 646, [53]. Their Honours added: 'To complete the metaphor, the rug and the floor must run the same way. The Bennion explanation is subject to the obvious qualification that the statute serves similar goals to the common law rule': *Ibid*.

(p 199)   **After Example 32.9, insert–**

Example 32.9A The common law offences of blasphemy and blasphemous libel were abolished by the Criminal Justice and Immigration Act 2008 ss 79, 149 and 153(2) and Sch 28. See further Francis Bennion, '*Farewell to the Blasphemy Laws*' (2008) 172 JPN 448.

(p 200)   **Toward bottom of page, after 'Companies Act 1985 s 36C(1)',
insert–**

(repealed)

S 33

(p 205)   **At the end of text, insert–**

Further, a Secretary of State may take some preparatory steps for the promotion of new legislation in advance of its enactment. However, the source and scope of this power, including a qualification of consistency with existing legislation, is controversial.[9A]

(p 205)   **In newly created footnote 9A, insert–**

R (Shrewsbury) v Secretary of State for Communities and Local Government [2008] 3 All ER 548. Compare *R (Raphael) v Highbury Corner Magistrates Court* [2010] EWHC 1502 (Admin). See also, generally, B V Harris, '*The "Third Source" of Authority for Government Action Revisited*' (2007) 123 LQR 225.

S 34

(p 208)   **In the second paragraph, at end of first sentence, insert footnote indicator 2A.**

(p 208)   **In newly created footnote indicator 2A, insert–**

This would explain why, according to some judges, a legitimate expectation created by one Secretary of State, as an emanation of the Crown, may not be disappointed by another such Secretary: *R (Bapio Action Ltd) v Secretary of State for the Home Department* [2008] 1 AC 1003, 1017–1018 (Lord Rodger), 1026 (Lord Mance). Compare 1016 (Lord Scott). As to this doctrine of legitimate expectation, see pp 1056–1057, 1060.

S 48

(p 238)   **In footnote 2, at end of first sentence, insert–**

See, generally, *R (Shields) v Secretary of State for Justice* [2010] QB 150.

(p 238)   **At the end of the second full paragraph, insert a new paragraph–**

While an exercise of prerogative legislative power is primary rather than subordinate, legislative power, it is, unlike a statute enjoying the principle of Parliamentary sovereignty, reviewable on ordinary principles of legality, rationality and procedural impropriety.[9A] Further, even where it has the effect of creating legal rights, a prerogative instrument may not be legislative in nature. In particular, it may comprise administrative policy as the future exercise of a prerogative power. A prerogative instrument, at least of this kind, may be made by a minister on his own authority.[9B] Controversy exists over whether there is a 'third power' which, apart from legislation and the prerogative, authorises state action.[9C]

(p 238)   **In newly created footnote 9A, insert–**

R (Bancoult) v Secretary of State for Foreign and Commonwealth Affairs [2009] 1 AC 453. As to the status of prerogative legislative power under the Human Rights Act 1998, see p 1374.

(p 238)   **In newly created footnote 9B, insert–**

Odelola v Secretary of State for the Home Department [2009] 1 WLR 1230.

(p 238)   **In newly created footnote 9C, insert–**

R (Shrewsbury) v Secretary of State for Communities and Local Government [2008] 3 All ER 548. See also, generally, B V Harris, *'The "Third Source" of Authority for Government Action Revisited'* (2007) 123 LQR 225.

(p 238)   **Under sideheading 'Acts of State', at end of second sentence, insert–**

Such jurisdiction as the courts have over the former is exceptional.[11A]

(p 238)   **In newly created footnote 11A, insert–**

See, in relation to acts of a foreign sovereign state, *R (on the application of Hilali) v City of Westminster Magistrates' Court* [2010] 1 WLR 241, 256. For the rule that municipal courts lack jurisdiction to entertain an action which is founded on an act of state, or which seeks to enforce the penal, fiscal or other public law of a foreign state, see *United States Securities and Exchange Commission v Manterfield* [2009] EWCA Civ 27, [2009] 2 All ER 1009. Compare, in relation to the conduct by the Crown of overseas affairs, *R (Gentle) v Prime Minister* [2007] QB 689, 713, affd: *R (Gentle) v Prime Minister* [2008] 1 AC 1356, 1367.

(p 238)   **Under sideheading 'Acts of State', at beginning of third sentence, delete 'The courts retain jurisdiction' and insert–**

However, the courts undoubtedly possess

(p 238)   **In footnote 12, at end insert–**

Compare *Christian v R* [2007] 2 AC 400, 409, 415, 419.

S 49

(p 242)   **In footnote 8 at end insert–**

See also *Government of Canada v Aronson* [1990] 1 AC 579, 610 where
the House of Lords felt 'it may be permissible to derive some slight
assistance' from the same.

S 58

(p 256)   **In footnote 8, at end insert–**

Similarly, where there is no duty to consult, but the delegate or other
decision-maker chooses to do so, 'the consultation must be carried out
properly. It must be undertaken at a time when the proposals are still at a
formative stage. Sufficient reasons [for the proposals] must be given to
allow those consulted to give intelligent consideration and an intelligent
response. There must also be adequate time for such a response': *R
(Boyejo) v Barnet LBC* [2009] EWHC 3261 (Admin), [67]. Again, the
product of the consultation must receive 'conscientious consideration':
R v North and East Devon Health Authority; Ex parte Coughlan [2001]
QB 213, 258.

(p 260)   **In footnote 2, delete text and insert–**

[2006] Ch 337. See also the discussion in *Oyarce v Cheshire County
Council* [2008] 4 All ER 907, [17], [59] regarding whether it would be
ultra vires for delegated legislation implementing a Community obligation go any wider than was required by that obligation.

S 59

(p 263)   **At beginning of Comment on Code s 59, insert–**

This section of the Code has twice been approved by the Court of
Appeal.

(p 263)   **In newly created footnote 1, insert–**

See *R v Secretary of State for Social Security; Ex parte Sarwar* [1997]
3 CMLR 648, 651–652; *Secretary of State for Work and Pensions v
Deane* [2010] EWCA Civ 699, [37]. It was also recognized, but not
applied to the facts, in *HM Revenue & Customs v Dunwood Travel Ltd*
[2008] EWCA Civ 174 at [14], [15], [23].

(p 263)   **Replace footnote indicators 1 to 9 with footnote indicators 2 to 10.**

(p 263)   **In renumbered footnote 10 at end, insert–**

This passage was applied by the Federal Court of Australia in *Re Aboriginal Development Commission* [1988] FCA 160, [37].

                                  S 60

(p 264)   **In footnote 1, at end insert–**

Indeed, there are instances where the courts have applied provisions of the Code to delegated legislation. See, for example, the decisions of the Federal Court of Australia in *Hanna v Migration Agents Registration Authority* (1999) 94 FCR 358, 363 (Code s 271) and *Ignatious v Minister for Immigration & Multicultural & Indigenous Affairs* (2004) 139 FCR 254, 268.

(p 265)   **In footnote 10, at end insert–**

This passage was considered in *Hertfordshire CC v Veolia Water Central Ltd* [2010] EWHC 278 (QB), [37]. The Court should also have considered other passages, including Code ss 157–160, 195 and 287.

(p 266)   **In footnote 1, at end insert–**

See also the discussion of Code s 60, and note of caution sounded, in *PNPF Trust Co Ltd v Taylor* [2010] EWHC 1573 (Ch), [479].

                                  S 64

(p 268)   **In Comment on Code s 64, insert at beginning of section–**

This section of the Code has been judicially approved.[5A]

(p 268)   **In newly created footnote 5A, insert–**

Law Society of Upper Canada v Ontario (Attorney-General) (1995) 21 OR (3d) 666, [19].

                                  S 78

(p 290)   **At end of paragraph beginning 'However it is submitted', insert footnote indicator 4A.**

(p 290)   **In newly created footnote 4A, insert–**

This sentence was applied by the Supreme Court of Victoria in *Shields v Chief Commissioner of Police* [2008] VSC 2 at [102]–[104].

(p 291)   **In footnote 3, delete '[2002] UKHL 27, [2002] 3 All ER 721 at [20]'**
and insert–

[2003] 1 AC 120, 133–134. Compare *Craftrule Ltd v 41–60 Albert Palace Mansions (Freehold) Ltd* [2010] EWHC 1230 (Ch), [28] where the above passage was considered inapplicable so long as 'the point of so doing is not to modify or contradict the meaning of [the relevant provision] as originally enacted, but merely to provide confirmation [through the fact] that Parliament [later] intended [the provision] to bear the same meaning as it always had'. This is difficult to reconcile with the authorities just mentioned, especially *Brown*, which rejected the use of the amending Act for assistance in any form, obviously including confirmation, subject only to Code s 234.

S 81

(p 294)   **In footnote 4, at end of second sentence, insert–**

It has been justified by reference to the 'primary law making role of Parliament', while also restricted as 'only appropriate where there is a genuine doubt about the effect of the statutory provision in question': *R (Spath Holme Ltd) v Secretary of State for the Environment, Transport and Regions* [2001] 2 AC 349, 383.

S 82

(p 297)   **In footnote 1, at end insert–**

and *Revenue and Customs Commissioners v Stringer* [2009] 4 All ER 1205, [28].

S 85

(p 301)   **At beginning of Comment on Code s 85, insert–**

This section of the code was approved by an Australian court in a 1995 case.

(p 301)   **In newly created footnote 1, insert–**

See the decision of the Full Court of the Supreme Court of Victoria in *R v Omarjee* (1995) 79 A Crim R 355, [46].

(p 301)   **Replace footnote indicators 1 to 9 with footnote indicators 2 to 10.**

(p 301)   **At end of fourth full paragraph, before sideheading 'Types of**
repeal', insert–

Thus, while it is possible for repealing legislation that contains successor provisions to those repealed to divide its work into repealing provisions and enacting provisions,[4A] the same can be achieved by a single set of new provisions expressed to be in substitution of the existing provisions.[4B]

(p 301)   **In newly created footnote 4A, insert–**

Macmillan & Co v Dent [1907] 1 Ch 107, 123–124.

(p 301)   **In newly created footnote 4B, insert–**

Such substitution was considered 'clearly an express repeal' by the Full
Court of the Supreme Court of Victoria in *R v Omarjee* (1995) 79 A
Crim R 355.

S 87

(p 304)   **In Comment on Code s 87, at end of second paragraph, before
Example 87.1, insert footnote indicator 3A.**

(p 304)   **In newly created footnote indicator 3A, insert–**

In previous editions of this work, the foregoing paragraph ended with the
sentence: 'Other interpretative criteria may indicate implied repeal, for
example the commonsense construction rule or the presumption that
Parliament wishes to avoid an anomalous result'. The sentence was
criticised by Buxton LJ (dissenting) in *O'Byrne v Secretary of State for
Environment, Transport & Regions* [1996] EWCA Civ 499, [26]. In
essence, his Lordship saw the sentence as contrary to the notion that the
'court will not lightly find a case of implied repeal, and the test for it is a
high one': *Ibid*, [22]. Accordingly, the sentence has been removed.

(p 305)   **Delete the third paragraph and replace it with the following, while
leaving the contents of footnotes 8 to 9 unchanged–**

In an unreported 1998 case, Popplewell J adopted Code s 87(1). He held
that the Firearms Act 1968 s 5(1A) (prohibition of ownership etc without
permission of a gun etc) impliedly 'gave the citizen the right to hold
arms'. In the latter respect, he was mistaken. The wording of the
provision in question, not included in the judgment, is:

> 'That the Subjects which are Protestants may have Arms for their
> Defence suitable to their Conditions *and as allowed by Law*'.

S 89

(p 309)   **In footnote 4, at end insert–**

See also *Majeau Carrying Co Pty Ltd v Coastal Rutile Ltd* (1973) 129
CLR 48, 51–52; *Oceania Manufacturing Co Ltd v Pang Kwong-Hon*
[1979] HKLR 445, 448–449, 452.

(p 309)   **In footnote 6, at end insert–**

See also the use to which the above discussion was put in *Radin v Vekic*
[1997] NSWSC 234.

S 91

(p 311)   **In Example 91.1, after 'Companies Act 1985 ss 736 and 736A',
insert–**

(repealed)

S 96

(p 314)   **At end of Code s 96, insert footnote indicator 2A.**

(p 314)   **In newly created footnote 2A, insert–**

Code s 96 was approved in *Quinlivan v Governor of Portlaoise Prison*
[1998] 2 IR 113. See also *Mullins v Harnett* [1998] 4 IR 426.

(p 314)   **In footnote 3, at end insert–**

The above discussion was approved in *Quinlivan v Governor of Portlaoise Prison* [1997] IEHC 181, [1998] 2 IR 113.

(p 315)   **In footnote 1, at end insert–**

See also *R v Cartwright* [2007] EWCA Crim 2581, [27]–[30].

S 97

(p 317)   **In footnote 3, at end insert–**

and by the British Columbia Court of Appeal in *S (L) v P (E)* (1999) 67
BCLR (3d) 254, [51].

(p 317)   **At the end of the second paragraph, after Example 97.2, insert a
new paragraph–**

Furthermore, some judges have suggested that the presumption does not
apply in relation to an executive statement of policy as to the future
exercise of statutory or prerogative powers.[4A]

(p 317)   **In newly created footnote 4A, insert–**

Odelola v Secretary of State for the Home Department [2009] 1 WLR
1230, 1240–1241, cf 1233, 1243.

(p 317)   **In passage beginning 'It is important to grasp', at end insert
footnote indicator 5A.**

(p 317)   **In newly created footnote 5A, insert–**

This passage has been approved by the New Zealand Court of Appeal:
Waitakere CC v Bennett [2008] NZCA 428, [52].

(p 319)   **At end of second complete paragraph, before Example 97.5, insert footnote indicator 4A.**

(p 319)   **In newly created footnote 4A, insert–**

This passage was approved in *Quinlivan v Governor of Portlaoise Prison* [1997] IEHC 181, [1998] 2 IR 113 and *Mullins v Harnett* [1998] 4 IR 426.

S 98

(p 320)   **In footnote 6, at end insert–**

; and *R v Tran Viet Tran* [1992] 2 HKLR 184, 188–189.

S 103

(p 329)   **In Comment on Code s 103, at beginning insert–**

This section of the Code has been judicially approved.[3A]

(p 329)   **In newly created footnote 3A, insert–**

See *Serious Organized Crime Agency v Perry* [2009] EWHC 1960 (Admin), [50], where Foskett J rightly recognised that a statement of the extent of an Act in terms of the territories of the United Kingdom to which the Act applied did not decide whether or not it had any application outside of those territories. See further Code ss 130–132.

S 104

(p 331)   **In footnote 8, at end insert–**

For an affirmation of this approach by the House of Lords, see *Davidson v Scottish Ministers* [2005] UKHL 74.

S 105

(p 335)   **In footnote 2, at end insert–**

Note, though, the criticism in *Bocardo SA v Star Energy UK Onshore Ltd* [2010] Ch 100, 122.

(p 335)   **In footnote 3, at end insert–**

As to the substrata beneath the surface of the land, see *Bocardo SA v Star Energy UK Onshore Ltd* [2010] Ch 100.

S 106

(p 336)   **In footnote 1, at end insert–**

See also the reference by the House of Lords to the 'well-established canon of construction that requires clear language if an Act is to be given extra-territorial effect': *King v Serious Fraud Office* [2009] 1 WLR 718, 725.

S 113

(p 343)   **In footnote 2, at end insert–**

See also, generally, *R (Barclay) v Secretary for Justice* [2009] 2 WLR 1205.

S 128

(p 360)   **In footnote 2, at beginning insert–**

Walker v New South Wales (1994) 182 CLR 45, 49; *Lawson v Serco Ltd* [2004] 2 All ER 200, [16].

(p 360)   **In footnote 2, at end insert–**

See also *Masri v Consolidated Contractors International Co SAL* [2010] 1 AC 90, 133, where Lord Mance, speaking for the House of Lords, approved of Code s 128, adding '[it] may not apply, at any rate with the same force, to English subjects ...but that is presently irrelevant'. The position of such subjects is in fact dealt with by Code s 131.

(p 362)   **In footnote 1, at end insert–**

See further *R (Bancoult) v Secretary of State For Foreign and Commonwealth Affairs* [2009] 1 AC 453, 488, 506–507, 512.

S 129

(p 366)   **In footnote 5, at end insert–**

See also *Walker v New South Wales* (1994) 182 CLR 45, 49–50.

S 131

(p 380)   **At end of first paragraph, delete '(repealed) and Anti-terrorism, Crime and Security Act 2001 s 109' and insert–**

(repealed); Anti-terrorism, Crime and Security Act 2001 s 109 and Sexual Offences Act 2003 s 72 (sex tourism).

S 133

(p 387)   **In 'Comment on Code s 133', at end of second sentence insert–**

This sentence and Code s 133 were considered by the Divisional Court in *Kennet District Council v Young & Ors* [1999] RTR 235, 242–243 and by the Federal Court of Australia in *Re: Luckins; Ex parte Columbia Pictures Industries Inc* (1996) 67 FCR 549, 556–557.

(p 388)   **In footnote 3, at end insert–**

In reaching this conclusion, Sedley J considered Code s 134: *Ibid*, 242–243.

S 136

(p 394)   **In footnote 4, at end insert–**

As to a limit on that function, see also *Mastercigars Direct Ltd v Withers LLP* [2009] 1 WLR 881, 919 where Morgan J revealed that his assessors did not agree with parts of his decision.

(p 394)   **In footnote 6, at end insert–**

and *Re: B (Children)* [2009] 1 AC 11, 38.

S 139

(p 403)   **At bottom of page, at the end of the sentence beginning 'For another example', insert–**

As to the use, in essence, of selective comminution by a trial judge when directing a jury and approval of his doing so on appeal, see *R v Ikram* [2009] 1 WLR 1419, 1432–1433.

S 144

(p 422)   **In footnote 6, delete text and insert–**

[2006] 2 AC 543.

(p 422)   **In footnote 7, delete text and insert–**

Ibid, 556, 569. Note that the accrual of a cause of action for a sum recoverable by virtue of an enactment is a question of a construction of that enactment. In general, though, accrual occurs notwithstanding that the sum remains to be quantified: *Hillingdon LBC v ARC Ltd (No 1)* [1999] Ch 139, 147, 153–154, 157; *Legal Services Commission v Rasool* [2008] 1 WLR 2711, 2722.

S 145

(p 426)   **At end of first sentence, before sideheading 'Law and fact', insert–**

Relevance may fall to be determined by implication.

> *Example 145.6* Section 91(1) of the Criminal Justice Act 1967
> says: 'any person who in any public place is guilty while drunk of
> disorderly behaviour, shall be liable on summary conviction to a
> fine not exceeding level 3 on the standard scale'. Under the
> ordinary and natural meaning of the relevant terms, this means that
> the defendant must be drunk by the voluntary consumption of
> alcohol and also that the disorderly behaviour must not be acci-
> dental. Accordingly, it is not relevant to ask whether the defendant
> had specific drunken intent or was reckless.[1A]

(p 426)   **In newly created footnote 1A, insert–**

Carroll v Director of Public Prosecutions [2009] EWHC 554 (Admin).

S 146

(p 427)   **In Comment on Code s 146, at end of second sentence, insert
footnote indicator 2A.**

(p 427)   **In newly created footnote 2A, insert–**

Re: B (Children) [2009] 1 AC 11, 17, 25.

(p 427)   **In footnote 3, after 'at 704', insert–**

Re: B (Children) [2009] 1 AC 11, 17, 25.

S 149

(p 434)   **In footnote 8, at end insert–**

Compare *Kay v Commissioner of Police of Metropolis* [2008] 1 WLR
2723, 2742.

(p 435)   **In footnote 3, at end insert–**

For an extraordinary failure by prosecuting counsel to assist the court
properly see *Attorney General's Reference (No 24 of 2008)* [2008]
EWCA Crim 2936, [2009] 3 All ER 839, [30], [37]–[39] (failure to
mention Criminal Justice Act 2003 ss 269, 270). Of course, all of the
foregoing remarks as to assistance cannot apply to litigants in person or
other lay person exercising a right of audience unless they happen to be
legal experts. See further p 112.

S 150

(p 442)   **In footnote 2, at end insert–**

The above passage was adopted by the High Court of Australia in *Project Blue Sky v Australian Broadcasting Authority* (1998) 194 CLR 355, 384.

(p 442)   **In footnote 6, after '384' insert–**

; *Spirerose Ltd v Transport for London* [2009] 1 WLR 1797; *Bocardo SA v Star Energy UK Onshore Ltd* [2010] Ch 100.

S 158

(p 458)   **In Comment on Code s 158, at beginning, insert–**

This Section of the Code has been applied in England and overseas.[4A]

(p 458)   **In newly created footnote 4A, insert–**

For s 158(a), see *Hyde Park Residence Ltd v Secretary for Environment, Transport & Regions* (2000) 80 P&CR 419, 425. As to s 158 in its entirety, see *Kok Cheng Weng v Wiener* (2007) 2 SLR 709, 731–732.

(p 461)   **At end of Example 158.4, insert–**

Example indicator 158.4A In New South Wales, the Crimes Act 1900 s 319 created an offence of perverting the course of justice. Section 312 defined such perverting as 'obstructing, preventing, perverting or defeating the course of justice or the administration of the law'. The Court of Criminal Appeal declined to give the words 'administration of the law' their literal meaning, especially as doing so would criminalise 'a very wide range of conduct, including conduct that was not previously unlawful'. Rather, their Honours understood those words as 'the administration of the civil and criminal law by courts and tribunals', even though this understanding 'differ[ed] little, if at all, from the expression 'the course of justice".[2A]

(p 461)   **In newly created footnote indicator 2A, insert–**

Einfeld v R (2008) 51 MVR 200, [97], [99].

S 159

(p 463)   **In Comment on Code s 159, at beginning, insert–**

This section of the Code and the Comment thereon has been judicially considered.[2A]

(p 463)   **In newly created footnote 2A, insert–**

See the decision of the Alberta Court of Appeal in *Purba v Ryan* (2006)
61 Alta LR (4th) 112, [56].

S 163

(p 470)   **In footnote 2, delete 'another reference' and replace with–**

other references

(p 470)   **In footnote 2, after 'at [11]', insert–**

Giles v Rhind [2009] Ch 191, 200. See also p 1091 n 3.

S 165

(p 474)   **In footnote 2, at end insert–**

Note, though, that Gleeson CJ's successor as Chief Justice of Australia
once described legislative intention as a 'convenient phantom': *Sloane v
the Minister of Immigration, Local Government and Ethnic Affairs*
(1992) 37 FCR 429, 443 (French J). See also *R v Hughes* (2000) 202
CLR 535, 563 (Kirby J). Fortunately, Gleeson CJ's successor as Chief
Justice of New South Wales shares his belief in legislative intention:
Spigelman CJ, 'The Principle of Legality and the Clear Statement
Principle' (2005) 79 ALJ 769.

S 167

(p 479)   **At end of final paragraph, insert footnote indicator 5A.**

(p 479)   **In newly created footnote 5A, insert–**

For effective judicial recognition of dynamic processing, see *Smith v
Northamptonshire CC* [2009] 4 All ER 557, [77]–[78].

S 171

(p 484)   **In footnote 3, at end insert–**

In this respect, see the comment by the Court of Appeal that the
Restrictive Trade Practices Act 1976 'clearly represents a compromise
between a variety of commercial and political considerations': *Dale
Farm Dairy Group Ltd (t/a Northern Dairies) v Akram & Ors* [1998]
ICR 349, 356.

S 172

(p 489)   **In footnote 2, at end insert–**

For a refusal to draw an implication from a provision on the basis of an
ellipsis, due to inconsistency with another provision, see *Re: UK Waste
Management* [1999] NICA 2, [24].

(p 489)   **In paragraph beginning 'In such cases', at end of first sentence insert footnote indicator 4A.**

(p 489)   **In newly created footnote 4A, insert–**

For a discussion of implication in this context, see *Electricity Supply Assoc of Australia Ltd v ACCC* (2001) 113 FCR 230, 258.

S 173

(p 491)   **In Comment on Code s 173, at beginning, insert–**

This section of the Code has been judicially approved in several jurisdictions.

(p 491)   **In newly created footnote 1, insert–**

Wang v Minister for Immigration & Multicultural Affairs (1997) 71 FCR 386, 396.

S 174

(p 491)   **Replace footnote indicators 1 to 5 with footnote indicators 2 to 6.**

(p 494)   **In Comment on Code s 174, at beginning, before sideheading 'Guides to legislative intention', insert–**

This section of the Code has been judicially approved.[2A]

(p 494)   **In newly created footnote 2A, insert–**

Frucor Beverages Ltd v Rio Beverages Ltd [2001] 2 NZLR 604, [36]; *Re: Application by the Local Government Auditor* [2003] NIQB 21, [11].

(p 494)   **In footnote 6, at end of second sentence, insert–**

Further, in *Jayasinghe v Minister for Immigration & Ethnic Affairs* (1997) 76 FCR 301, 315, the Federal Court of Australia remarked '[t]he threshold of "necessity" has been rejected in favour of the formulation that the implication be "proper" '. See also *Liu Pik Han v Hong Kong Federation of Insurers Appeals Tribunal* [2005] 3 HKC 242, [23].

(p 495)   **In footnote 6, delete text and insert–**

This paragraph has been adopted by the Full Federal Court of Australia: *Austereo Ltd v Trade Practices Commission* (1993) 41 FCR 1, 37.

(p 497)   **In footnote 4, at end insert–**

See also *Nguyen v Minister for Health & Ageing* [2002] FCA 1241 (express power to revoke an approval granted to two people carried implicit power of partial revocation affecting only one of those people)

and *A v Securities and Futures Commission* [2008] 1 HKLRD 591, [23] (power to conduct interview impliedly enabled audio recording of interview).

(p 497)   **In footnote 8, at end of first sentence, insert–**

Brent London Borough Council v Risk Management Partners Ltd [2010] PTSR 349.

(p 498)   **In footnote 2, at end of second sentence, insert–**

See also *Dolphin Quays Development Ltd v Mills* [2008] 1 WLR 1829. This sentence was adopted in *Re: Application by the Local Government Auditor* [2003] NIQB 21, [12].

S 176

(p 502)   **In footnote 4, at end insert–**

The common law referred to in the Criminal Justice Act 2003 s 166(3)(b), being the totality principle relevant to consecutive sentences, exemplifies the need for further processing referred to by Donaldson J. As to the principle, see *R v Raza* [2009] EWCA Crim 1413; [2009] Crim LR 820.

S 177

(p 504)   **At end of final paragraph, insert, as a new paragraph–**

It should be noted that an interstitial articulation is not concerned with improving the drafting of the enactment in question. It keeps to the official wording except so far as is needed to express clearly the rival legal meanings. Defects in that wording, such as unnecessary repetition, should therefore be ignored. An interstitial articulation is directed solely to bringing out a possible operative legal meaning of the enactment.

S 179

(p 508)   **After Example 179.9, insert–**

Example 179.9A The House of Lords held that a requirement in the Asylum and Immigration (Treatment of Claimants, Etc.) Act 2004 s 19(3)(b) for the written permission of the Secretary of State to marry in the United Kingdom was to be read as if there were appended to it 'such permission not to be withheld in the case of a qualified applicant seeking to enter into a marriage which is not one of convenience and the application for, and grant of, such permission not to be subject to conditions which unreasonably inhibit exercise of the applicant's right under article 12 of the European Convention'.[10A]

(p 508)   **In newly created footnote 10A, insert–**

R (Baiai) v Secretary of State for the Home Department [2009] 1 AC 287, 306.

(p 508)   **In footnote 11, at end of first sentence, insert–**

Perrin v Northampton BC [2008] 1 WLR 1307, 1329–1330; *JT (Cameroon) v Secretary of State for the Home Department* [2009] 1 WLR 1411, 1418.

S 180

(p 513)   **In footnote 6, at end insert–**

This statement and the above commentary were adopted in *Securities and Futures Commission v Stock Exchange of Hong Kong Ltd* [1992] 1 HKLR 135, 144.

S 182

(p 517)   **In final paragraph, at end of third sentence, insert footnote indicator 9.**

(p 517)   **In newly created footnote 9, insert–**

This passage was adopted in *Mullins v Harnett* [1998] 4 IR 426.

S 185

(p 521)   **In Comment on Code s 185, at beginning, insert–**

This section of the Code has been judicially approved.[5A]

(p 521)   **In newly created footnote 5A, insert–**

Nangles Nurseries v Commissioners of Valuation [2008] IEHC 73, 41.

S 193

(p 544)   **In Comment on Code s 193, at beginning, insert–**

This section of the Code has been judicially approved.[6A]

(p 544)   **In newly created footnote 6A, insert–**

Medical Council of Hong Kong v Chow Siu Shek [2000] 2 HKLRD 674, 683.

(p 546)   **After sideheading 'The basic rule', at end of first sentence, insert footnote indicator 7.**

(p 546)   **In newly created footnote 7, insert–**

Note that different rules, including a rule of generous construction, may apply in jurisdictions with a written constitution. See, for example, *Ng Ka Ling & Others v Director of Immigration* (1999) 2 HKCFAR 4; *Department of Land Affairs v Goedgelegen Tropical Fruits* [2007] ZACC 12, [53], [55].

S 195

(p 549)   **In footnote 3, at end insert–**

This statement has been judicially approved: *R (RD) v Secretary of State for Work and Pensions* [2010] EWCA Civ 18, [47].

S 197

(p 552)   **In Comment on Code s 197, at beginning, insert–**

This section of the Code has been judicially approved.

(p 552)   **In newly created footnote 1, insert–**

Quinlivan v Governor of Portlaoise Prison [1998] 2 IR 113; *Mullins v Harnett* [1998] 4 IR 426.

(p 552)   **Replace footnote indicators 1 to 9 with footnote indicators 2 to 10.**

(p 553)   **At end of first complete paragraph, before Example 197.1, insert–**

On the meaning of 'accident' s 2(1) of the Road Traffic Offenders Act 1988: 'the word "accident" [is] to be given a commonsense meaning and [is] not restricted to untoward or unintended consequences having an adverse physical effect.'[3A]

(p 553)   **In newly created footnote 3A, insert–**

R v Currie (Paul Alan) [2007] 2 Cr App R 18, [24].

(p 554)   **In paragraph beginning 'Drafters are often silent', at end of second sentence insert footnote indicator 2A.**

(p 554)   **In newly created footnote 2A, insert–**

This paragraph has been judicially approved: *A v Securities and Futures Commission* [2008] 1 HKLRD 591, [20].

(p 554)   **In footnote 5, at end insert–**

Note, though, that where a period ends on Sunday or other *dies non* it is common sense to treat it as extended to include the next *dies utilis* or working day: see *Mucelli v Government of Albania* [2009] 1 WLR 276, 298.

(p 555)   **In footnote 7, at end insert–**

For judicial approval of this passage, see *New Zealand Customs Service v Wang* [2010] NZAR 322, [32].

                                      S 199

(p 562)   **In footnote 7, at end insert–**

The sentence to which this footnote relates has been judicially approved: *Wealthcare Financial Planning Pty Ltd v Financial Industry Complaints Service Ltd* (2009) 69 ACSR 418, [37].

(p 562)   **In footnote 8, at end insert–**

See also the approval of the Full Federal Court of Australia in *Minister for Immigration and Multicultural Affairs v Hu* (1997) 79 FCR 309, 324 ('usual occupation') and the NSW Court of Appeal in *Manly Council v Malouf* (2004) 61 NSWLR 394, [8] ('shop').

(p 562)   **In footnote 9, at end insert–**

; *R (Heffernan) v Rent Service* [2008] 1 WLR 1702, 1720–1721 ('locality').

(p 565)   **In third paragraph, at end of third sentence, before Example 199.14, insert footnote indicator 6A.**

(p 565)   **In newly created footnote 6A, insert–**

This passage was approved by an Australian intermediate appellate court in *Munn v Agus* (1997) 6 NTLR 84 and by the Federal Court of Canada in *Hrushka v Canada (Minister of Foreign Affairs)* [2009] FC 69, [16].

(p 569)   **In footnote 6, at end insert–**

See also *Re: Dairy Farmers of Britain Ltd* [2010] Ch 63.

(p 569)   **In footnote 7, at end insert–**

See also the decision of the Federal Court of Australia in *Re: Interchase Corp Ltd (in liq) (No 2)* (1993) 47 FCR 253, 260–261.

(p 570) <h3 align="center">In footnote 5, at end insert–</h3>

This dictum was applied in *Health Service Executives v Commissioners for Valuation* [2008] IEHC 178, [9].

(p 573) <h3 align="center">In footnote 8, at end insert–</h3>

It is submitted that Lord Hoffmann NPJ, speaking for the Hong Kong Court of Final Appeal, effectively recognised enlarging definitions in *Penny's Bay Investment Co Ltd v Director of Lands* [2010] HKCFA 12, [38].

(p 573) <h3 align="center">In third complete paragraph, at end insert–</h3>

In particular, the presence of X does not, apart from the operation of its ordinary meaning, normally affect the width of the ordinary meaning of T.[8A] Despite the typical form, it is possible for an enlarging definition to appear alongside a definition of the term subject to the enlarging definition. Instead of comprising 'T includes X', the enactment will state 'T means X and includes Y', with Y being the enlarging definition.[8B]

(p 573) <h3 align="center">In newly created footnote 8A, insert–</h3>

Revenue & Customs v Premier Foods Ltd [2007] EWHC 3134 (Ch), [17]. Note that the opposite may be true, in the sense that T may affect the width of the ordinary meaning of X under the potency of the term defined: see pp 562–564. For an example of an enlarging definition arguably attracting the latter, see Female Genital Mutilation Act s 6(1) ('girl includes woman').

(p 573) <h3 align="center">In newly created footnote 8B, insert–</h3>

Begg v Commissioner of Inland Revenue [2009] 3 NZLR 353, [18]–[19]; *Moweno Pty Ltd v Stratis Promotions Pty Ltd* [2003] NSWCA 376, [61].

<h3 align="center">S 200</h3>

(p 576) <h3 align="center">In first complete paragraph, at end of first sentence, before Example 200.1, insert footnote indicator 3A.</h3>

(p 576) <h3 align="center">In newly created footnote 3A, insert–</h3>

It has been said of this sentence 'That holds weight in respect of Interpretation Acts where the purpose is to collect generally applicable definitions and terms. Provisions of the [Irish] Interpretation Act 2005, however, go much further than this "traditional" function of Interpretation Acts': D Dodd Statutory Interpretation in Ireland (Tottel, 2008) p. 254.

(p 576)   **At bottom of page, insert new paragraph–**

However, the effect of the Interpretation Act is that an unincorporated association may be criminally liable, at least for offences involving strict liability. The Crown may, at its discretion, in light of relevant considerations and subject to oppression involving abuse of process, bring a prosecution against either the association in its own name or its members.[9A]

(p 576)   **In newly created footnote 9A, insert–**

R v L [2009] 1 Cr App R 16.

(p 579)   **At end of second sentence, insert–**

Further, damage to a substance from or part of the body of a person, where the substance or part has previously been separated from the body without unlawful injury to the person, cannot give rise to such injury.[3A]

(p 579)   **In newly created footnote 3A, insert–**

Yearworth v North Bristol NHS Trust [2010] QB 1, 11–12. See, generally, R Hardcastle, Law and the Human Body: Property Rights, Ownership and Control (Oxford, Hart Publishing, 2007).

(p 579)   **In footnote 4, at end insert–**

As to contrary intention see Example 200.10A below.

(p 580)   **At top of page, at end of quotation, before paragraph beginning
               'As so often happens', insert new paragraph–**

Care must be taken to ensure that recourse to the rule is necessary. A challenge to conduct by reference to the rule could fail because the conduct is lawful regardless of whether a particular term is pluralised.

> *Example 200.10A* Section 6(4) of the Local Government and Public Involvement in Health Act 2007 says that the Boundary Committee must, before making an alternative proposal as to the structure of local government for an area to the Secretary of State under s 5(3)(c) of the Act, publish and facilitate representations as to a draft of the alternative proposal. The Secretary of State had a discretion to implement the alternative proposal under s 7(1)(b) of the Act. The Committee acted on the basis that it could only consult in respect of and transmit to the Secretary of State one draft alternative proposal. The trial judge upheld a challenge to this course, ruling that s 6(c) of the Interpretation Act 1978 applied, emphasising that 'any contrary intention must be garnered not simply from one statutory provision but from a consideration of the legislation as a whole and the purposes behind it'. The Court of Appeal endorsed this analysis. However, the Court suggested that the assistance of s 6(c) was unnecessary. The Committee could consult on various draft alternative proposals. Further, the Secretary of State could receive and consider all of those, but

could only implement one. The Court seems to be saying that, even if the relevant terms were read in the singular, the powers to which they relate could be exercised more than once. If so, functus officio should have been discussed. In short, though, the Committee and the Secretary could act *intra vires* even without pluralisation.[1A]

(p 580)   **In newly created footnote 1A, insert–**

East Devon District Council v Electoral Commission (The Boundary Committee for England) [2009] EWHC 4 (Admin) [37]–[38], reversed on other grounds: *R (Breckland District Council) v Electoral Commission Boundary Committee for England* [2009] PTSR 1611, [78]–[80]. See also F A R Bennion, ' *"Never On The Cards": Fighting For Two-Tier Local Government'*, 173 CL&J (31 Jan 2009) pp 72–75, www. francisbennion. com/ 2009/005.htm, [15]–[23]. For a more restrictive approach to the ascertainment of contrary intention in this context, see *C & E Pty Ltd v CMC Brisbane Pty Ltd (Administrators Appointed)* [2004] QCA 60, [20].

S 201

(p 585)   **At beginning of Comment on Code s 201, after Subsection (1), insert–**

This section of the Code was recently considered by the Supreme Court of the United Kingdom.

(p 585)   **In newly created footnote 1, insert–**

R (BA (Nigeria)) v Secretary of State for the Home Department [2010] 1 AC 444, 458. Regrettably, the Court reduced s 201 and Part XIV of the Code to the *Barras* principle, as to which see Code s 210(3). The Court then said one should look beyond Code s 201 and Part XIV to the 'elementary principle ... that the words of the statute should be construed in the context of the scheme of the statute as a whole'. This is something plainly embraced by Code ss 201(2) and 202. Thus, it was necessary for the Court to look not beyond but further within the informed interpretation rule. For broader recognition of Code s 201, see *Chan Ching Kit v Lam Sik Shi* [2002] HKCFI 132, [18]–[19] and *Lee Yiu Kee v Chinese University of Hong Kong* [2010] HKCA 218, [73].

S 202

(p 588)   **In Comment on Code s 202, at beginning, insert–**

This section of the Code has been judicially approved.[1A]

(p 588)   **In newly created footnote 1A, insert–**

Lee Yiu Kee v Chinese University of Hong Kong [2010] HKCA 218, [73].

(p 589)   **In second complete paragraph, at end of sentence 'The words are not deployed in a vacuum', insert–**

Rather, as Lord Steyn has said, 'in law, context is everything'.[3A]

(p 589)   **In newly created footnote 3A, insert–**

R (Daly) v Secretary of State for Home Department [2001] 2 AC 532, 548.

S 205

(p 593)   **In footnote 3, at end insert–**

The above passage was approved in *Transpower New Zealand Limited v Taupo District Council* [2007] NZHC 999, [13] and *Avowal Administrative Attorneys Ltd v District Court at North Shore* [2007] NZHC 714, [7].

S 210

(p 600)   **In footnote 6, at end, insert–**

For other judicial consideration of Code s 210(3), see *Ward v Chief Adjudication Officer* [1998] EWCA Civ 1552; *BBC Scotland v Souster* 2001 SC 458, [28].

(p 601)   **In footnote 1, after 'construed in the same way)', insert–**

Commissioner of Inland Revenue v N Evans [2008] NZHC 1017, [34] (repeated appearance of concept of aiding and abetting in criminal legislation).

(p 603)   **At bottom of page, in the last line, after 'was intended', insert footnote indicator 10A.**

(p 603)   **In newly created footnote 10A, insert–**

These words were considered by the Court of Appeal in *Ward v Chief Adjudication Officer* [1998] EWCA Civ 1552 and by the Irish High Court in *Action Aid Ltd v Revenue Commissioners* [1997] IEHC 196.

S 211

(p 604)   **In footnote 7, at end insert–**

See also *R (Friends of the Earth) v Secretary of State for Business, Enterprise and Regulatory Reform* [2009] EWCA Civ 810, [25].

(p 606)   **In second paragraph, at end of fourth sentence, insert footnote
indicator 5A**

(p 606)   **In newly created footnote 5A, insert–**

This passage was approved by the Divisional Court in *Staff Side of the
Police Negotiating Board & Anor v Secretary of State for the Home
Department* [2008] EWHC 1173 (Admin), [44].

(p 607)   **In footnote 1, at end insert–**

For a case where a consolidation with amendments was effected and was
considered in support of an interpretation of the legislation as it stood
before the consolidation, see *Isle of Anglesey CC v Welsh Ministers*
[2010] QB 163, 177–180. In that case, the Court of Appeal also
considered the history of consolidations with amendments.

S 213

(p 610)   **In footnote 2, at end insert–**

This could extend to preparatory steps taken by the Executive for the
promotion of new legislation in advance of its enactment, to the extent
that they shed light on its meaning. As to such steps, see *R (Shrewsbury)
v Secretary of State for Communities and Local Government* [2008]
3 All ER 548. See also p 205 n 10.

S 217

(p 621)   **At end of first passage, before paragraph beginning 'It has been
suggested', insert–**

Lord Neuberger has also recently exhibited a similar lack of enthusiasm
for the use of Hansard, albeit without reference to the *Pepper v Hart*
conditions.[3A]

(p 621)   **In newly created footnote 3A, insert–**

See *Malcolm v Lewisham LBC* [2008] 1 AC 1399, where Lord Neuberger was 'in insufficient doubt as to the correct answer to justify
looking at the parliamentary material' and thought doing so was only in
'rare cases ...appropriate' (at 1446) and an 'exceptional course' (at
1447). On the other hand, Baroness Hale considered the *Pepper v Hart*
conditions to be met (at 1427) and referred to parliamentary material
'[f]or what it may additionally be worth' and to 'confirm the [relevant]
construction' (at 1428). See also *Yarl's Wood Immigration Ltd v Bedfordshire Police Authority* [2010] 2 WLR 1322, 1347.

S 219

(p 642)   **In footnote 1, at end insert–**

See also *Davidson v Scottish Ministers (No 1)* [2005] UKHL 74, [50].
Note, however, the more recent disapproval of their use in *R (Public and*

Commercial Services Union) v Minister for Civil Service [2010] EWHC 1027 (Admin), [55] where Sales J said 'it is fundamental that all materials which are relevant to the proper interpretation of such an instrument should be available to any person who wishes to inform himself about the meaning of that law. That is not the position in relation to notes on clauses and for that reason I do not consider they are a legitimate aid to construction of an Act of Parliament'.

S 220

(p 682)   **In footnote 2, at end insert–**

See also *R v Zafar (Aitzaz)* [2008] QB 810, 822. A similar approach prevails in Hong Kong: *HKSAR v Cheung Kwun Yin* (unreported, Hong Kong Court of Final Appeal, FACC 11/2008), [14]–[17].

S 221

(p 683)   **After Example 221.3, insert–**

Example 221.3A The current statute governing the validity of patents is, of course, the Patents Act 1977, which must be read together with the European Patent Convention ('the EPC'). Indeed, all the provisions of the 1977 Act of central relevance for present purposes have been specifically framed 'as nearly as practicable' to have 'the same effects in the United Kingdom as the corresponding provisions of the [EPC] have in the territories to which [it applies]': see section 130(7) of the 1977 Act.[10A]

(p 683)   **In newly created footnote 10A, insert–**

Generics (UK) Ltd and others v H Lundbeck A/S [2009] RPC 407, [68].

(p 684)   **In footnote 4, delete text and insert–**

See the Australian case *Commissioner of Taxation v Lamesa Holdings BV* (1997) 77 FCR 597, 603–605 and authority discussed there.

(p 684)   **In footnote 6, at end insert–**

See also *FA (Iraq) v Secretary of State for Home Department [2010] EWCA Civ 696* (Refugee Convention and Qualification Directive (2004/83/EC).

(p 685)   **In footnote 4, at end insert–**

See also *Hatzl v XL Insurance Company Ltd* [2010] 1 WLR 470, 478–479.

(p 685)   **At end of first full paragraph, before sideheading 'Subsection (2)', insert–**

Another such limitation may be imposed in the course of indirect enactment or by any other enactment.

Example 221.5A Section 54 of the Immigration, Asylum and Nationality Act 2006 says that in the 'construction and application' of Art 1(F)(c) of the Refugee Convention the 'reference to acts contrary to the purposes and principles of the United Nations shall be taken as including' certain conduct related to terrorism, with the last term being defined by the Terrorism Act 2000 s 1. An English court would be obliged to approach the Refugee Convention in this way, regardless of whether it would do the same by independent interpretation.[5A]

(p 685)   **In newly created footnote 5A, insert–**

See further *MH (Syria) v Secretary of State for the Home Department* [2009] EWCA Civ 226, [29].

S 232

(p 703)   **At end of first passage, before paragraph beginning 'The administration of every Act', insert sentence–**

Nonetheless, the Court of Appeal has recently emphasised the limits of Code s 232. In particular, 'the judiciary, not the executive, decide the meaning and effect of legislation.' An official statement 'may be of assistance for some purposes, for example, if it throws light on the background to the legislation and thereby enables the court to understand better its general purpose.' Further, 'insofar as the views expressed in such a document are inherently persuasive they may be taken into account.' However, 'that is as far as it goes'.[2A]

(p 703)   **In newly created footnote 2A, insert–**

R (Risk Management Partners Ltd) v Brent LBC [2010] PTSR 349, [227]. See also *Yemshaw v Hounslow LBC* [2009] EWCA Civ 1543, [28].

(p 703)   **Toward end of page, at end of sentence beginning 'Its significance was a matter of weight', insert footnote indicator 9A.**

(p 703)   **In newly created footnote 9A, insert–**

For other instances of confusion of these concepts, see *Sharratt v London Central Bus Co* [2002] EWHC 9006 (Costs), [46]–[49]; *Grays Timber Products Ltd v Revenue and Customs (Scotland)* [2010] 1 WLR 497, 514–515.

(p 704)   **In footnote 8, at end insert–**

; *Boyle v SCA Packaging Ltd* [2009] UKHL 37, [2009] 4 All ER 1181, [67]; *R (Risk Management Partners Ltd) v Brent LBC* [2010] PTSR 349, [110]–[111], [227]. Compare *R (Bapio Action Ltd) v Secretary of State for the Home Department* [2008] 1 AC 1003.

(p 705)   **In footnote 7, at end insert–**

; and *BBC v Information Commissioner* [2009] EWHC 2348 (Admin), [75].

(p 706)   **At end of second complete paragraph, before paragraph beginning 'On statutory and judicial guidelines', insert new paragraph–**

The Court of Appeal recently indicated that, while such guidelines would attract Code s 232, and be taken into account by and even be of assistance to the judiciary when interpreting the legislation to which the guidelines relate, they 'need not be authority, or even persuasive authority, but what [they] purport[] to be, that is, guidance'.[7A]

(p 706)   **In newly created footnote 7A, insert–**

R (Risk Management Partners Ltd) v Brent LBC [2010] PTSR 349, [111].

S 233

(p 707)   **In footnote 8, at end insert–**

See also *Scottish & Newcastle plc v Raguz* [2008] 1 WLR 2994, 2504, cf 2497. As to forms prescribed under an enactment, see p 242 n 8.

S 234

(p 708)   **In footnote 4, delete text and insert–**

This sentence was judicially considered in *Ward v Chief Adjudication Officer* [1998] EWCA Civ 1552.

(p 709)   **In footnote 3, at end insert–**

Revenue and Customs Commissioners v Halcyon Films LLP [2010] EWCA Civ 261, [27].

(p 709)   **In footnote 9, at end insert–**

The sentence to which this footnote relates was applied by the Full Federal Court of Australia in *Kalway v Secretary, Department of Social Security* (1992) 38 FCR 295, 299.

(p 710)   **After Example 234.3, insert sideheading and new paragraph as follows–**

Redundant enactments The Court of Appeal recently declined to apply s 234 in relation to an enactment that was never brought into force and, shortly after its passage, was repealed and replaced by another enactment.[4A]

(p 710)   **In newly created footnote 4A, insert–**

Revenue and Customs Commissioners v Halcyon Films LLP [2010] EWCA Civ 261, [27].

S 235

(p 710)   **In Comment on Code s 235, at beginning before sideheading Sub-rules, insert new paragraph with text as follows–**

This section of the Code has been judicially approved.[6A]

(p 710)   **In newly created footnote 6A, insert–**

JF v Minister for Health and Children [2008] IESC 16.

(p 711)   **After Example 235.3, insert text as follows–**

However, the implication may not be drawn where the context otherwise requires. This has arisen where a legislature altered an enactment in light of a judicial decision in a very specific way, without any suggestion that it considered any other aspects of the operation of the enactment.

> *Example 235.3A* In Hong Kong, the *ratio* of a decision of an intermediate appellate court had been that, under the Employment Ordinance (Cap 57), the remedy for unlawful dismissal was unliquidated damages subject to a duty to mitigate. The Legislative Council inserted a new provision into the Ordinance, s 8A, with the intention, as stated in the Second Reading, of reversing the decision. The decision had also contained *obiter*, of a majority and minority, as to the meaning of Ordinance s 7. In a subsequent case before the Court of Final Appeal, including Lord Scott of Foscote NPJ, it was argued that the Legislative Council had implicitly approved the majority *obiter*. Ribeiro PJ said, for the Court, that there was 'no basis for taking the legislature to have considered in any shape or form the divided views … on the *obiter* question'. It was 'therefore impossible to suggest that the legislature's intent was tacitly to confer legislative force on [those views].'[7A]

(p 711)   **In newly created footnote 7A, insert–**

Kao Lee & Yip (a firm) v Lau Wing (2008) 11 HKCFAR 576, [36].

S 236

(p 712)   **In Comment on Code s 236, at beginning, insert–**

This section of the Code has been judicially approved.

(p 712)   **In newly created footnote 1, insert–**

R (Public and Commercial Services Union) v Minister for Civil Service [2010] EWHC 1027 (Admin), [38]. The Court added: 'That is especially

the case where, as here, an Act is being introduced specifically to regulate relations between certain persons and it is those persons who have the understanding in question'.

S 243

(p 725)   **In Comment on Code s 243, at end of third sentence after 'shall ...', insert–**

This passage, and Code s 243, has been judicially approved: *Comptroller and Auditor General v Ireland* [1997] 1 IR 248.

S 250

(p 740)   **Toward end of page, at end of sentence beginning 'Examples were given in', insert–**

and s 44(6) of the Criminal Justice Act 2003.

S 255

(p 746)   **In footnote 1, at end of first sentence insert–**

; *ETI Euro Telecom International NV v Republic of Bolivia* [2009] 1 WLR 665, 682 (citing Code s 255 et seq).

(p 746)   **At end of first full sentence insert footnote indicator 1A.**

(p 746)   **In newly created footnote 1A, insert–**

This sentence has been applied by a Northern Irish court: See also *Re Application by the Local Government Auditor [2003] NIQB 21*, [16].

(p 746)   **In footnote 6, at end insert–**

In any event, the same cannot be said of delegated legislation such as the Civil Procedure Rules: *Brown v Innovatorone Plc* [2009] EWHC 1376 (Comm), [17].

S 256

(p 748)   **In footnote 9, at end insert–**

In any event, the same cannot be said of delegated legislation such as the Civil Procedure Rules: *Brown v Innovatorone Plc* [2009] EWHC 1376 (Comm), [17].

S 257

(p 749)   **In Comment on Code s 257, at beginning, insert–**

This section of the Code has been judicially approved.[2A]

(p 749)   **In newly created footnote 2A, insert–**

Australian Securities Commission v Lucas (1992) 36 FCR 165, 170–171.

S 258

(p 751)   **In Comment on Code s 258, at end of first sentence, insert footnote indicator 1.**

(p 751)   **In newly created footnote 1, insert–**

This sentence has been judicially approved: *Official Bay Heritage Protection Society Incorporated v Auckland City Council and another* [2007] NZCA 511, [33].

S 259

(p 758)   **In footnote 3, at end insert–**

This sentence has been approved by the Ontario Court of Appeal: *R v St Lawrence Cement Inc* (2002) 60 OR (3d) 712, [18]. See also *BCGEU v British Columbia* (2007) 283 DLR (4th) 307, [34]–[36].

S 260

(p 761)   **At end of page insert new paragraph–**

The contrary intention referred to in Code s 260(2) has been found to be present where a constitutional statute of an overseas common law jurisdiction imports English common law into the jurisdiction on a specific date. Doing so does not preclude the subsequent development of that law by the courts of the jurisdiction, including by the application of decisions of English courts after the relevant date.[7A]

(p 761)   **In newly created footnote 7A, insert–**

Lai v Chamberlains [2007] 2 NZLR 7, [86]. See also *China Field Ltd v Appeal Tribunal (Buildings) (No 2)* [2009] 5 HKLRD 662, 668–670, 688–690.

S 263

(p 773)   **In footnote 9, at end insert–**

For a perspective extending beyond the United Kingdom, see M Kirby, *Judicial Activism: Authority, Principle and Policy in the Judicial Method* (55th Hamlyn Lectures, Sweet & Maxwell, 2004), Ch 2.

(p 778)   **In footnote 3, at end insert–**

Note that maintenance and champerty were abolished as crimes and torts by Criminal Law Act 1967 s 14, but had their relevance to the law of contract, including public policy, preserved. For a recent example, see

Ruttle Plant Ltd v Secretary of State for Environment, Food and Rural Affairs (No 2) [2008] EWHC 238 (TCC), [2009] 1 All ER 448.

S 264

(p 790)   **Toward top of page, at end of sideheading Conflicting interests insert footnote indicator 1A.**

(p 790)   **In newly created footnote 1A, insert–**

This discussion has been judicially approved: *Li Wang Pong v Medical Council of Hong Kong* [2009] HKCFI 2, [59].

(p 793)   **In footnote 9, at end insert–**

As to the meaning of fraud, see generally *Giles v Rhind* [2009] Ch 191, 207.

S 265

(p 795)   **In Comment on Code s 265, at beginning, insert–**

This section of the Code has been judicially approved.[3A]

(p 795)   **In newly created footnote 3A, insert–**

R (Hampstead Heath Winter Swimming Club) v Corporation of London [2005] 1 WLR 2930, [33].

(p 797)   **In footnote 4, at end insert–**

Similarly, public policy may require that an injustice be tolerated, as where the need for the maintenance of an order for the adoption of children outweighed the need to redress injustice in the making of the order: *Webster v Norfolk CC* [2009] 1 FLR 1378.

(p 805)   **In footnote 1, at end insert–**

See, generally, F A R Bennion, '*Is Law Still A Learned Profession?*', www.francisbennion.com/2008/016.htm and "*Writing Like a Lawyer*" (2010) 19 *Commonwealth Lawyer* 24–27, available at http://www.francisbennion.com/pdfs/fb/2010/2010–017-coml-writing-like-a-lawyer.pdf.

S 267

(p 807)   **In Comment on Code s 267, at beginning, insert–**

This section of the Code has been judicially approved.[4A]

(p 807) **In newly created footnote 4A, insert–**

See the decision of Kiefel J (as she then was) of the Federal Court of Australia *Insurance and Superannuation Commissioner v Hiscock* (1995) 59 FCR 1, 3.

S 268

(p 808) **In Comment on Code s 268, at beginning, insert–**

This section of the Code has been judicially approved.[1A]

(p 808) **In newly created footnote 1A, insert–**

See the decision of New Zealand Supreme Court in *Elders New Zealand Ltd v PGG Wrightson Ltd* [2009] 1 NZLR 577, [30] and the majority of the Singapore Court of Appeal in *Lee Chez Kee v Public Prosecutor* [2008] SGCA 20 at [93]–[94]. As to the reasoning in the latter case, see also Example 355.9.

S 269

(p 812) **In Comment on Code s 269, at beginning, insert–**

This section of the Code has been judicially approved.[3A]

(p 812) **In newly created footnote 3A, insert–**

Re: Joseph's Estate (1993) 14 OR (3d) 628, [10]; *Jade City International Ltd v Director of Lands* [2002] 3 HKLRD 33, 47. See also *Medical Council of Hong Kong v Chow Siu Shek* [2000] 2 HKLRD 674.

(p 814) **In footnote 2, at end insert–**

See also *Re: P* [2010] Ch 33.

(p 816) **In footnote 3, at end insert–**

See further the reasons of French J (as he then was) in the Full Federal Court of Australia in *Commissioner of Taxation v Citibank Ltd* (1989) 20 FCR 403, 432–433.

S 270

(p 819) **In footnote 3, at end insert–**

For a broader approach see *Sellers v Maritime Safety Inspector* [1999] 2 NZLR 44, 61, 62 discussed in P Sales and J Clement, '*International Law in Domestic Courts: the Developing Framework*' (2008) 124 LQR 388, 393. See also *Zaoui v Attorney-General (No 2)* [2006] 1 NZLR 289, [90]. Compare *R v Hape* [2007] 2 SCR 292, [53]–[56].

(p 823)   **At end of first complete sentence, insert footnote indicator 1A.**

(p 823)   **In newly created footnote 1A, insert–**

This remark has been noticed by Lord Phillips of Worth Matravers PSC
and apparently applied by the Supreme Court of New Zealand: *Ahmed v
HM Treasury* [2010] 2 WLR 378, 423; *Cropp v A Judicial Committee*
[2008] 3 NZLR 774, [27].

(p 823)   **In second complete paragraph, at end of sentence beginning 'This
            so-called principle of legality', insert–**

The previous sentence has been questioned by Lord Phillips of Worth
Matravers PSC on the ground that the majority found ambiguity to be
present. He did 'not consider that the principle of legality permits a court
to disregard an unambiguous expression of Parliament's intention'.[8A] It
is suggested that the requisite ambiguity should, in general terms, be
explained. It seems to go beyond ambiguity under Code s 151(3), which
excludes general words. It may arise by necessary implication.[8B] Quite
how it embraces the view of the above majority of the House should be
clarified.[8C]

(p 823)   **In footnote 5, at end insert–**

So much has been acknowledged by the House of Lords: *R (Morgan
Grenfell & Co Ltd) v Special Cmr of Income Tax* [2003] 1 AC 563, 607.

(p 823)   **In newly created footnote 8A, insert–**

Ahmed v HM Treasury [2010] 2 WLR 378, 423. Lord Phillips saw this as
a point of departure from interpretation under the Human Rights
Act 1998 s 3(1). See further Code s 421, including p 1324 n 3.

(p 823)   **In newly created footnote 8B, insert–**

W (Algeria) v Secretary of State for Home Department [2010] EWCA
Civ 898, [45].

(p 823)   **In newly created footnote 8C, insert–**

See generally Code s 153 and *Bowers v Gloucester Corporation* [1963]
1 QB 881, 886–887.

(p 823)   **Replace 'Yet in 2006' with–**

In this respect, a degree of progress has already been made. In 2006

(p 823)   **In paragraph beginning 'This so-called principle of legality', at
            end insert–**

In 2008, the Supreme Court of the United Kingdom reaffirmed that the
principle can displace general or ambiguous words and, on this basis,
held delegated legislation to be in excess of its enabling power.[11A] That

year, the Court of Appeal applied the principle in the context of statutory regulation of judicial fact-finding, refusing to convert 'shall take account' into may do so, but reading 'damaging the claimant's credibility' as potentially damaging the same.[11B]

(p 823)   **In newly created footnote 11A, insert–**

Ahmed v HM Treasury [2010] 2 WLR 378, 406–407, 438–439, 462. This reflects the recognition by the Supreme Court of New Zealand that the principle of legality naturally applies to words which authorise subordinate legislation': *Cropp v A Judicial Committee* [2008] 3 NZLR 774, [27].

(p 823)   **In newly created footnote 11B, insert–**

JT (Cameroon) v Secretary of State for the Home Department [2008] EWCA Civ 878, [2009] 2 All ER 1213. See also Code s 281.

S 271

(p 825)   **In Comment on Code s 271, at beginning, insert–**

This section of the Code has been judicially approved.[1A]

(p 825)   **In newly created footnote 1A, insert–**

HKSAR v Tang Hoi On [2003] 3 HKC 123, [32].

(p 828)   **At bottom of page, at end of sentence 'A denial of this must be clearly stated', insert footnote indicator 10.**

(p 828)   **In newly created footnote 10, insert–**

See, for example, *Mount Lawley Pty Ltd v Western Australian Planning Commission* [2004] WASCA 149; (2004) 136 LGERA 16, [296].

S 273

(p 837)   **In footnote 6, at end insert–**

R (G) v Chief Constable of West Yorkshire Police [2008] 1 WLR 550, 559.

(p 839)   **At end of first paragraph, before sideheading 'Technicalities' insert–**

Further, the House of Lords recently held that, where an appeals process under the Extradition Act 2003 was available, habeas corpus would be excluded. This was due to the 'clear and unequivocal wording' of the Act s 34, which provided for the exclusivity of the process, as well as the European law implemented by the Act, which had the purpose of promoting recognition of extradition requests by member states and removing complexity and delay from extradition procedures.[4A]

(p 839)   **In newly created footnote 4A, insert–**

Hilali v Governor of Whitemoore Prison [2008] 1 AC 805, 840–841.

S 278

(p 846)   **In footnote 5, at beginning insert–**

This sentence has, together with Code s 278, been judicially approved: *Independent Committee for the Supervision of Standards of Telephone Information Services v Andronikou & Ors* [2007] EWHC 2307 (Admin), [25].

(p 846)   **In footnote 6 at end of first sentence, before sentence beginning 'See also Examples', insert–**

Registrar of Liquor Licences v Iliadis (1988) 19 FCR 311, 315–316 (statutory licence for sale of liquor not to amenable to cancellation).

(p 846)   **At bottom of page, at end of last complete sentence, before Example 278.1 insert footnote indicator 7.**

(p 846)   **In newly created footnote 7, insert–**

This sentence was approved by the Federal Court of Canada in *Society Promoting Environmental Conservation v Canada (Attorney-General)* (2002) FTR 236, [31].

(p 848)   **At bottom of page, at end of final sentence insert footnote indicator 9.**

(p 848)   **In newly created footnote 9, insert–**

This sentence has been judicially approved: *Re: Landlord's Association for Northern Ireland* [2005] NIQB 22, [41].

(p 850)   **In footnote 5, at end insert–**

Compare *Grays Timber Products Ltd v Revenue and Customs Commissioners* [2010] 1 WLR 497, 509 '[t]he principle that tax is to be charged only by clear words may be less potent than it was, but it is still relevant to the construction of taxing statutes'.

S 281

(p 854)   **After sideheading 'Trial by jury', at end of quotation insert–**

Further, where an Act of Parliament unequivocally restricted the right of trial by jury in certain circumstances, it was held the right was 'so deeply entrenched in our constitution' that the presence of the circumstances had to be established to the 'highest possible forensic standard of proof [being] the criminal standard'.[5A]

(p 854)   **In newly created footnote 5A, insert–**

R v T [2010] 1 WLR 630, 637–638.

S 282

(p 858)   **At end of first paragraph, insert–**

Nonetheless, a person not a party to first instance proceedings may, in appropriate cases, appeal from a decision in the proceedings, especially where the person has a real interest in the matter.[4A]

(p 858)   **In newly created footnote 4A, insert–**

George Wimpey UK Ltd v Tewkesbury BC [2008] 1 WLR 1649.

S 285

(p 864)   **In Comment on Code s 285, at beginning, insert–**

This section has been judicially approved.[3A]

(p 864)   **In newly created footnote 3A, insert–**

Jeffrey v Sawyer (1993) 16 OR (3d) 75, 78; *Maguire v Director of Public Prosecutions* [2004] 3 IR 241, [45].

(p 868)   **At bottom of page at end of last sentence, insert footnote indicator 7.**

(p 868)   **In newly created footnote 7, insert–**

This can, of course, produce differences of judicial opinion: see, for example, *Knowsley Housing Trust v White* [2009] 1 AC 636, 651, 675.

S 286

(p 871)   **In footnote 8, at end insert–**

Sinclair Gardens Investments (Kensington) Ltd v Poets Chase Freehold Co Ltd [2008] 1 WLR 768.

S 287

(p 876)   **In footnote 1, at end insert–**

This case has recently been applied in England and overseas: *Gibson v Secretary of State for Justice* [2009] QB 204; *OTC International AG v Perfect Recovery Ltd* [2009] 3 HKLRD 13. The latter expressly approved of this Code's description of the process as 'rectifying construction': at [48]. See also *Taylor v Centennial Newstan Pty Ltd* [2009] NSWCA 276.

S 288

(p 890)   **In Comment on Code s 288, at beginning, insert–**

This section of the Code has been judicially considered.

(p 890)   **In newly created footnote 1, insert–**

Ackland v Yonge-Esplanade Enterprises Ltd (1992) 10 OR (3d) 97, [25];
Fong Yau Hei v Gammon Construction Ltd [2008] 3 HKLRD 604, 613.

(p 890)   **In footnote 4, at end insert–**

For overseas approval of Code s 288(2), see *Osborne v Chief Executive
of Ministry of Social Development* [2010] 1 NZLR 559, [64].

(p 899)   **In footnote 2, at end insert–**

Compare *Sonea v Mehedinti District Court, Romania* [2009] EWHC 89
(Admin), [2009] 2 All ER 821.

(p 908)   **In first complete paragraph at beginning replace 'The
                  decision' with–**

The decision ('*Munks*')

(p 908)   **In first complete paragraph, at end of sentence beginning
                  'However, the italicised passages', insert–**

In any event, the Court of Appeal has recently retreated from this
conclusion.

> *Example 288.37A*[5A] The accused had attached a sharp metal
> object to the roof frame of a shed. In the event that a person
> opened the door to the shed, the object would, through the
> combination of a wire attached to the door and the force of gravity,
> descend and strike the person. When this occurred, the accused
> was charged with the same offence as that in *Munks*. He submitted
> that there had been no mechanical contrivance, as that case
> required. *Held*: *Munks* had no such effect. It had not replaced
> 'other engine' with 'other mechanical contrivance'. In any event,
> the latter words should not be applied restrictively. In each case, it
> was necessary that 'the object itself as well as the manner, if any,
> in which it may be activated … be examined pragmatically to see
> whether, looked at overall, it falls within the statutory language'.
> The object in the present case, which was a mechanical contriv-
> ance, did so unquestionably.[5B]

> Thus, while purporting not to depart from *Munks*,[5C] the Court gave
> the decision a flexible operation. As to 'engine', the Court added
> that:

> 'Something of the breadth of its meaning at the time when the
> 1827 Act came into force is identified in the [OED] where, among
> other references, we find a pair of scissors described as a 'little

engine' in the Rape of the Lock (1712–1714) and a description of 'engines of restraint and pain' at the victim's feet in Death Slavery (1866). Indeed at much the same time, in *Barnard v Ford* [1869] LR 4Ch App. 247, the court rejected a proposition which would turn it 'into an engine of fraud'. None of these references dilutes or could dilute the authority of *Munks*, although they suggest that the Crown's argument in that case was more constrained than it perhaps should have been.'[5D]

This is even more disappointing than *Munks*. The Court built upon that decision by considering the historic meaning of engine but then failed to interpret the enactment under the box principle accordingly.

(p 908)   **In newly created footnote 5A, insert–**

R v Cockburn [2008] QB 882.

(p 908)   **In newly created footnote 5B, insert–**

At 885–887.

(p 908)   **In newly created footnote 5C, insert–**

At 886. The Court, being in its Criminal Division, would have been able to do so: see, for example, *Gibson v United States* [2007] 1 WLR 2367, 2375.

(p 908)   **In newly created footnote 5D, insert–**

At 886.

(p 909)   **In first sentence after 'police', insert–**

rent,[7A]

(p 909)   **In newly created footnote 7A, insert–**

Rent has come to mean not only periodic monetary consideration for the tenant's right to possession of land but such consideration inclusive of VAT: *Mason v Boscawen* [2009] 1 WLR 2139, 2155–2156.

(p 909)   **In footnote 1, at end insert–**

The passage to which this footnote relates has been approved by two judges of the High Court of Australia: *Byrne v Australian Airlines Ltd* (1995) 185 CLR 410, 459–460.

(p 914)   **In footnote 6, at end insert–**

See also the cautionary words as to Code s 288 in *R (Hammersmith & Fulham LBC) v Secretary Of State For Health* [1998] EWCA Civ 1300.

S 294

(p 929)   **In footnote 1, at end insert–**

See generally F A R Bennion, '*Law Churning and the Sociologists*' (2008) 172 JPN 228, available at http://www. francisbennion. com/ 2008/010.htm.

PART XXI

(p 963)   **In Comment on Code s 308, at beginning, insert–**

This section of the Code has been judicially approved.[2A]

(p 963)   **In newly created footnote 2A, insert–**

Commissioner of Inland Revenue v Common Empire Ltd [2006] 1 HKLRD 942, [17].

S 310

(p 965)   **In Comment on Code s 310, at beginning, insert–**

This section of the Code has been judicially approved.[4A]

(p 965)   **In newly created footnote 4A, insert–**

Commissioner of Inland Revenue v Loganathan [2000] 1 HKLRD 914, 917.

(p 966)   **In footnote 3, insert–**

Compare *Grays Timber Products Ltd v Revenue and Customs Commissioners* [2010] 1 WLR 497, 509 '[t]he principle that tax is to be charged only by clear words may be less potent than it was, but it is still relevant to the construction of taxing statutes'.

PART XXI – S 311

(p 969)   **At end of first paragraph, insert–**

Part XXI as a whole been judicially described as 'most instructive'.

(p 969)   **In newly created footnote 1, insert–**

QBE Worker's Compensation (Vic) Ltd v Freisleben [1999] 3 VR 401, [19].

(p 969)   **In footnote 2, at end insert–**

See also the concurring opinion of Lord Scott of Foscote in *Gumbs v Attorney-General (Anguilla)* [2009] UKPC 27, [44].

S 312

(p 969) **In Comment on Code s 312, at beginning, insert–**

Section 312(1) has been judicially approved.[1A]

(p 969) **In newly created footnote 1A, insert–**

Frucor Beverages Ltd v Rio Beverages Ltd [2001] 2 NZLR 604, [28]; *Wicken (Litigation Guardian of) v Harssar* (2004) 73 OR (3d) 600, [28]; *Boardwalk Reit LLP v Edmonton* (2008) 91 Alta LR (4th) 1, [78].

S 313

(p 971) **In Comment on Code s 313, at beginning, insert–**

This section of the Code has been judicially approved.[1A]

(p 971) **In newly created footnote 1A, insert–**

Braganza v Minister for Immigration and Multicultural Affairs (2001) 109 FCR 364, 376.

(p 971) **In footnote 2, at end insert–**

See also *Scottish & Newcastle Plc v Raguz* [2008] 1 WLR 2994, 2498 where the House of Lords rejected an interpretation adopted by the courts below on the ground that it produced 'some remarkably silly consequences'.

(p 974) **In footnote 7, at end insert–**

See also *Pang Yiu Hung v Commissioner of Police* [2003] 2 HKLRD 125, 161 (mere difficulty does not suffice).

S 314

(p 979) **In footnote 4, at end insert–**

Lord Shaw's dictum was applied by a Canadian appellate court, in light of the Code, in *Wicken (Litigation Guardian of) v Harssar* (2004) 73 OR (3d) 600, [29].

(p 982) **In footnote 3, at end insert–**

Compare *Mason v Boscawen* [2009] 1 WLR 2139, 2156–2157.

(p 983) **In footnote 3, at end insert–**

As to the courts' general desire to avoid fragmentation of legal and other proceedings, see *Beoku-Betts v Secretary of State for Home Department* [2009] 1 AC 115, 128.

(p 986)   **In footnote 4, at end insert–**

This dictum and preceding sentence in the Comment on Code s 315 were approved in *Wicken (Litigation Guardian of) v Harssar* (2004) 73 OR (3d) 600, [30].

S 315

(p 998)   **In footnote 1, at end insert–**

In such situations, the courts may overcome anomaly by other means, for example by staying proceedings as oppressive: *R v Morgan* [2008] EWCA Crim 1323, [2008] 4 All ER 890.

(p 999)   **In footnote 6, at end insert–**

Similarly, the courts may consider the invocation of anomaly by counsel as inapt: *Re: WD* [2007] Scot CS CSOH 139.

S 316

(p 1001)   **In footnote 4, at end insert–**

This extends to beyond court-based proceedings to arbitration: *Mason v Boscawen* [2009] 1 WLR 2139, 2152–2153.

S 318

(p 1006)   **In Comment on Code s 318, at beginning, insert–**

This section of the Code has been judicially approved.[1A]

(p 1006)   **In newly created footnote 1A, insert–**

See the decision of the Alberta Court of Appeal in *R(W) v Alberta* (2006) 62 Alta LR (4th) 6, [44].

S 319

(p 1009)   **In Comment on Code s 319, after sideheading 'Subsection (1)', insert–**

This subsection of the Code has been judicially approved.

(p 1009)   **In newly created footnote 1 insert–**

Niagara-on-the-Lake (Town) v Gross Estate (1993) 12 OR (3d) 1, [73].

(p 1013)   **In footnote 1, at end insert–**

For a case where counsel failed to raise fraud on an Act and the court declined to apply a strained construction, saying Parliament should deal

with the problem, see *Welwyn Hatfield Council v Secretary of State for Communities and Local Government & Anor* [2010] EWCA Civ 26 at [35], [36], [44]–[47].

(p 1013)   **In footnote 8, at end insert–**

As to evasion by a tribunal, see *Repatriation Commission v Morris* (1997) 79 FCR 455, 461.

S 324

(p 1025)   **In Comment on Code s 324, at beginning, insert–**

This section of the Code has been judicially approved.[1A]

(p 1025)   **In newly created footnote 1A, insert–**

Equuscorp Pty Ltd v Belperio [2006] VSC 14 at [248]–[251].

S 326

(p 1025)   **In passage following Example 325.4, after 'Companies Act 1985 s 726(1)', insert–**

(repealed)

(p 1030)   **In paragraph beginning 'A construction will not be allowed', at end of first sentence, insert footnote indicator 1A.**

(p 1030)   **In newly created footnote 1A, insert–**

This sentence has been judicially approved: *Wang v Minister for Immigration and Multicultural Affairs* (1997) 71 FCR 386, 394; *Byrne v Transport Accident Commission* [2008] VSC 92, [52].

S 327

(p 1033)   **In Comment on Code s 327, at beginning, insert–**

This section of the Code has been judicially approved.

(p 1033)   **In newly created footnote 1, insert–**

Re: King's Application for Judicial Review [2003] NI 43, [58].

(p 1033)   **In footnote 4, at end insert–**

For judicial discussion as to why Parliament does so, see, for example, *Revenue & Customs v BUPA Purchasing Ltd & Ors* [2007] EWCA Civ 542 at [46].

(p 1035)   **In footnote 6, at end insert–**

See also the decision of the Ontario Court of Appeal, citing Code s 327, in *Ward-Price v Mariners Haven Inc* (2001) 57 OR (3d) 410, [24] (statutory trust subject to equitable remedies for breach of trust).

S 329

(p 1050)   **In Comment on Code s 329, at beginning, insert–**

This section of the Code has been judicially approved.[3A]

(p 1050)   **In newly created footnote 3A, insert–**

Re: King's Application for Judicial Review [2003] NI 43, [58].

(p 1055)   **In last complete paragraph, after 'implicit in the Act', insert–**

This is all the more so because, in the words of Sir John Dyson, '[t]he rules of natural justice are one of the most important pillars of the common law'.[10A]

(p 1055)   **In newly created footnote 10A, insert–**

McNally v Secretary Of State For Education & Anor [2001] EWCA Civ 332, [39].

(p 1056)   **In footnote 10, at end insert–**

For an excellent summary of the law in this area, see *R (Niazi) v Secretary of State for Home Department* [2008] EWCA Civ 755.

(p 1057)   **In footnote 2, at end insert–**

See also *Odelola v Secretary of State for the Home Department* [2009] 1 WLR 1230, 1238, 1244, 1245.

(p 1057)   **In footnote 4, at end insert–**

; and *R (Bancoult) v Secretary of State for Foreign and Commonwealth Affairs* [2009] 1 AC 453, 490–491.

(p 1062)   **In footnote 4, at end insert–**

As to when a court can reopen its decision, see, generally, *HKSAR v Tin's Label Factory Ltd* (2008) 11 HKCFAR 637.

S 330

(p 1067)   **In footnote 5, at end insert–**

; *Poets Chase Freehold Co Ltd v Sinclair Gardens Investments (Kensington) Ltd* [2008] 1 WLR 768, 786–788.

(p 1069)   **At top of page, at end of quotation, before Code s 331, insert new paragraph as follows–**

Procedure Where equitable doctrines arise in a case, there may be a need for the case to be determined by a judge with specialist knowledge of those doctrines. In that event, the case will need to be adjourned to enable its determination by a specialist Chancery Circuit judge, a High Court judge of the Chancery Division or a Crown Court judge with the relevant experience and expertise.[1A]

(p 1069)   **In newly created footnote 1A, insert–**

Serious Fraud Office v Lexi Holdings Plc [2009] QB 376, 405–406.

S 331

(p 1069)   **In footnote 2, at end insert–**

Contract law may so arise in a field based partly on contract and partly on statute: see, for example, *Buckland v Bournemouth University Higher Education Corp* [2010] EWCA Civ 121 (employment law). Further, the court may apply contract law in appropriate situations notwithstanding that, due to the interposition of statute, a true contract is not in question: *Warren v Random House Group Ltd* [2009] QB 600, at [17] (case under Defamation Act 1996 ss 2–4).

(p 1070)   **After sideheading 'Effect of Act on existing contracts', at end of sentence insert footnote indicator 1A.**

(p 1070)   **In newly created footnote 1A, insert–**

This passage was approved in *Australasian Correctional Management Limited v Corrections Association of New Zealand (Inc)* [2002] 3 NZLR 250.

S 334

(p 1079)   **In footnote 5, at end insert–**

See also *Hin Lin Yee v HKSAR* [2010] 2 HKLRD 826. For the abolition of the doctrine of *doli incapax*, and the criminal liability of persons who have not attained the age of discretion (14), see *R v T* [2009] 1 AC 1310 and F A R Bennion, '*Mens rea and defendants below the age of discretion*' [2009] *Criminal Law Review* 757–770, www.francisbennion.com/2009/031.htm

(p 1083)   **In footnote 13, at end insert–**

As to autrefois acquit see *Coke-Wallis v Institute of Chartered Accountants in England and Wales* [2009] EWCA Civ 730.

(p 1084)   **At end of first passage, before sideheading 'Statement of offence', insert–**

Further, the principle does not apply where the first 'jeopardy' was vitiated by a procedural defect, such as a conviction inadvertently obtained on unsworn evidence.[3A] In any event, the principle has been modified by statute, so as to enable a person acquitted of an offence to be retried for the offence where there is 'new and compelling evidence'.[B]

(p 1084)   **In newly created footnote 3A, insert–**

Green & Green Scaffolding Ltd v Staines Magistrates' Court [2008] EWHC 1443 (Admin), [10].

(p 1084)   **In newly created footnote 3B, insert–**

Criminal Justice Act 2003 s 78. See further *R v A* [2009] 1 WLR 1947; *Re: Attorney-General's Reference (No 3 of 1999)* [2010] 1 AC 145. See also Code s 342.

S 335

(p 1086)   **In footnote 3, at end insert–**

R v Athwal [2009] 1 WLR 2430; *R v Horncastle* [2010] 2 WLR 47. Implied rules of evidence are taken to be imported in their latest form, unless the implication is to the contrary. For a fundamental change regarding the admissibility of infant evidence see *R v Barker* [2010] EWCA Crim 4, [33]–[52].

(p 1088)   **In footnote 3, at end insert–**

The wording of Example 335.6 has been judicially approved: *Iarnroid Eireann v Social Welfare Tribunal* [2007] IEHC 406. 8.1.

(p 1088)   **In footnote 4, at end insert–**

This sentence has been applied by the Bokhary PJ and Lord Scott of Foscote NPJ, speaking for the Hong Kong Court of Final Appeal. They said 'if a statutory shortcut to the proof of essential matters is to be taken advantage of it is essential that the conditions of the statutory shortcut be strictly observed': *Tse Mui Chun v HKSAR* (2003) 6 HKCFAR 601, [53].

(p 1090)   **At end of page, insert–**

Fortunately, the view of Lord Hoffmann has since prevailed in the House of Lords,[10A] as it earlier had in the Hong Kong Court of Final Appeal.[10B]

(p 1090)   **In newly created footnote 10A, insert–**

Re: B [2009] 1 AC 11. See also *Re: D* [2008] 1 WLR 1499.

(p 1090)   **In newly created footnote 10B, insert–**

Solicitor 24/07 v Law Society of Hong Kong [2008] 2 HKLRD 576.

(p 1093)   **In footnote 3, at end insert–**

See the important judgment in *Director of Public Prosecutions v Wright*
[2009] EWHC 105 (Admin), [2009] 3 All ER 726 (prosecution under
Hunting Act 2004 s 1), particularly as to Art 6 of the European
Convention on Human Rights and the distinction between the 'persuasive' and 'evidential' burdens on an accused.

(p 1094)   **In footnote 9, at end insert–**

As to quasi-estoppel, see *AAA v ASH* [2009] EWHC 636 (Fam), [2009]
4 All ER 641, [81].

(p 1097)   **In footnote 4, at end insert–**

See also *Ofulue v Bossert* [2009] 1 AC 990.

S 342

(p 1116)   **In footnote 9, at end insert–**

In this context, 'the double jeopardy rule cannot be resuscitated under
the guise of the interests of justice': *R v A* [2009] 1 WLR 1947, 1958.
See further p 1084.

S 343

(p 1117)   **After Example 343.2, insert–**

Example 343.2A The Court of Appeal had to decide whether a
variant of poker was a 'game of chance' under the Gaming
Act 1968 s 52(1). The variant involved both chance and skill.
'Game of chance' was defined by s 52(1) to include a game of
chance and skill combined. The defendant argued that, in such a
case, the element of chance had to predominate over that of skill.
The Court rejected this argument. Referring to the *de minimis*
principle, it said the element of chance should only be ignored
'where it is so insignificant as not to matter'.[6A]

(p 1117)   **In newly created footnote 6A, at end insert–**

R v Kelly [2009] 1 WLR 701, 711.

(p 1118)   **At end of first sentence, insert–**

It has even received recognition in the interpretation of a written
constitution.[1A]

(p 1118)   **In newly created footnote 1A, insert–**

Prem Singh v Director of Immigration [2003] 1 HKLRD 550, 575.

(p 1119)   **In footnote 4, at end insert–**

Note that the de minimis principle can be applied in a criminal case in
favour of the prosecution: *Briere v Hailstone* [1969] Crim LR 36.

(p 1122)   **In footnote 2, at end insert–**

See also, with approval of Code s 343, *Farnell Electronic Components
Pty Ltd v Collector of Customs* (1996) 72 FCR 125; *Roberts v Secretary
of State for Social Security* [2001] EWCA Civ 910 at [8]–[15].

S 346

(p 1129)   **In Common on Code s 346, at beginning, insert–**

This section of the Code has been judicially approved.[2A]

(p 1129)   **In newly created footnote 2A, insert–**

R (Winchester College) v Hampshire CC [2009] 1 WLR 138, 152. See
also the decision of the Alberta Court of Appeal in *Boardwalk Reit LLP
v Edmonton* (2008) 91 Alta LR (4th) 1, [75]. The Court added (at [76]):
'[c]ourts interpret statutes to relieve against more than total physical
impossibility. They demand of the citizen neither extreme ingenuity,
superhuman effort, nor massive unusual resources to comply with an
Act. All practical endeavours and a fair trial suffice'.

S 347

(p 1134)   **In footnote 9, at end insert–**

R v S Ltd [2009] EWCA Crim 85; [2009] 2 Cr App R 11.

S 350

(p 1144)   **In Comment on Code s 350, at beginning, insert–**

This section of the Code has been judicially approved.[1A]

(p 1144)   **In newly created footnote 1A, insert–**

See the decision of the Full Federal Court of Australia in *Re Sandvik
Australia Pty Limited v Commonwealth of Australia* [1990] FCA 386,
[12].

(p 1145)   **In footnote 1, at end insert–**

R (Thomas) v Greenwich Magistrates' Court [2009] EWHC 1180
(Admin); [2009] Crim LR 800 [18].

(p 1146)   **After sideheading 'Agency principle' at end of paragraph, but before Example 351.1 insert footnote indicator 1A.**

(p 1146)   **In newly created footnote 1A, insert–**

This passage was approved in *Midlands Co-Operative Society Ltd v HM Revenue & Customs* [2008] EWCA Civ 305, [14].

S 352

(p 1149)   **At bottom of page, insert–**

Indeed, the vigilance principle has been taken so far as to mean that, as in the law of contract, a statutory requirement must, in the absence of an express time limit, by implication be performed within a reasonable time.[5A]

(p 1149)   **In newly created footnote 5A, insert–**

See the decision of the Federal Court of Australia in *Boswell v Secretary, Department of Foreign Affairs and Trade* (1993) 46 FCR 434, 441. As to the law of contract, see, for example, *Behzadi v Shaftesbury Hotels* [1992] Ch 1, 12 and the decision of Lord Millett NPJ, for the Hong Kong Court of Final Appeal in *Lau Suk Ching Peggy v Ma Hing Lam* [2010] HKCFA 20, [40]–[43].

(p 1152)   **At bottom of page, insert–**

Similarly, an Act may exclude liability in the event of 'voluntary assumption of risk'.[1A] The present view is that, where an Act employs a concept similar to the *volenti* principle, the words it uses 'must be given their ordinary meaning, and not be complicated by fine distinctions or by reference to the old common law doctrine'.[1B]

(p 1152)   **In newly created footnote 1A, insert–**

See, for example, Animal Act 1971 s 5(2).

(p 1152)   **In newly created footnote 1B, insert–**

Freeman v Higher Park Farm [2008] EWCA 1185, [48].

S 355

(p 1160)   **After Example 355.13, insert new paragraph–**

On occasions, legislatures engage in cross-referencing between overlapping enactments. For example, in Australian federal statutes, where a provision enactment deals with a criminal matter, a note will direct the reader to related federal criminal legislation.[5A] However, the note is not part of the Act.[5B] In a 2003 case, the Ontario Court of Appeal had to decide whether a reference in one statutory provision to another statute was such a cross-reference or had some free-standing effect. It decided

on the former, citing the Comment on Code s 355 and describing the provision as 'deliberate redundancy'.[5C] Had the Australian approach been taken, the question would not have arisen. In any event, the provision, being part of its Act, was better classified as a declaratory enactment.[5D]

(p 1160)   **In newly created footnote 5A, insert–**

See, for example, Healthcare Identifiers Act 2010 s 15.

(p 1160)   **In newly created footnote 5B, insert–**

Interpretation Act 1901 s 13(3).

(p 1160)   **In newly created footnote 5C, insert–**

Guelph (City) v Wyndham Street Investments Inc (2003) 63 OR (2d) 481, [16].

(p 1160)   **In newly created footnote 5D, insert–**

See further Code p 188.

(p 1160) **After sideheading 'Different words to be given different meanings', at end of first sentence insert footnote indicator 10A.**

(p 1160)   **In newly created footnote 10A, insert–**

This sentence has been judicially approved: *Omagh District Council, Re Judicial Review* [2007] NIQB 61, [50].

(p 1161)   **In footnote 1, at end insert–**

; *Re James* [2005] NIQB 38, [21]; *Davidson v M* [2009] CSIH 70, [15]. See also *Speciallaser Tech Inc v Specialloy Industries Ltd* [1999] 12 WWR 139, [12].

(p 1164) **After sideheading 'Generalibus specialia derogant', at end of third sentence, insert footnote indicator 2A.**

(p 1164)   **In newly created footnote 2A, insert–**

See also *Henry Boot Construction (UK) Ltd v Malmaison Hotel Ltd* [2001] QB 388.

(p 1164)   **In footnote 5, at end insert–**

The passage from Pearce and preceding passages of the Code were applied in *Secretary for Justice v Tang Bun* [1999] 3 HKC 647, 652, 658. See also *Secretary for Justice v Lau Suk Han* [1998] 2 HKLRD 14, 22.

S 363

(p 1190)   **In footnote 11, at end insert–**

Compare *Majorstake Ltd v Curtis* [2008] 1 AC 787, 790–791, 804; *R (M) v Slough BC* [2008] 1 WLR 1808, 1825; *R (Aweys) v Birmingham CC* [2009] 1 WLR 1506.

(p 1192)   **In footnote 5, at end insert–**

This passage was applied in *Blackpool Council Licensing Authority v Howitt* [2008] EWHC 3300 (Admin), [17]–[20]. See also *Pilling v Reynolds* [2008] EWHC 316 (QB), [2009] 1 All ER 163, [21] and *Fairfax v Ireton* [2009] 1 NZLR 540.

(p 1193)   **After first paragraph, including Example 363.28 insert**
new paragraph–

Even so, a reference to a collective noun, such as a 'woodland', which includes things *in posse* as well as things *in esse* has been taken to include both.[2A]

(p 1193)   **In newly created footnote 2A, insert–**

Palm Developments Ltd v Secretary of State for Communities and Local Government [2009] EWHC 220 (Admin), [42] (tree preservation order).

S 364

(p 1195)   **In footnote 1, at end insert–**

See further *Palm Developments Ltd v Secretary of State for Communities and Local Government* [2009] EWHC 220 (Admin), [26], where Cranston J said that such provisions 'avoid the need for unprofitable disputes'.

(p 1197)   **In footnote 2, at end insert–**

See further *Victims Compensation Fund Corp v Brown* (2003) 201 ALR 260, [34].

(p 1198)   **In footnote 6, at end insert–**

For evidential issues raised by the foregoing, see, for example, *Distribution Group v Commissioner of Taxation* (2000) 45 ATR 494, 500–502.

(p 1200)   **In footnote 4, at end insert–**

In *Schanka v Employment National (Administration) Ltd* (2000) 97 FCR 186, the Full Federal Court was 'not persuaded that *"duress"* in [the provision] is used in a context dealing with the same branch of the law as the cases in which courts have [generally] been concerned to apply it ... Accordingly, we do not regard the expression as *"a free-standing legal*

term" as that phrase is used in [Code, p 1199]'. So much may be accepted. However, care must always be taken not to confuse the presence of contrary intention with the outright absence of a free-standing legal term.

S 370

(p 1215)   **At end of first full paragraph, insert–**

The Divisional Court accepted criticism of the expression 'saving life or limb' in Police and Criminal Evidence Act s 17(1)(e) as 'colourful [and] slightly outmoded' but explained that it 'indicates a serious matter – that ... would involve some serious injury to an individual'.[2A]

(p 1215)   **In newly created footnote 2A, insert–**

Syed v DPP [2010] 1 Cr App Rep 480, [11].

S 374

(p 1219)   **At top of page, after passage in inverted commas but before paragraph beginning 'Where an artificial meaning', insert–**

Example 373.5A Section 22(2)(a) of the Immigration Act 1971 (repealed) enabled rules of procedure to be made so as to enable 'the Tribunal, on an appeal from an adjudicator, to remit the appeal for determination by him in accordance with any directions of the Tribunal'. In context, 'appeal' was a homonym as the proceeding before the adjudicator grounding the appeal to the Tribunal was also called an appeal. Counsel argued that 'appeal' in s 22(2)(a) had a consistent meaning, being 'appeal from an adjudicator', with the result that the Tribunal could delegate the task of determining a particular appeal to an adjudicator. The Court rejected the argument, effectively reading the second reference to appeal as 'the appeal [that had been] to [the] adjudicator'. After referring to the Comment on Code s 373, Scott Baker J (as he then was) said there was 'no absolute rule that one word cannot have two different meanings within the same section or subsection. True, it will only rarely occur but the ultimate question is what did Parliament intend'.[1A]

(p 1219)   **In newly created footnote 1A, insert–**

R (Secretary of State for Home Department) v Immigration Tribunal [2001] QB 1224, 1233. The judge also said (at 1227) that successor legislation was 'not materially different' and '[f]or convenience ... annexed to this judgment a table that shows the corresponding provisions in the old and new law'.

S 384

(p 1242)   **In Comment on Code s 384, insert at beginning–**

This section of the Code has been judicially approved.[2A]

(p 1242)   **In newly created footnote 2A, insert–**

See the decision of the Queensland Court of Appeal in *Pepper v Attorney-General (No 2)* [2008] QCA 207, [32].

S 389

(p 1250)   **After Example 389.1, insert–**

Example 389.1A Section 11 of the Public Order Act 1986 required notice to be given of a proposal to hold a public procession, including the route of the procession, except where the procession was 'commonly or customarily held'. The issue arose: could a procession attract the exception without having a predetermined route? If not, the procession could not be held, as notice thereof could not properly be given. This implied prohibition would operate alongside an express prohibition elsewhere in the Act. The House of Lords applied the exception. Lord Rodger (Baroness Hale agreeing) said 'Where the Act contains a specific provision prohibiting certain processions, there is no room for implying into another provision a requirement which would have the effect of prohibiting a different type of procession'.[2A]

(p 1250)   **In newly created footnote 2A, insert–**

Kay v Commissioner of Police [2008] 1 WLR 2723, 2735.

S 393

(p 1255)   **In Comment on Code s 393, at beginning, insert–**

This section of the Code has been judicially approved.[5A]

(p 1255)   **In newly created footnote 5A, insert–**

See the decision of the Full Federal Court of Australia in *Eastman v Commissioner of Superannuation* (1987) 15 FCR 139, 148.

S 397

(p 1268)   **In footnote 2, at end insert–**

R (Kaupthing Bank HF) v HM Treasury [2009] EWHC 2542 (Admin), [37].

S 412

(p 1292)   **At top of page, after quotation, insert new paragraph–**

English judges have, on occasion, lamented the adoption of substantial effect where copyout would clearly do.[1A]

(p 1292)   **In newly created footnote 1A, insert–**

Spencer-Franks v Kellogg Brown and Root Ltd and others [2008] UKHL 46, [2009] 1 All ER 269, [26]. For discussion of an error in transposing see *Marks & Spencer plc v Revenue and Customs Commissioners* [2009] UKHL 8, [8].

S 413

(p 1299)   **In footnote 2, at end insert–**

For a recent application of the Marleasing principle, see *R (on the application of Irving) v Secretary of State for Transport* [2008] EWHC 1200 (Admin).

S 417

(p 1309)   **At end of Comment on Code s 417, before Code s 418, insert–**

A claim for Francovich damages against the government for failing to implement Community law is a claim in tort to which the Limitation Act 1980 s 2 applies.[2A]

(p 1309)   **In newly created footnote 2A, insert–**

Spencer v Secretary of State for Work and Pensions [2009] QB 358.

INTRODUCTION TO PART XXX

(p 1312)   **In footnote 2, at end insert–**

See further *AS (Somalia) v Entry Clearance Officer (Addis Ababa)* [2009] 1 WLR 1385, 1391–1392.

S 420

(p 1321)   **In Comment on Code s 420, at end of second paragraph, insert–**

Nonetheless, the court may, on rare occasions, decline to follow a particular Strasbourg decision where the court has concerns as to whether the decision insufficiently appreciates or accommodates particular aspects of the domestic process.[3A]

(p 1321)   **In newly created footnote 3A, insert–**

R v Horncastle [2010] 2 WLR 47, 97. Compare *Manchester CC v Pinnock* [2010] 3 WLR 1441.

S 421

(p 1324)   **In footnote 3, at end insert–**

For a similar rule of interpretation relating to compatibility with a written constitution, see, for example, *HKSAR v Lam Kwong Wai* [2006] 3 HKLRD 808.

(p 1325)   **In footnote 4, at end insert–**

See further *Corporate Officer of the House of Commons v The Informa-tion Commissioner & Ors* [2008] EWHC 1084 (Admin), [2009] 3 All ER 403, [2] where the Divisional Court said 'It is a fundamental principle of our constitutional structures that Parliament should not normally be subject to judicial scrutiny or supervision. The House of Commons is answerable to its collective conscience, and in the ultimate analysis, to the electorate.'

(p 1325)   **In footnote 3, at end insert–**

More gratifying is the holding by the High Court of Justiciary, after referring to the discussion above, 'I consider that it is possible to come to a Convention compatible construction of [the provision at issue] without imposing such a degree of strain on the language as to require justifica-tion by reference to section 3 of the Human Rights Act': *M v Watson* [2009] HCJ 3, [26]–[27].

S 422

(p 1331) **At end of fourth passage, after quotation ending 'instead to grant a declaration of incompatibility' insert, as a new paragraph–**

Fortunately, in a 2009 case, the House of Lords allowed an appeal against a decision of the Court of Appeal purporting to write words into the Standards Act 2000 s 82(4)(b) under the Human Rights Act 1998 s 3(1). The House substituted a declaration of incompatibility, with the House remarking 'it is not for us to attempt to rewrite the legislation'. To the extent this represents a shift away from s 3(1) and toward a declaration, it is welcome.[8A]

(p 1331)   **In newly created footnote 8A, insert–**

R (Wright) v Secretary of State for Health [2009] 1 AC 739, 748, 755.

S 428

(p 1335)   **In footnote 2, at end insert–**

For an instance where a Minister indicated he was unable to make a statement of compatibility as envisaged by Code s 426(1)(b) see *R (Animal Defenders International) v Secretary of State for Culture, Media and Sport* [2008] 1 AC 1312, 1340.

S 443

(p 1352)   **Under sideheading 'Meaning of 'court', at end of paragraph, insert–**

Nonetheless, in the case of a determinate sentence, the power of the Home Secretary under s 35(1) to accept or reject a recommendation by

the Board to release prisoners on licence is not incompatible with Art 5(4), as the foregoing does not give rise to a new issue affecting the lawfulness of their detention.[5A]

(p 1352)   **In newly created footnote 5A, insert–**

R (Black) v Secretary of State for Home Department [2009] 1 AC 949.

S 444

(p 1356)   **In footnote 2, delete text and insert–**

[2003] 2 AC 430, 445–447. See also *R (A) v Croydon LBC* [2009] 1 WLR 2557.

(p 1356)   **At bottom of page, insert–**

It is uncontroversial that Art 6 'does not require a right of appeal, let alone an appeal by way of rehearing'.[14A]

(p 1356)   **In newly created footnote 14A, insert–**

R (Langley) v Preston Crown Court [2009] 1 WLR 1612, 1619.

S 446

(p 1360)   **Under sideheading 'Police powers', at end of sentence insert–**

It also applies to the retention and release by the police of criminal records and related information.[11A]

(p 1360)   **In newly created footnote 11A, insert–**

R (L) v Commissioner of Police [2010] 1 AC 410.

S 447

(p 1362)   **In footnote 7, at end insert–**

Thus, Art 9 'does not always guarantee the right to behave in the public sphere in a way which is dictated by [religion]': *Ladele v London Borough of Islington* [2009] EWCA Civ 1357; [2010] 1 WLR 955.

(p 1363)   **In footnote 1, at end insert–**

and *Ladele v London Borough of Islington* [2009] EWCA Civ 1357; [2010] 1 WLR 955.

(p 1369)   **In footnote 1, at end insert–**

As to the scope of personal rights, see *Hanchett-Stamford v Attorney-General* [2009] Ch 173 (right of sole surviving member of unincorporated association to assets of association).

S 462

(p 1373)   **In footnote 8, at end insert–**

See also *Corporate Officer of the House of Commons v The Information Commissioner & Ors* [2008] EWHC 1084 (Admin), [2009] 3 All ER 403, [43].

(p 1376)   **In footnote 5, at end insert–**

In relation to the words 'as it has effect for the time being in relation to the United Kingdom' see *R (on the application of Bancoult) v Secretary of State For Foreign and Commonwealth Affairs* [2009] 1 AC 453.

Appendix C

Updated Text of Interpretation Act 1978

(p 1391)   **In section 20A:**

replace 'Community Instruments' in heading and 'Community Instrument' in body of section with 'EU instruments' and 'EU instrument' respectively.

In annotations insert–

(p 1395)   Amended by European Union (Amendment) Act 2008 s 3(3), Sch Pt 2.

Definitions–

(p 1397)   In definitions beginning 'The Communities', replace 'The Communities' with 'The EU' and 'the Community treaties' with 'the EU treaties'.
In definition '["The Immigration Acts"]' delete, 'section 64 of the Immigration, Asylum and Nationality Act' and replace with 'section 61 of the UK Borders Act 2007'].

(p 1398)   In definition 'London borough', replace '[or Part II of the Local Government Act 1992]' with '[, Part II of the Local Government Act 1992 or Part I of the Local Government and Public Involvement in Health Act 2007]'

After definition of 'registered medical practitioner', insert–

(p 1400)   'Registered provider of social housing' and 'private registered provider of social housing' have the meanings given by section 80 of the Housing and Regeneration Act 2008 (and 'non-profit' and 'profit-making' in connection with a registered provider are to be read in accordance with section 115 of that Act).'

In between definitions of 'Committed for trial' and 'The Corporation Tax Acts', insert–

'Definition beginning "The Communities" amended by European Union (Amendment) Act 2008 s 3(3) Sch Pt 2.'

(p 1401)   Date in force: 1 December 2009: see SI 2009 / 3143 art 2.

In annotation regarding definition ['The Immigration Acts'] insert at end of first sentence–

Definition amended by UK Borders Act 2007 s 61(4).
Date in force: 30 October 2007 (date of the Royal Assent of the UK Borders Act 2007) in the absence of any specific commencement provision.

In annotation regarding definition "London borough', insert at end of first sentence–

, words '[, Part II of the Local Government Act 1992 or Part I of the Local Government and Public Involvement in Health Act 2007]' substituted by Local Government and Public Involvement in Health Act 2007, s 22, Sch 1, Pt 2, para 14"

(p 1402)   Date in force: Local Government and Public Involvement in Health Act 2007: 1 November 2007: see SI 2007/3136, art 2(b).

Definition beginning 'Registered provider of social housing' inserted by Housing and Regeneration Act 2008 s 277 Sch 9 para 5. Amended by SI 2010/844, art 6, Sch 2, para 1.

Date in force: 1 April 2010: see SI 2010/844 art 1(2), SI 2010/862, art 2.

Index

Note An item not found in this Index may be included either in the list set out in Appendix E (pages 1419 to 1424) or in the Bibliography (pages 1475 to 1507).

Abbott CJ   1010, 1070
abbreviations   37, 1216
Abinger, Lord   869, 879
absolute liability – *see* strict liability
absurdity
    anomaly   521, 841–842, 917, 986–999,
        1021–1022
    artificiality   969–971, 1003–1006
    and see counter-mischief;
        evasion of Act
    futility   969–971, 999–1003
    illogicality   986–999
    impracticality   388n, 969–979
    inconvenience, avoidance of   382, 526,
        527, 870, 969–971,
        979–986
    literal construction and   459
    logical impossibility   973–974
    meaning of   969–971
    Pepper v Hart, rule in, and   616, 618–621
    presumption against   325–326, 527, 529,
        870, 969–971
    trivial acts – *see de minimus non*
        curat lex
    unreasonable dilemma   974
    – *and see* counter-mischief;
        evasion of Act
abuse of process – *see* process
academic point   143, 144, 175, 418, 780,
        1269
accidental fit – *see* intention,
    legislative
Ackner, Lord   177, 1270
acquis communautaire   1283, 1285
'acronymania'   737
act in law – *see* judicial act
act of God   1104–1105, 1176
Act of Parliament – *see* Bill,
    parliamentary; enactment;
    free-standing Act, doctrine of;
    heading; Parliament;

Act of Parliament – *contd*
    Parliament Roll; punctuation;
    section; statute; taxing Acts;
    treaty
    acting 'in execution of' an   95
    acting 'under' an   183
    administration of – *see* enforcement
        agencies
    adoptive – *see* adoptive Act
    'always speaking'   891
    amending   186
    amendment of – *see* amendment to
        Act
    amnesty, conferring   184, 189
    ancient – *see* statutes
    application of – *see* application of
        Act
    Appropriation   191
    assent to – *see* Royal assent
    atmosphere analogy   365
    attainder, of   189
    bad faith, whether vitiated by   234
    Bill for – *see* Bill, parliamentary
    chapter number of – *see* chapter
        number of Act
    citation in other Act   1391
    Clauses – *see* Clauses Act
    code of practice under – *see* codes
        of practice
    codifying – *see* codification
    commencement of – *see*
        commencement of Act or
        enactment
    components of – *see* functional
        construction
    consolidation – *see* consolidation
        Act
    constitution, incorporating   910
    constitutional   189, 305
    contravention of – *see* disobeying
        Act; statutory duty
    conveyancing   190

All references are to page numbers

Act of Parliament – *contd*
copyright in   183, 226–227
Crown, when bound by – *see*
    Crown
declaratory – *see* **declaratory**
    enactment
definition of   179–183
desuetude   15, 102, 277, 312–314, 572,
                888
    – *and see* **Scotland**
disproprietory   846–847
duplication of application – *see*
    application of Act
editions, published official, of   230–232
enabling   241, 256
enactment procedure   213–216, 714–715
    – *and see* **enacting formula;**
       Royal assent
enforcement of – *see* **enforcement**
    agencies; legal policy;
    prosecution of offences
Estate   1072
evasion of – *see* **evasion of Act**
exemplification of   229
Expiring Laws Continuance Act –
    see **Expiring Laws**
    Continuance Acts
expiry of – *see* **temporary Act**
extent of – *see* **territorial extent of**
    Act
failure of   942
financial   190–191
    – *and see* **taxing Acts**
fixed-time   184, 187, 890, 909–911
floodlight analogy   192, 194, 196, 308,
                316, 325, 365
fraud, not vitiated by   233
general   183, 185–186
guidelines issued under   706
in pari materia – *see* **in pari**
    materia, Acts
Indemnity Act   184, 189, 909
integrity of   1028–1029
interpretation of – *see*
    interpretative criteria;
    interpretative factors;
    statutory interpretation
invalidity, grounds of   232–236
judicial notice of – *see* **judicial**
    notice
law reform   184, 187
    – *and see* **Law Commission;**
       Statute Law Revision Act
local – *see* **local Act**
long title of – *see* **long title**
mistake in – *see* **mistake**
model Act – *see* **adoptive Act**
modern statute – *see* **statutes**
naming of   735–739

Act of Parliament – *contd*
nature of   5, 191–194
non-homogeneous   1165
oblivion, of   184, 189
ongoing   184, 187, 890–910
overriding effect of   197–204, 304–305
'passing' of   744
permanent   183, 186
personal – *see* **personal Act**
personal application of – *see*
    application of Act
preparation of – *see* **Bill,**
    parliamentary
prerogative and – *see* **prerogative,**
    Royal
principal   183, 186, 607
private – *see* **private Act**
promulgation of – *see*
    promulgation of Act
public general   183–186
publication of – *see* **promulgation**
    of Act
purpose of – *see* **purposive**
    construction
references to   230–232
regulatory   829–830, 1006, 1066
remedial   207
renaming of   738–739
repeal of – *see* **repeal**
reprinting clause   228
residual powers in   256
retrospective – *see* **retrospectivity**
rewrite Act – *see* **tax law rewrite**
    Acts
Royal assent to – *see* **Royal assent**
rug analogy   198
self-applying   183
short title of – *see* **short title**
specialty, as – *see* **specialty**
split   710
Statute Law Revision – *see* **Statute**
    Law Revision Act
suspensory   225
tax law rewrite – *see* **tax law**
    rewrite Act
temporal aspect of – *see* **time**
temporary – *see* **temporary Act**
territorial extent of – *see* **territorial**
    extent of Act
text of   213, 215–216, 225–230
three-fold consent, doctrine of   179–182,
                212–213, 223, 224,
                232–236, 407
transitional provisions of – *see*
    transitional provisions
treaty, implementing   190
types of   183–191
uniqueness of   204–206
validation   184, 189

Act of Parliament – *contd*
  validity, challenge to   232–236
    – *and see* **enactment; natural
      law**
act of state
  judicial notice of   823–824
  nature of   238, 369
    jurisdiction of courts   238
  sovereign immunity – *see* **privileges
    and immunities**
  territory, relating to   329, 406
  war   238, 369
    – *and see* **Minister of the
      Crown**
*acta exteriora indicant interiora
  secreta* – *see* **intention,
  ascertainment of**
acte clair   1306
action, cause of – *see* **cause of action**
actus curiae neminem gravabit   984
actus dei nemini facit injuriam – *see*
  act of God
actus reus – *see* **criminal law**
adjudicating authorities
  appellate jurisdiction, with   142–154
  original jurisdiction, with   138–142
    – *and see* **enforcement agencies**
administration of Act – *see*
  **enforcement agencies; statutory
  power**
Administrative Court   154, 155, 163
administrative law – *see*
  **decision-making rules; judicial
  review; public law**
Admiral, the   140, 141, 330, 351, 357, 368,
       913
Admiralty – *see* **Admiral, the;
  jurisdiction**
Adoptive Act   183, 186–187
  – *and see* **Clauses Act**
adversarial system – *see* **court**
adviser, legal – *see* **advocate;
  solicitors; subject, the**
Advisory Committee on Statute Law   231
advocate
  adoption of text as part of argument   29,
       34, 693
  adviser, as   35, 42, 438
  alternative arguments, presented by   433
  checklist for   1383–1385
  conduct of case, rights regarding   617–618,
       692–693, 854, 1087
  court technique   593–594, 1381–1382
  court, interpretative function of, and   434–
       435, 443
  cross-examination by   777
  duty of   435, 620, 623–627
  facts, preparation and presentation
    of, by   426–427

advocate – *contd*
  interpretative factors and   528, 575–576,
       583, 955–956
  interstitial articulation by   505, 534–537
  lay   112–113
  legislative history, use of, and   617–618,
       620, 623–627, 693
    – *and see* **legislative history;**
       ***Pepper v Hart*, rule in**
  Parliamentary Bar   184
  parliamentary procedure, duty to
    know   626–627
  plausible   26
  privilege regarding legal advice   244
  role of   436–437, 443
  specially appointed (SAA)   112
    – *and see* **Brandeis brief;
      central function of
      practitioner; hairsplitting;
      McKenzie friend;
      pleading; skeleton
      arguments; solicitors;
      subject, the**
affirmative resolution procedure –
  see **delegated legislation**
Agag   485
age   200, 948n, 992
  – *and see* **children**
agency   200, 1146–1149
  – *and see* **employment; vicarious
    liability**
aircraft, law prevailing on   386–387
airspace   334
Alderson, B   206
Aldous LJ   1185
aliens   366–367, 371, 383, 922
  – *and see* application of Act;
    foreign; European Convention
    on Human Rights
Allan, T R S – *see* **Bibliography (pp
  1475 to 1507)**
*allegans suam turpitudinem non est
  audiendus* – *see* **illegality**
allegiance, duty of   379
Allen, Carleton Kemp   182, 203n, 241n,
       392, 407n, 488, 865
  – *and see* **Bibliography (pp 1475
    to 1507)**
Allen, Layman – *see* **Bibliography
  (pp 1475 to 1507)**
Allgemeines Landrecht   170
Alsatia   105
alter ego **doctrine** – *see* *Carltona*
  principle
**Alternative Dispute Resolution
  (ADR)**   102
Alverstone, Lord   732
ambiguity
  contextual   445–446

All references are to page numbers

ambiguity – *contd*
ejusdem generis *principle and* 1233–1234
grammatical – *see* **ambiguity**
(**grammatical**)
noscitur a sociis *principle and* 1230
resolving – *see* **interpretative**
criteria
semantic 445–446
syntactic 445–446
unrecognised 446–447
vagueness and, contrasted 445–446
ambiguity (grammatical)
general 447–448, S46
interpretative factors, application of 444–
447, 515, 521–523,
529–531, 551
judgment or discretion, and 127–129, 444
literal meaning, relation to 952–954
nature of 443–444, 1190
opposing constructions, and 257, 263,
429–438, 448–450,
972–973
punctuation and 757–758
relative 447–448
syntactical or formal 557
– *and see* **ambiguity; broad**
terms; differential
readings; doubtful
penalisation, principle
against; legal meaning;
noscitur a sociis **principle;**
obscurity, semantic; politic
uncertainty; repugnancy
amendment to Act
commencement of 288
consequential 295–297
consolidation Acts and 604–607
construction of 288, 1166
defective 413n
delegated legislation, by 245, 293–295
enactment procedure, mistake in 235–236
– *and see* **mistake**
extra-statutory concession – *see*
extra-statutory concession
implied 293, 295
indirect express 145–146, 292–293, 295n,
301
meaning 195, 214, 287–288
Official Table 295
power to propose, statutory 978–979
printing corrections – *see* **printing**
corrections
reference to amended Act 298–199
referential definitions and 572
repeal and 288
– *and see* **repeal**
same session, in 287, 288, 1387
substantive and temporal provisions 195–
196

amendment to Act – *contd*
textual 146, 288–292, 300
– *and see* **punctuation**
transfer of Minister's functions, on 85–86,
288–292
transitional provisions – *see*
transitional provisions
– *and see* **free-standing Act,**
doctrine of; Henry VIII
clause; repeal;
retrospectivity
amendment to delegated legislation 274–
275, 1390
Amos, Maurice Sheldon – *see*
Bibliography (pp 1475 to 1507)
analogy, statutory – *see* **statutory**
analogy
ancillary powers, implied – *see*
implied ancillary powers
ancillary rules of law
express application of 1033, 1042
implied application of 254, 1033–1042
meaning 1033
vacant provisions 1039
'and', use of 1192
Andrews, J – *see* **Bibliography (pp**
1475 to 1507)
Anisminic **principle** – *see*
decision-making rules
anomaly – *see* **absurdity**
anonymity
criminal cases, in 121
drafting defect 567n
Anson, W – *see* **Bibliography (pp**
1475 to 1507)
anti-social behaviour order 94, 1356
anti-social behaviour order (*ASBO*) 1356
appeal
academic point, on 144
additional grounds of 56
appellate courts 102, 116–118
case stated, by 55, 146–147, 159
consent order, against 1260–1261
contempt of court and 148, 255
county court, from 149
county court, to 145
Court of Appeal 113, 116, 139, 148–151,
392, 1396
criminal 94, 149–151, 993
Crown court, from 146–147, 149
Crown court, to 146–147
decision on appeal, against 149
facts and 427
'final' decision, against 109, 147, 414
High Court, from 147–148
High Court, to 146–147
Human Rights Act 1998 – *see*
Human Rights Act 1998

All references are to page numbers

appeal – *contd*
judicial and administrative
discretion compared   144
'leapfrogging'   148, 151
leave to   106, 148–152
    – *and see Scherer* **principle**
Lords, House of, to   151–152
magistrates, to   145
mistake of law, and   41
nature of   143, 392
point of law, meaning of   148
references to European Court and   1307
review and   102, 116–118, 1054n
right of   857–858
tribunals, from   147–148
    – *and see* **county court;**
       Divisional Court;
       evidence; jurisdiction;
       Lords, House of;
       magistrates; mandatory
       and directory
       requirements; mistake;
       notice; retrospectivity;
       time; tribunals
appearance *gratis*   58
Appellate Committee of House of
    Lords   152–153
application of Act
aliens, to   392
deemed location of omission   387–389
duplication of   393
extra-territorial   364
    – *and see* **extra-territoriality**
foreign elements within the territory,
    and   364–371
'foreign' elements and   362–363
    – *and see* **private international law**
matters both within and outside
    jurisdiction   381
non-resident Britons, to   378–384
non-resident foreigners, to   371–378
overseas property of resident
    foreigners   367
Parliament, to   1049
principles governing   193, 194–196, 327,
       360–364, 1098–1099
resident foreigners, to   364–371
sovereign immunity – *see* **privileges**
    and immunities
    – *and see* **aliens;**
       exterritoriality;
       extra-territoriality;
       uniform statutes
appropriate forum test   333
Arbab-Dehkordi, B   720
    – *and see* **Bibliography (pp 1475**
       to 1507)
arbitration   54, 120, 270, 294, 447, 448,
       449, 478, 781, 782,

arbitration – *contd*
       800, 812, 974, 988,
       1087, 1193, 1260
archaisms   1181, 1213
Archbold, J F – *see* **Bibliography**
    (pp 1475 to 1507)
archival drafting – *see* **incorporation**
    by reference
Arden LJ   27, 200, 547, 1300n
Arizona, constitution of   171
Arnold P   980
arson   374, 896, 991, 1124, 1125
artificial person
appearance by   112
company   87
creation of   239, 577, 903
included in 'person'   577
location, deemed, of   389–390
piercing the veil   389
powers of   239
rights of   103
    – *and see* **absurdity;**
       commercial enactments;
       Crown; local authority;
       public authority; *qui facit*
       *per alium facit per se***;**
       vicarious liability
artificiality – *see* **absurdity; artificial**
    person
ASBO – *see* **anti-social behaviour**
    order (ASBO)
Ashworth J   993
Ashworth, Andrew   94
    – *and see* **Bibliography (pp 1475**
       to 1507)
'asifism'   146, 386, 759n
    – *and see* **deeming**
Asquith of Bishopstone, Lord   910
assessor   30, 394, 1355n
associated state, meaning of   339, 340, 345,
       1394, 1396
Astill J   90
Aston J   654
Atiyah, P S   418
    – *and see* **Bibliography (pp 1475**
       to 1507)
Atkin, Lord   29, 32, 42, 142, 418, 419, 467,
       473, 563, 936, 956,
       965, 1126
Atkinson, Lord   658, 813, 829
Attorney General
consent of   74
functions of   73–74, 97, 100, 435n, 623
prosecutions, role of in   96–98, 660, 1083
public interest immunity and   1095–1097
relator actions – *see* **relator action**
    – *and see* **Crown Prosecution**
       Service; Director of Public
       Prosecutions; Minister of

All references are to page numbers

Attorney General – *contd*
  relator actions – *contd*
    – *and see* Crown Prosecution Service;
      Director of Public Prosecutions;
      Minister of – *contd*
      the Crown; prosecution of
      offences; relator action
Attorney General v Great Eastern
  Railway Co, rule in   256, 497
Attorney General v Lamplough, rule
  in   x, 289–290
audi alteram partem principle   120, 1055–
                              1056, 1061, 1111–
                              1115, 1137, 1286
Auld LJ   506, 1040, 1196
Australia
  amendments to Bill, interpretative
    use of, in   640
  Australia Act 1986   338–339
  ejusdem generis principle, in   1236n
  Hansard, use of, in   618, 673–677
  hendiadys, use of, in   1197
  independent Crown dominion, an 338–339
  legislative history, use of, in   590, 592n,
                        611–612, 613n, 669n
  mischief   929
  Parts, division of Act into, in   749–750
  'plant', meaning of, in   1215
  punctuation, in   757
  purpose clause, in   734
  purposive construction in   944
  self-defence, law of, in   556
autrefois acquit   374, 555, 810, 1083, 1084
autrefois attaint   889
autrefois convict   810, 1083, 1084
avoidance – *see* evasion of Act
Avory J   715, 746, 748, 1084, 1085, 1454
Bacon, Francis   1102, 1226 –
  and see Bibliography (pp 1475 to
    1507)
Bacon, Matthew – *see* Bibliography
  (pp 1475 to 1507)
Baggallay LJ   656
bailiff – *see* enforcement agencies
Baker, K   206n
Baker, (Sir George) P   661
Balcombe LJ   51, 55, 106, 294n, 937, 1307
Bankes LJ   1265
Bank of England   1394
Bank of Ireland   1395
bankruptcy   46, 371, 378n, 503, 772, 847,
                  947, 994, 1004, 1005,
                       1067, 1100
Barber principle   1279–1280
Barnes, Jeffrey W   6n, 124n, 431n, 547,
                 651n, 652n, 944 –
  and see Bibliography (pp 1475 to
    1507)
Barras principle   599–604, 694n, S35

Barrington, Daines   7, 118, 477, 917, 1240
  – *and see* Bibliography (pp 1475
    to 1507)
Barwick CJ   640, 734
  – *and see* Bibliography (pp 1475
    to 1507)
baseline
  meaning of   340–341
  UK   340–341, 358
Bates, T St J N   475n, 723n
  – *and see* Bibliography (pp 1475
    to 1507)
Bayley J   1190
Beatson J   499n, 1291n, 1459
  – *and see* Bibliography (pp 1475
    to 1507)
Beaulac, Stéphane – *see*
  Bibliography (pp 1475 to 1507)
Beldam LJ   1305
Bell, John   8n, 135
  – *and see* Bibliography (pp 1475
    to 1507)
Bell, W E – *see* Bibliography (pp
  1475 to 1507)
Bellamy, J G – *see* Bibliography (pp
  1475 to 1507)
belt-and-braces phrase   1157n, 1189
benefit from own wrong – *see nullus*
  commodum capere potest de
  injuria sua propria
benefit, statutory – *see* statutory
  right
Bennett principle   100
  – *and see* process
Bennion, F A R – *see* Bibliography
  (pp 1475 to 1507)
Bennion's Gloss   828n
Bentham, Jeremy   24, 118, 397, 507, 527n,
                  564, 805, 922, 1173
  – *and see* Bibliography (pp 1475
    to 1507)
Berwick upon Tweed   42, 341–342
Best CJ   1239
Better Regulation Commission   91
Better Regulation Task Force   91
Bevan, Aneurin   592
bias   1061
  – *and see nemo debet esse judex in*
    propria causa
bilingual systems – *see* legal
  meaning
Bill of Rights [1689]   181, 236, 305, 836,
                   853, 1047, 1048, 1050
Bill, parliamentary
  amendment to – *see* amendment to
    Bill
  Civil List   191
  commentary on   592
  Consolidation Fund   191, 221

All references are to page numbers

Bill, parliamentary – *contd*
copyright in   183, 226–227
draft   180
enactment procedure – *see* **Act of Parliament**
endorsements on   214–215
enrolment of   227
explanatory material on, published by Government   641–644, 1454–1455
explanatory memorandum   641, 1454–1455
financial   191, 221
form of   180
hybrid   186, 1073
interpretation of enactment by reference to   180
judicial notice of – *see* **judicial notice**
legal status of   182, 205
money bill   223–224
notes on clauses   641–642
printing corrections – *see* **printing corrections**
private   184, 724, 733,
– *and see* **Private Act**
private member's   621
Royal Assent to – *see* **Royal assent**
'scope', doctrine of   728
sessional carry-over   180
statutory effect of   205
textual memorandum on – *see* **textual memorandum**
– *and see* **legislative history**
Bingham of Cornhill, Lord   101n, 125, 130, 131, 153, 202, 278, 369n, 415, 420, 550, 632, 688, 706, 783, 788, 806, 812, 823, 826, 837, 1006, 1090, 1200, 1201, 1311, 1312, 1314, 1324, 1327, 1348, 1360
– *and see* **Bibliography (pp 1475 to 1507)**
Birkenhead, Lord LC   640, 1128
Birks, Peter   12, 14
– *and see* **Bibliography (pp 1475 to 1507)**
Blackburn, Lord   335n, 497, 585, 614n, 677n, 775, 870, 899, 912, 1202
Blackburne J   244n, 494, 708
Blackett-Ord V-C   901
Blackstone, William   7, 30, 39, 40, 41, 46, 63, 64, 93, 96, 103, 139, 167, 182, 229, 238, 343, 344, 346, 347, 352, 356, 359, 365, 372, 408, 426,

Blackstone, William – *contd*
458, 464, 471, 477, 478, 484, 491, 495, 513, 516, 559, 655, 668, 671, 760, 761, 773, 801, 802, 804, 806, 808, 838, 846, 875, 889, 895, 898, 920, 921, 924, 926, 948, 1002, 1009, 1072, 1083, 1125, 1133, 1135, 1137, 1172, 1175, 1176, 1198, 1246, 1247
– *and see* **Bibliography (pp 1475 to 1507)**
blasphemy and blasphemous libel   S15
Blom-Cooper, Louis   1196n
– *and see* **Bibliography (pp 1475 to 1507)**
body corporate – *see* **artificial person**
Bokhary PJ   S58
Bologna, law of   170
bona fides non patitur ut bis idem exigatur – *see* **double jeopardy**
Bond, M F – *see* **Bibliography (pp 1475 to 1507)**
Book, this
nature of   ix, 12–14
philosophy of   1–5, 544–548
practitioner's bible   ix
substance of   5
updating of   x
– *and see* **Code, the**
Bouvier, John   751
– *and see* **Bibliography (pp 1475 to 1507)**
Bowen LJ   46, 423n, 427, 491, 681n, 979n, 1187, 1245
Bowles, Gibson   191n, 205
box principle   907, 908–909
– *and see* **updating construction; words**
Brabazon CJ   653
Bracewell J   87, 436n
Bracton   30, 801n
– *and see* **Bibliography (pp 1475 to 1507)**
Bradley, A W – *see* **Bibliography (pp 1475 to 1507)**
Bramwell, B   870
Brandeis brief   595
Brandon, Lord   686n, 1029, 1131
Bray CJ   675
Brazil, P   652n
– *and see* **Bibliography (pp 1475 to 1507)**

All references are to page numbers

breach of statutory duty, tort of
class intended to benefit   76
common law and   71
damage intended to be covered   77–79, 939
difficulty of determining   69
European Community law, under   71
exclusive remedy, where   75
general remedies for   67, 72
Law Commissions' recommendation   70
legislative intention and   68, 69, 70, 73–82
mental element and   79
misfeasance in public office and   72
negligence and   68, 72, 82–84
personal safety, high risk to, and   78–79
private law remedies for   67, 68, 70, 71
public law remedies for   67, 68
relator actions and   73–74
vicarious liability and   67, 72–73
volenti non fit injuria and   1150–1151
   – *and see* **contempt of statute; disobeying Act; magistrates; relator action; tort**

Brett LJ   79

Bridge of Harwich, Lord   106, 403, 619, 636, 1297

Brightman, Lord   117, 127, 321, 392, 800, 850, 1024

'British Islands', meaning of   342, 1395

British overseas territory   1395

'British possession', meaning of   343, 1395

broad terms
consistent interpretation of, required   803–804
examples of   125, 146n, 419–421, 429, 445, 1167–1170
fact and degree, question of – *see* **fact**
guidelines as to meaning of   129
interpretation of   448, 803, 1167
mobile in space   1170
mobile in time   1169
mobile in time and space   1170
multiple   425, 1170
narrowing by implication   1168–1169
nature of   129
processed   1169
static   1169

Brooke LJ   107, 187, 605, 632, 642, 709, 776, 782, 806, 822, 831n, 856, 1075, 1117, 1215, 1311, 1314, 1318, 1319, 1367
   –*and see* **Bibliography (pp 1475 to 1507)**

Broom, Herbert   39n, 62, 63n, 408, 464, 601n, 647, 864, 865, 888, 889, 1129, 1250
   – *and see* **Bibliography (pp 1475 to 1507)**

Brougham, Lord   184n, 228, 373, 398, 412, 493, 576, 718, 719, 1047, 1410, 1414, 1418

Brown (Simon) LJ   332n, 402n, 414n, 576, 580, 596n, 826, 838, 924, 1135, 1136, 1238

Brown (Stephen) P   461, 681, 811, 1137, 1294

Brown of Eaton-under-Heywood, Lord   950, 1367

Browne LJ   299, 796

Browne-Wilkinson, Lord   71, 72, 80, 81, 83, 84, 126, 260n, 410, 506, 563, 582, 617, 620, 621, 622, 623, 631, 632, 633, 634, 635, 637, 646, 648, 667, 669n, 670, 671, 685, 695, 706, 707, 788, 814, 828, 857, 868, 971, 982, 1014, 1020, 1050, 1053, 1065, 1111, 1276n, 1313
   – *and see* **Bibliography (pp 1475 to 1507)**

Brownlie, I – *see* **Bibliography (pp 1475 to 1507)**

Brussels Convention on Jurisdiction and the Enforcement of Judgments in Civil and Commercial Matters   1354

Bryson J   673, 674n, 675
   – *and see* **Bibliography (pp 1475 to 1507)**

Buckland, W W – *see* **Bibliography (pp 1475 to 1507)**

Buckley LJ   846, 996, 998, 1065, 1184, 1221

building regulations   1395

burden of proof
evidential burden   1091–1092, 1329
general   1091–1092
legal or persuasive burden   1091–1092, 1329

Burn, R – *see* **Bibliography (pp 1475 to 1507)**

Burrow, James   757
   – *and see* **Bibliography (pp 1475 to 1507)**

Burrows, J F – *see* **Bibliography (pp 1475 to 1507)**

burthysack   1136n

All references are to page numbers

---

business
facilitating   55, 980–981, 1204
Moorcock The, doctrine of   1070
– *and see* **Law Merchant;**
     restraint of trade
Butler-Sloss P   118n, 787, 1008n, 1314,
     1331, 1379
Buxton LJ   88, 435, 600, 811, 822, 855, 891,
     909, S20
byelaws
breach of   78, 492–493, 1025
confirmation of   269–271
display of invalid, unlawfulness of   262
enforcement of   74
interpretation of   270, 1130
invalidity of   176n, 261–262
judicial review of   262
local authority, made by   269–271
ministerial control of   246, 269
nature of   269–271, 413
non-legislative   271
ultra vires   260–262
uncertainty, void for   270, 448
unreasonable, void if   269–270
– *and see* **delegated legislation;**
     ***ultra vires*, doctrine of**
Byles J   647, 654, 1017n, 1033, 1034, 1036,
     1056

Cadogan v Morris principle   871
Cairns, Lord   34, 231, 308, 656, 736, 833,
     1025, 1038, 1165
Calvert, H G – *see* **Bibliography (pp**
     1475 to 1507)
Campbell, Lord   47, 108, 261n, 331, 332,
     347, 988, 1007, 1187,
     1212, 1239, 1245,
     1252

Canada
aborigines' rights   1034–1035
acts in *paria materia*   1167
Canada Act 1982   338–339
delegated legislation in   247n
discrimination, legislation against   518
Hansard, use of, in   677–679
human rights   518
legislative history, use of   651n
liberal construction requirement   519
multilingual jurisdiction   25
statements of compatibility with
     Charter of Rights and
     Freedoms   1335
Westminster Parliament and   338–339
canon law – *see* **ecclesiastical law**
canons of construction, linguistic
broad terms – *see* **broad terms**
construction as a whole – *see*
     construction as a whole
deductive reasoning, use of – *see*
     logic, use of in interpretation

canons of construction, linguistic – *contd*
nature of   1155
– *and see* **composite**
     expressions; ordinary
     meaning; technical terms;
     words
Cantley J   1161
capacity, legal – *see* **incompetents**
Cardozo J   849, 873, 874, 987
Cardus, Neville – *see* **Bibliography**
     (pp 1475 to 1507)
***Carltona* principle**   88–89, 273
Carnwath J   42n, 258n, 306, 681
– *and see* Bibliography (pp 1475 to
     1507)
Carr, Cecil Thomas – *see*
     Bibliography (pp 1475 to 1507)
Carruthers J   669n
Carswell, Lord   45, 781
Carter, Ross – *see* **Bibliography (pp**
     1475 to 1507)
Carus, Sjt   801
Casement, Roger   234n, 876n
castle, person's home is – *see*
     domestic sanctuary, principle of
casus male inclusus – *see* **rectifying**
     construction
casus omissus – *see* **rectifying**
     construction
causation   552–553, 953–954, 1162, 1269
cause of action   70, 77, 78, 81, 83, 84, 198,
     422–423, 553, 627,
     669, 711, 790, 809,
     811, 848, 951, 993,
     1035n, 1105, 1106,
     1107, 1108, 1116,
     1141, 1379
accrual   S24
– *and see* **legal proceedings;**
     procedure, civil
caution, judicial review   S9
central function of practitioner   438
central funds   1395
'Centrebinding'   923
certainty of law – *see* **predictability**
     of law
certiorari **(quashing order)** – *see*
     judicial review
cessante ratione legis cessat ipsa lex   888,
     889
Chadwick LJ   772, 821, 827, 1281
Chalmers, Mackenzie   549, 718n, 1172
– *and see* **Bibliography (pp 1475**
     to 1507)
chameleon word   1226, 1228
champerty   199, 777, 781, S43
Chancery Roll – *see* **Roll**
Chandos clause   720
Channel Islands   194, 343–344, 347

All references are to page numbers

Channel Tunnel 346
chapter number of Act
  interpretative use of 741–743
  post-1962 practice 741–743
  pre-1963 practice 741–743
  type-face, significance of 185, 741–743
  use of 185
Charity Commission 1395
Chaucer, Geoffrey 752
  – *and see* **Bibliography (pp 1475 to 1507)**
children
  abduction of 816, 1119
  access to 1112
  adoption of 51, 835–836, 894
  application of enactment to 577–579
  care of 543–544
  care proceedings 883, 886, 957–958
  court, role of, in respect of 105
  custody of 780, 787–788
  disciplining of 1317
  education of 835
  evidence by 461, 901, S52
  guardian ad litem of 1137–1138
  identity, restrictions on publication
    of 130n, 867–868
  immigration of 51, 809
  legitimacy of 990
  medical or psychiatric examination
    of 1234–1235
  open court principle and 120
  parents and 841, 1317
  passports of 1045–1046
  protection of 80, 461, 790, 845
  welfare of 543–544, 841
    – *and see* **evidence; foetus; incompetents; minor; wardship**
Chitty LJ 1250
  – and *see* **Bibliography (pp 1475 to 1507)**
chose in action 953, 1035, 1072
Christianity 780–781, 842–843, 1259
  – *and see* **religion**
church court – *see* **ecclesiastical court**
Church Commissioners 1395
Cicero 1126, 1203
  – *and see* **Bibliography (pp 1475 to 1507)**
circulars, official – *see* **legislative history**
citizen, the – *see* **doubtful penalisation, principle against; legislation; subject, the**
civil law and criminal law contrasted – *see* **criminal law**
civil law, the – *see* **Roman law**
Clarke LJ 314, 839, 1269

clause – *see* **section**
Clauses Act 186, 187, 269, 758
  – *and see* **adoptive Act**
Clauson J 1001
clausula derogatoria 405
clausula generalis non referta ad expressa 1164
Cleasby, B 1217
Clerk of the Crown 217, 219
Clerk of the House of Commons 617
Clerk of the Parliaments
  appointment of 226
  Crown, as agent of 217, 227
  enactment procedure, and 217, 745
  settling text of Act by 225, 227–228, 745
cloning 906n, 907n
closure order (premises used for drugs) 45, 360, 702
Clyde, Lord 904, 955, 967
Cockburn CJ 565, 656, 751, 885, 1011, 1239
Cockburn, Lord 10
  – *and see* **Bibliography (pp 1475 to 1507)**
Cocks, Ray – *see* **Bibliography (pp 1475 to 1507)**
Code for Crown Prosecutors 99
  – *and see* **prosecution of offences**
Code, the
  philosophy of 1, 10
  summary of 14–18
  terms defined in, list of 1419–1424
  – *and see* **Book, this**
codes of practice 704, 706
codification
  custom and 608–609
  interpretation of codifying Act 608–609
  interstitial articulation and 509
  Lord Hershell's rule 608
  nature of 187, 201, 421, 608–609
  non-statutory law, effect on 1250
  prerogative and 608–609
  – *and see* **plain meaning rule; practice; sub-rules**
coffee bars, licensing of 185, 1016
Cohen LJ 1184, 1242
Cohen question, the 1184
Cohen, M D – *see* **Bibliography (pp 1475 to 1507)**
Coke, Edward 26n, 30, 32, 41, 57, 62, 63, 68, 128, 134, 180, 203, 232, 304, 331, 337, 347, 356, 372, 393, 433, 471, 490, 654, 655, 668n, 697, 792, 801, 806, 814, 832, 888, 912, 945, 979, 982n, 1023, 1101, 1104, 1105, 1112,

All references are to page numbers

Coke, Edward – *contd*
1124, 1128, 1141,
1144, 1146, 1156,
1246, 1247, 1251,
1252
– *and see* **Bibliography (pp 1475
to 1507)**
Coleridge, Lord 72, 655, 656, 669, 1011,
1222
collective noun, reference to S63
collective title
interpretative use 764–765
nature of 184, 603, 763, 764–765
short title, descriptive words of,
differing from 764–765
updating, by implication 764–765
Collins (Lawrence) J 1264
Collins J 415, 1024, 1057
Collins MR 657, 1121
colonial legislature 1395
colony
meaning of 345, 1395
nature of 406
comity
court and court, between 174, 332,
see Scotland
international 328, 361, 367–368, 371–372,
376, 818–819
Parliament and courts, between 157, 233n,
445, 647–648, 695,
776, 781, 965
– *and see* **tacit legislation**
commencement of Act or enactment
anticipatory delegated legislation 286–287
– *and see* **delegated legislation**
commencement provisions 277–287, 717
court, adjourning, and 279
different days for different
provisions 283–286
early rule on 280, 719
European Community law and 279
mandatory and directory
requirements 285
meaning of 277–279, 1395
nature of 194, 325–326
on date specified by order 281, 283–286
on date specified in Act 280–283
on event specified in Act 282
on lapse of period specified in Act 282
on passing of Act 280, 744
parliamentary session, on
commencement of 280, 719
postponement of 280–281
repeal before – *see* **repeal**
retrospective – *see* **retrospectivity**
textual amendment and 289–292
time of 1387
– *and see* **commencement
order; judicial review;**

commencement of Act or enactment –
contd
time of – *contd*
– *and see* **commencement order;
judicial review;** – *contd*
political factors;
retrospectivity;
transitional provisions
commencement order 239, 253, 263, 278,
283–286, 287, 1052n
commercial enactments 332
comminution
examples of 451–452, 522, 532, 755–756
meaning 391
selective – *see* **selective
comminution**
**Commissioners for Her Majesty's
Revenue and Customs** 190
committee reports – *see* **legislative
history**
common law
abolition of common law rules by
Act 75, 198, 504, 1459–1460
basis of 29, 917
codification of – *see* **codification**
criminal law concepts of 504, 1078
custom and, compared 203
declared by Act – *see* **declaratory
enactment**
developed by reference to Act 504, 695,
816, 1314, 1459–1460
enacting common law rule 201–202,
1459–1460
European Community directive and 1069
European Convention on Human
Rights and 819–822, 1314
interpretative criteria as part of 513–514
justice of 1033
mischiefs, examples of 920
modified by Act 75, 197–204, 304, 501,
812, 814, 1010–1011,
1459–1460
nature of 347, 499n, 848, 926
precedent and 177
presumption as to statutory
alteration of 504, 814–816, 829,
1459–1460
revival of 309
rights under, statutory interference
with 504, 848, 1459–1460
statute law, relation to 504, 589, 771,
812–816, 848, 919,
926, 1038, 1041,
1199–1200, 1255,
1459–1460
technicalities of – *see* **technicalities**
torture forbidden by 1348–1349
– *and see* **implied ancillary
rules; contempt of statute;**

All references are to page numbers

common law – *contd*
torture forbidden by – *contd*
– *and see* implied ancillary rules;
contempt of statute; – *contd*
contract; criminal law;
custom; equity, rules of;
negligence; nuisance; tort
Commons, House of
delegated legislative power of   251
history of   719
journals of   234
legislative procedure of   213–216
money, control over   251, 745, 1047–1049
orders of   251
resolutions of   186, 191, 205, 248–249,
617, 666–673
time, expressions of, and   868–869
– *and see* **Parliament**
**commonsense construction
rule**
application of converse   555
examples of application of   55, 178, 387,
882–883, 908, 1099n,
1194, 1267
failure to apply   554
greater includes less   555–557
implied repeal and   557
incommensurable elements and   556
lay interpretation, apposite to   558
nature of   178, 527, 551–558, 986, 1267
per incuriam decisions   554
– *and see* **absurdity; ambiguity
(grammatical)**
Commonwealth, the   333, 339–340, 348,
406
– *and see* **exclusionary rule, the**
communis error facit jus   913
Community law, definition of   1274
– *and see* **European Community
Law**
company – *see* **artificial person**
compatible construction rule – *see*
Human Rights Act 1998
composite act or omission   327, 387, 388–
389, 389
composite acts or omissions   387
composite expressions   551, 557, 1181,
1193–1197
composite restatement   402n, 453
Community law, definition of   1396
conceptualism   987
conditional fee agreement (CFA)   36, 781–
782, 925, 1117
conditions – *see* **description,
statutory; statutory duty;
statutory power; statutory right**
confidence, law of   75, 119, 852
– *and see* **good administration,
duty of**

conflation of texts   292–293, 1166
conflict of laws – *see* **private
international law**
consent – *see* **appeal; criminal law;
Gillick test; order, court; *volenti
non fit injuria***
consequential amendments – *see*
amendment to Act
consequential construction
'adverse' consequences of   517, 871
'beneficent' consequences of   871, 874
consequences, weighing, and   871
European Community law, in   1284
examples of   388, 835n, 869–875
'floodgates' argument   872
mandatory and directory provisions,
and   48–49
nature of   459, 869–875
– *and see* **absurdity; evasion of
Act; strict and liberal
construction**
consolidation Act
Acts consolidating with
amendments   604–607
Acts solely consolidating   604–607
commencement of   281
difficulty in drafting   199
error in   880
– *and see* **rectifying
construction**
inadequate, example of   809
interpretation of   604–607, 1161, 1166,
1251–1252
Lord Herschell's rule   605
nature of   189, 604–607
preliminary 'tidying up'   282
references to re-enacted provision   310–
311
savings in – *see* **saving**
– *and see* **plain meaning rule**
conspiracy – *see* **criminal law**
constable – *see* **police**
Constitution for Europe   1276, 1315
constitutional enactment – *see* **Act of
Parliament; constitutional law**
constitutional law
Act, constitutional   189–190
Act, unconstitutional   406
legal proceedings, rights as to   858
mandatory and directory
requirements   49–50
Pepper v Hart, rule in, and   618
presumed application of rules of   1042–
1050

– *and see* **Act of Parliament;
Crown; law; Minister of
the Crown; Prime
Minister**

constitutional rights   190, 773, 1323
   – *and see* **legality, principle of**
construction as a whole– *see*
    Attorney General v Lamplough,
    rule in; composite expressions;
    conflation of texts; European
    Convention on Human Rights;
    free-standing Act, doctrine of;
    functional construction; *in para*
    materia, **acts;** *noscitur a sociis*
    principle; repugnancy;
    transitional provisions; words
   amendments to Act and   288
   comminution and   402–403
   conflicting statements in one
     instrument, and   1163
   conflicting statements in separate
     instruments, and   1163
   different words to be given different
     meanings   1160–1163
   different words to be given same
     meaning   1161
   every word to be given meaning   1157–
     1160
    – *and see* **tautology**
   ex visceribus actus construction   1156
   nature of   192, 465, 1155–1167
   need for   89
   overlap and   1160
   provisos and   723–725
   punctuation and   755
   same words to be given same
     meaning   1160
   Schedules and   721–723
   specific and general provisions   1165
   statutory requirement to disregard
     use of different words   1161
   words with no meaning   1158–1159
    – *and see* **meaningless terms**
construction as one – *see*
    incorporation by reference
construction in good faith – *see*
    illegality
construction summons   114, 847
construction, consequential – *see*
    consequential construction
construction, equitable   170
    – *and see* **equitable construction**
construction, linguistic – *see* **canons**
    of construction, linguistic
construction, rectifying – *see*
    rectifying construction
construction, rules of – *see* **rules of**
    construction
constructive meaning   1193
construe, meaning of   23–24
Community law, definition of – *see*
    European Community Law
consular officer   1396

consultation   247, 1057n, S17
contemporanea expositio   34, 702, 890, 912,
    914
contempt of court
   appeal, right of   148
   committal for   839
   court, by   970
   execution and   166
   face of court, in   497–498, 754
   fine for   975n
   powers of court   140, 497–498, 754, 958
   prerogative orders and   165–166
   prisoners and   255
   reports of legal proceedings,
     restrictions on – *see* **open**
     court, the
   right to bring proceedings   S9
   strict liability rule   900
   undertaking, breach of   116
contempt of statute   62, 63, 65, 66–67
context – *see* **construction as a**
    whole; informed interpretation;
    noscitur a sociis **principle**
continental shelf   335, 364
continuity, presumption of   913
contract
   agency – *see* **agency**
   application of law of   116, 1069–1071
   breach of promise, action for   198
   consent order   116
   court's jurisdiction, and   S7
   existing, effect of Act on   1069
   frustration of   1070
   illegal – *see* **illegality**
   private Act as   1071
   proper law of   1098
   society's original   39
   statutory modification of law of   200
    – *and see* **arbitration; business;**
     common law
contracting out – *see* **statutory right**
contradiction, principle of – *see*
    logic, use of in interpretation
contravention of Act – *see*
    disobeying Act
Convention on Jurisdiction and the
    Enforcement of Judgments   1309–
    1310
conviction   374
Cooke J   679
Cooke of Thorndon, Lord   777, 1155n,
    1156, 1164, 1298n,
    1312, 1331
Coté, Pierre André   1457–1458
copyout – *see* **transposition of**
    European Community law
coroner   50, 250, 436, 501, 905–906, 975n,
    1214–1215

All references are to page numbers

---

corporation – *see* **artificial person; Crown; local authority; public authority**
Corporation Tax Acts 1396
correctness, presumption of 715, 1144–1145
Corry, J A 677
 – *and see* **Bibliography (pp 1475 to 1507)**
costs
 burden of, duty to mitigate 112
 capping 925–926
 central funds, payment out of 894
 conditional fee agreements 925
 contributors to ('funders') 774n
 follow the event, should 774
 insurance against 508
 non-party, payment by 499
 order for 436, 499, 894
 references to European Court and 1307
 relator action, in 74
 security for 1027
 taxation of 117, 203n
 trial, and legislative history 612, 624
 – *and see* **Pepper v Hart, rule in; Scherer principle; solicitor**
Côté, Pierre-André – *see* **Bibliography (pp 1475 to 1507)**
Cottenham, Lord 169, 723, 1137
counsel – *see* **advocate; Parliamentary Counsel**
counter-intuitive readings 470, 1091n
counter-mischief 118–119, 620n, 890, 911–912, 915, 942, 969, 1006, 1007–1008
county court 73, 102, 112, 113, 116, 117, 121, 141, 145–146, 149, 172, 229, 307, 478, 528, 792, 974, 996, 1007, 1184, 1226, 1253, 1254, 1396, 1406, 1415, 1437, 1438
court
 access to 110
 – *and see* **European Convention on Human Rights; justice; open court**
 Administrative Court 138–139
 Admiralty 140
 – *and see* **jurisdiction**
 adversarial system 426, 434–435, 1087
 advocate and interpretative function of 434–435, 443
 Appeal, court of – *see* **appeal**
 appellate 102
 – *and see* **appeal**
 cassation, of 158
 Chivalry, high Court of 926

court – *contd*
 Commercial 140
 Companies 138–139
 County – *see* **county court**
 criminal, presumption against civil jurisdiction in 1049
 Crown – *see* **Crown Court**
 decisions of, statutory modification of – *see* **processing of enactments, dynamic**
 definition of 103
 delegation by 107, 1115
 doubt, treatment of , by 867, 871
 – *and see* **doubt as to legal meaning**
 ecclesiastical – *see* **ecclesiastical court**
 European Court of Human Rights – *see* **European Court of Human Rights**
 European Court of Justice – *see* **European Court of Justice**
 evasion of Act by 1013
 first instance, of 102, 1302–1303
 function of 36, 103–104, 122
 functus officio, when 1062
 guidelines by 129
 High – *see* **High Court**
 illegality, duty to notice – *see* **illegality**
 implied delegation of interpretation to, by Parliament 479
 inferior 101, 116, 1038, 1226
 inherent powers of – *see* **inherent judicial powers**
 inquisitorial proceedings 436
 inspection of Rolls by – *see* **Roll**
 interpretative function of 27, 122–123, 479, 489
 interstitial articulation by – *see* **interstitial articulation**
 judgment, reopening of 114
 jurisdiction of – *see* **jurisdiction**
 leave of 62
 legal meaning, duty to determine 24–25, 403
 – *and see* **non liquet principle**
 legislator, as 479, 785, 803, 1137
 magistrates – *see* **magistrates' court**
 open – *see* **open court, the**
 order of – *see* **order, court; inherent judicial powers**
 overruling of precedents 172, 173, 177
 Patents Court 140
 private hearings – *see* **open court, the**
 prize court 140, 148

All references are to page numbers

court – *contd*
 procedure of – *see* **inherent**
  judicial powers; procedure,
  civil; procedure, criminal
 proceedings to be conducted in
  public – *see* **open court, the**
 reasons, duty to give 1062–1064
 record, of 134, 139–140, 162
 remedies – *see* **enforcement**
  agencies
 reviewing 102, 116–118
 rules of 49, 59, 246, 268, 807, 1398
  – *and see* **Civil Procedure Rules**
 Senior Courts 1398
 small claims 54, 112
 statute book, responsibility for 509
 'statutory attorney', acting as 105
 superior 101, 111–114, 139, 527–528
 'Supreme court', definition of 1399
 Technology and Construction Court 138–
  139
 treaties, citation of, before 824
 undertaking to 997–998, 1131
  – *and see* **advocate; appeal;**
   comity; contempt of court;
   county court; criminal
   law; European Court of
   Justice; Crown Court;
   discretion; enforcement
   agencies; High Court;
   judges; judicial power of
   the state; judicial review;
   jurisdiction; legal policy;
   magistrates;
   non-justitiable matters;
   per incuriam **decisions;**
   practice; precedent,
   doctrine of; treaty;
   tribunals
Court of Appeal – *see* **appeal**
Court of Judicature 1396
Court of Justice of the European
  Communities (CJEC) – *see*
  European Court of Justice
Courts Service, Her majesty's
  (HMCS) 121
Coventry Act 555
Cowen, D V – *see* **Bibliography (pp**
  1475 to 1507)
Cowley, David – *see* **Bibliography**
  (pp 1475 to 1507)
Cox, Archibald 651
Cozens-Hardy, Lord 383, 1065n
CPS 98, 1013, 1096–1097

Craies, W F 7, 46n, 63, 228, 318n, 331,
  332, 333, 411n, 663,
  736, 1010, 1151, 1242,
  1284n
 – *and see* **Bibliography (pp 1475**
  to 1507)
Craig, Paul – *see* **Bibliography (pp**
  1475 to 1507)
Cranworth, Lord (Rolfe B) 373, 1158
Cretney, Stephen – *see* **Bibliography**
  (pp 1475 to 1507)
criminal conversation, abolition of 198
criminal injuries compensation
  scheme 251
criminal law
 accessories 1080
 actus reus 416, 417
 civil law, distinguished from 69, 94, 1353
 common law offences altered or
  replaced by statute 201
 composite crime 388
 concepts of 1078
 consent and 1150
 conspiracy 201
 crime, definition of 63, 94
 Crown, and 1083
 defences 1085
 direct action 201, 1135–1136
  – *and see* **pressure groups**
 felony, abolition of term 64
 fraud 202
 hi-jacking 376
 hybrid orders 94
 implied application of 1077–1086
 mens rea 41–42, 416, 417, 555, 1078–
  1080
  – *and see* **strict liability**
 misdemeanour, abolition of term 64
 nature of 92, 1354
 new offences, creation of by courts 1085
 nuisance 201–202
 peace, Queen's – *see* **peace,**
  Queen's
 prosecutions – *see* **prosecution of**
  offences
 provocation 504, 578
 statutory alteration of 200
 subliminal images, broadcasting of 65–66
 terrorism 376, 1135
 uniform application of 332
 war crimes 189n, 238n
  – *and see* **age, anti-social**
   behaviour orders
   (ASBOs), attorney
   General; contempt of
   statute; criminal
   procedure; doubtful
   penalisation, principle
   against; greater includes

All references are to page numbers

criminal law – *contd*
  war crimes – *contd*
    – *and see* age, anti-social behaviour
        orders (ASBOs), attorney
        General; contempt of statute;
        criminal procedure; doubtful
        penalisation, principle against;
        greater includes – *contd*
        less; legal policy; *mala in
        se*; *mala prohibita*; offence;
        public international law;
        public mischief;
        retrospectivity; strict
        liability; suicide; Taafe
        defence; erritorial extent
        of Act
criminal procedure
  abuse of process – *see* process
  accused, naming of   121
  appeals – *see* appeal
  arraignment   1013n
  code   187–188
  committal for trial   306, 318–319, 489,
                               948, 949, 1395
  Crown Court, in – *see* Crown
      Court
  de minimis principle and   1122–1123
  defences   91, 178, 274, 286, 1085
    – *and see* defences
  duplicity rule   810, 1084–1085
  evidence – *see* evidence
  exceptions rule – *see* evidence
  fitness to plead – *see* incompetents
  'indictable offence', definition of   1399
  indictment   64, 160, 230, 295, 403, 811,
                           1084, 1162, 1168
  magistrates' court, in – *see*
      magistrates' court
  natural justice and   1081–1083
  'offence triable either way',
      definition of   1399
  oral hearing, right to   1352
  preparatory hearing   114
  retrospectivity and   807–808
  Royal Commission 1981 on   99
  self-incrimination   527, 1081–1083, 1355
  sentencing   170, 803, 807, 1086,
                                 see appeal
  'sent for trial', definition of   1398
  silence, right of   59, 527, 1081–1083
  'standard scale', definition of   1398
  'statutory maximum', definition of   1399
  'summary offence', definition of   1399
  trial   1081
  waiver of steps in   62
    – *and see* anonymity;
        application of Act;
        criminal law; Crown
        Prosecution Service;

criminal procedure – *contd*
  waiver of steps in – *contd*
    – *and see* anonymity; application of
        Act; criminal law; Crown
        Prosecution Service; – *contd*
        double jeopardy;
        European Convention on
        Human Rights; judicial
        review; jurisdiction; jury;
        legal proceedings; open
        court, the; prosecution of
        offences; retrospectivity
criteria, interpretative – *see*
    interpretative criteria
Croke, George – *see* Bibliography
    (pp 1475 to 1507)
Cross of Chelsea, Lord   995
Cross, Rupert   7, 12, 418n, 499, 517n, 587,
                                          592
  – *and see* Bibliography (pp 1475
    to 1507)
crossheading – *see* heading
'Crossman catalogue', the   681
Crown
  ambit of concept   207–208
  bound by Act, when   206–212, 239
  can do no wrong   206–212
  charter   239
  Commonwealth and – *see*
      Commonwealth, the
  courts, jurisdiction of, derived from 104
  criminal law and – *see* criminal law
  declaration by   250
  dispensing power of   300
  extra-statutory payments by   251
  financial initiative of   251
  franchise   165, 204, 209–210
  immunity, doctrine of   206–212
    – *and see* Crown immunity,
        doctrine of
  indivisibility of   96, 208, 406
  joinder of, in proceedings where
      declaration of incompatibility
      anticipated – *see* Human
      Rights Act 1998
  justice, and   103, 128–129
    – *and see* judicial power of the
        state
  letters patent of   217
  meaning   206–208
  orders of court and   209
  overseas territories, in   349–350
  parens patriae doctrine   814, 1044–1046
    – *and see* wardship
  privilege – *see* public interest
      immunity
  proclamation by   250, 271, 548

All references are to page numbers

Crown – *contd*
prosecutions, in name of   96
  – *and see* **prosecution of**
    offences
regnal year   742–743
suspending power of   300
taking advantage of Act by   211–212
time, does not run against   1083
warrant of   783, 846, 1045
  – *and see* **act of state; Channel**
    Islands; Clerk of the
    Crown; Clerk of the
    Parliaments; delegated
    legislation; enacting
    formula; enforcement
    agencies; feudal tenures;
    forfeiture rule; Her
    Majesty's dominions; Her
    Majesty's independent
    dominions; Man, isle of;
    Minister of the Crown;
    Order in Council; Order
    of Council; peace,
    Queen's; precision
    drafting; prerogative,
    royal; Prime Minister;
    royal assent; saving;
    Sovereign, references to;
    taxing Acts; tort
Crown Court   140–141, 146–147, 149, 1396
– *and see* **appeal**
Crown Estate Commissioners   1396
Crown immunity, doctrine of
Crown taking benefit of an
  enactment, where not bound
  by it   211–212
expressio unius principle and   210
implied intention to bind Crown   208–209
indirect application of   209
nature of   206–212
overseas territories and   212
private Acts and   212
subjects, rights conferred on by
  prerogative, and   209–210
Crown Office – *see* **Administrative**
  Court
Crown Prosecution Service   95–100, 1013,
    1096–1097
– *and see* **prosecution of offences**
'**culprit**'   1216
Cumming-Bruce LJ   476, 1023
Curtis, Charles P   651
– *and see* **Bibliography (pp 1475**
  to 1507)
custom   135, 152, 198, 203, 360n, 608, 1250
'**Daily List**' – *see* **Statutory**
  Instruments Issue List

damages   77, 627, 1030–1031
– *and see* **Human Rights Act 1998;**
  judicial review; tort
Darling J   462
Davidson Review of implementation
  of European legislation (2006)   1295
Davis, G R C – *see* **Bibliography (pp**
  1475 to 1507)
Dawson J   676
day, fractions of – *see* **time**
de bene esse – *see* **evidence**
De Burca, Grainne – *see*
  Bibliography (pp 1475 to 1507)
de facto office   241, 1356
de minimis non curat lex   1003, 1101, 1116,
    1117, 1118, 1119,
    1122, 1123, 1167,
    1265, 1286
De Tocqueville, Alexis   406
death   64, 72, 164, 847–848, 983, 988, 1183,
    1192–1193, 1258–
    1259
debt – *see* **statutory right**
decision-making rules
Anisminic principle   110, 1050–1053
benefit from own wrong – *see*
  nullus commodum capere
  potest de injuria sua propria
consultation   247, 1057n, S17
decision endangering life   832
delegation of powers   166, 324–325
  – *and see* **delegated legislation**
due process, procedural   853, 1055–1059
failure to decide   1064
fairness – *see* **natural justice**
'final' decision   109
hearing both sides – *see* *audi*
  alteram partem **principle**
implied application of   1050–1064
intention, ascertainment of – *see*
  intention, ascertainment of
judge in own cause – *see* *nemo*
  debet esse judex in propria
  causa
legal policy, influence of – *see* **legal**
  policy
legality and   1052–1053
legitimate expectation   161,1056–1057,
    1278–1279, S15
natural justice – *see* **natural justice**
policy decisions   1061
procedural propriety   1055–1059
  – *and see* **irregularity,**
    procedural
proportionality – *see*
  proportionality
rationality and   1053–1055
reasons for decision   1062–1064, 1254–
    1255

decision-making rules – *contd*
  Wednesbury principle   125n, 144, 260,
                         1054–1055, 1312
  – *and see* **Carltona principle;
    discretion; doubtful
    penalisation, principle
    against; judicial review;
    jurisdiction; Minister of
    the Crown;** *ultra vires*,
    **doctrine ofdeclaration,
    judicial**
  discretionary, whether   128
  grant of, statute affecting   75
  guidelines, as to   130
  human rights incompatibility – *see*
    Human Rights Act 1998
  medical treatment, consent to   810n, 834,
                   1045
  nature of   102, 163
  offence, as to existence of   809–810
  ultra vires enactment   260
declaration, Royal   250
declaratory enactment 188, 293, 709, 718n,
                   923
  – *and see* **statutory exposition**
deductive reasoning – *see* **logic, use
  of in interpretation**
deeming 297, 389–390, 582–583, 949, 950–
         951, 1003–1005, 1072,
              1080, 1292
  – *and see* **absurdity; artificial
    person; asifism; location,
    deemed**
defences 58, 83–84, 286, 1108–1109
  – *and see* **pleading; procedure,
    criminal**
defendant, identity of   38
definite article   954, 1190
definition, statutory
  abandonment of, effect of   568–569
  Acts in *pari materia*, application to   708–
                 710, 1200
  ancillary documents, application to   566
  circular   568
  clarifying   561, 570–571
  common law meaning and   563–564
  compound   561
  comprehensive   561, 574–575
  contrary intention and   561, 570, 978
  delegated legislation and   265, 561–564,
                575
  dictionary meaning and   562
  different definitions of a term   465
  ejusdem generis principle and   1231–1245
  enlarging   561, 573–574, 1255–1256
  exclusionary   561, 572–573
  failure to define, or define correctly   567,
                1168, 1183
  failure to keep to, in drafting   566

definition, statutory – *contd*
  free-standing   561, 1000
  general   561, 569
  in pari materia Acts   708–710
  inclusionary   1227
  Interpretation Act **1978**   561
  – *and see* **Interpretation
    Act 1978**
  judicial gloss on   575
  labelling   561, 571–572
  list of   575
  literal meaning of, and
    purpose-and-strained
    construction   959
  nature of   561–575, 1211
  non-free standing   1211
  noscitur a sociis principle, use in
    construction of   1227
  potency of term defined   183, 562–564,
                575
  purpose of   561
  referential   561, 572
  restricted   561
  simple   561, 562
  substantive effect, having   565
  technical terms of – *see* **technical
    terms**
  unexpected meaning and   464–465
delay – *see vigilantibus non
  dormientibus leges subveniunt*
delegated legislation
  Act, amending   245
  Act, conflict with   244
  Act, does not override   244
  Act, modifying effect of   246
  affirmative resolution procedure   248
  amendment of – *see* **amendment to
    delegated legislation**
  annulment of   249
  anticipatory   243, 286–287
  'as if in Act'   244–245
  byelaws – *see* **byelaws**
  commencement of   273–274
  components of   716
  consult, duty to, on   247, 256
  contravention of   66
  declaration of incompatibility – *see*
    Human Rights Act1998
  delegate, types of   250–252
  disobeying – *see* **disobeying Act**
  drafting, quality of   264, 410, 413
  duty to exercise delegated powers   253–
               254, 285–286
  effect of   241–247
  enabling Act and   241, 243, 256, 598,
              706–708, 886
  – *and see* **Act of Parliament**
  enactments in   399–400

All references are to page numbers

delegated legislation – *contd*
executive instrument – *see*
executive instrument
exercise of power to make 243
explanatory notes 265–266
expressions in, have same meaning
as in enabling Act 265
general law, does not override 244
implied ancillary powers to make 256
interpretation of 257–258, 263–266, 716,
1388
interpretation of Act, by reference to 242n
intra vires interpretation to be
preferred 257–258
invalid provision, purported
confirmation of 257
issue by Stationery Office, effect of 274
judicial notice of – *see* **judicial
notice**
judicial review of 247, 260
laying before Parliament of 248
legislative history, use of, in
construction of 266, *295*
– *and see* **legislative history**
legislative intention of 269–270
mandatory or directory 253
nature of 237, 241–247
negative resolution procedure 249
notice of 274
orders 267–268
– *and see* **order; Order in
Council; Order of
Council; provisional
order; special procedure
order**
parliamentary control of 243, 248–249
primary intention, rule of 262–263
– *and see* ***Padfield* approach**
quashing of – *see* **judicial review**
ratification of, by Parliament 257
reasons for 242
regulations 268
repeal and re-enactment of enabling
provision, effect on 311
retrospectivity and 324–325
– *and see* **retrospectivity**
revocation of 275, 301
rules – *see* **court; legal
proceedings; rules**
scrutiny, parliamentary, of 249, 264
severance – *see* **severance**
statute modified by 182, 325–326
statutory instruments 241–247, 266–267
sub-delegation 246, 272–273
terminology of 246
types of 266–272

delegated legislation – *contd*
ultra vires – *see **ultra vires*,
doctrine of**
– *and see* **amendment to Act;
delegation of powers;
Henry VIII clause;
statutory power**
delegation of powers – *see Carltona*
**principle; court;
decision-making rules;
enforcement agencies; Minister
of the Crown**
democracy 2, 39, 474
Denman, Lord 109, 323n, 388, 654, 668,
736, 1199
Denning, Lord 33, 51, 55, 109n, 135, 165,
207, 208, 270, 434,
458, 465, 485, 500n,
507, 524, 593, 659,
662, 664, 668, 669n,
684, 685, 691, 692,
698n, 732, 739, 761,
775, 777, 784, 790,
793, 800, 803, 818,
839, 865, 903, 904,
936, 949, 966, 967,
975, 984, 1034, 1035,
1051, 1055, 1066,
1075, 1105, 1113,
1136, 1210, 1211,
1257, 1295
– *and see* **Bibliography (pp 1475
to 1507)**
description, statutory
construction in bonam partem – *see*
illegality
exceeded, where – *see* **greater
includes less**
mechanical etc apparatus 957, 1263, 1267
only partly met, where 1262–1270
– *and see* **evasion of Act;
severance**
desuetude – *see* **Act of Partliament;
Scotland**
**Developmental method of statutory
interpretation** – *see* **statutory
interpretation**
Devlin, Lord 97, 134, 150, 197, 379, 776,
780, 781, 790, 798,
813, 977, 986, 1015,
1196, 1233
– *and see* **the Bibliography (pp
1475 to 1507)**
devolution 6, 328, 1100, 1202
Diamond, Aubrey L – *see*
Bibliography (pp 1475 to 1507)
Dias, R W M 23, 407n, 472, 795n
– *and see* **Bibliography (pp 1475
to 1507)**

All references are to page numbers

Dicey, A V   406, 407, 843, 1044, 1192
  – and see **Bibliography (pp 1475
    to 1507)**
Dickerson, Reed   433, 446, 473
  – and see **Bibliography (pp 1475
    to 1507)**
dictionary, reference to – see **judicial
    notice; reference, works of**
different words, construction of –
    see **words**
differential readings
  examples of   132–133, 618n, 623, 952,
                                        1170
  nature of   122, 130–133
  – and see **impression, matters of**
Dilhorne, Viscount   448, 568, 649, 650, 663,
                      696n, 699, 700, 707,
                      809, 940, 945, 978,
                      998n, 1007, 1182,
                      1212, 1227, 1239
Dillon LJ   169, 508, 839, 1070, 1188, 1191,
                                        1214
Dingwall, Gavin: – see **Bibliography
    (pp 1475 to 1507)**
Diplock, Lord   35, 125, 627, 807, 1054
  – and see **Bibliography (pp 1475
    to 1507)**
direct action – see **criminal law**
direction   272
Director of Public Prosecutions   96
Director of Revenue and Customs
    Prosecutions   96, 97
directory requirements – see
    **mandatory and directory
    requirements**
disciplinary committee   104
discovery   119, 526, 852
  – and see **public interest immunity**
discretion
  administrative   81, 89, 144, 820–821, 850
  anomaly, avoidance of, by exercise
    of   999
  appeal from exercise of   142, 145
  appellate court or body, exercise by
    – see **appeal**
  delegated legislation, as to making
    of   253
  discovery, as to ordering – see
    evidence
  'discretionary area of judgment',
    so-called   1327
  duty, as to enforcement of   45, 51
  estoppel and   1094
  European Convention on Human
    Rights   1321
  extra-statutory   51
  fettering of   90
  guidelines, as to exercise of   130, 145,
                                        1140

discretion – contd
  implied restriction of   820–821, 1130
  interpretation, as factor in   80, 521, 533,
                                872–873, 999
  judgment, distinguished from   80, 122,
                            123, 127–129, 619
  judicial   144, 313, 900
  justly, to be exercised   798–799
  nature of   55, 126–127, 253, 313, 396,
                                521, 949
  party-political mischief and – see
    mischief
  policy and operational contrasted   68, 81
  prosecution of offences and   97
  rationality and   1054–1055
  reasons, duty to give   1062–1064
  review of   117
  – and see **common law;
      decision-making rules;
      judicial notice; judicial
      review; margin of
      appreciation; *Padfield*
      approach; *Scherer*
      principle; statutory power**
discrimination, legislation against
  interpretation of   518–519, 600
  race, on grounds of   726, 740, 873, 978–
                                979, 1041
  religion, on grounds of   842–843
  sex, on grounds of   61, 740, 978–979,
                                        1328
  – and see **Canada; European
      Convention on Human
      Rights**
discrimination, legislation against
    sexual orientation, on grounds
    of   1328
disobeying Act
  civil sanctions for – see **breach of
      statutory duty, tort of; tort**
  consequence of disobedience
    unstated, where   45–46
  criminal sanctions for   62–67
  delegated legislation and   66
  general   62–64, 68–69
  impecuniosity as excuse for   126–127
  – and see **public authority**
  Law Commission, recommendation
    with respect to   66
  persistent disobedience, treatment of   74
  – and see **Act of Parliament;
      contempt of statute; *de
      minimis non curat lex*;
      evasion of Act; *ignorantia
      juris neminem excusat*;
      judicial review; law**
disorganised composition
  consequences, interpretative, and   1249,
                                        1250

All references are to page numbers

disorganised composition – *contd*
examples of   329–330, 451–455, 536, 614–
615, 970, 1159n
nature of   60, 409–413, 1250
provisos and   723–725
– *and see* **obscurity, semantic;
precision drafting**
dispensing power – *see* **Crown**
distance, measurement of   581, 1388
diversity   133
Divisional Court
appeal from   147–148
appeal to   146–147
Court of Appeal as   158
departure from own decisions   175
divorce   787–788
Dockray, M S – *see* **Bibliography (pp
1475 to 1507)**
document, service of – *see* **notice**
doli incapax, **abolition of doctrine of**   S57
domestic sanctuary, principle of   1007,
1124, 1125, 1126–
1127
– *and see* **doubtful penalisation,
principle against; European
Convention on Human
Rights**
dominant purpose test   1263
**domus sua cuique est tutissimum
refugium** – *see* **domestic
sanctuary, principle of**
Donaldson of Lymington, Lord   116, 174
Donoughmore Committee (1932)   271
Donovan, Lord   981, 1223
double detriment – *see* ***bona fldes
non patitur ut bis idem exigatur***
double jeopardy   788, 1083, 1116, 1286
doubt as to legal meaning
causes of   325–326, 391, 515–516
must be 'real'   25–26, 176, 437, 515, 591–
592, 624–625, 999
resolution of   391, 511, 591
– *and see* **doubtful penalisation,
principle against**
term with different meanings   466–468
**doubtful penalisation, principle
against**
citizenship rights, statutory
interference with   858–859
deprivation or restriction of rights
without compensation and   828–829,
849
family rights, interference with   840–842
– *and see* **domestic sanctuary,
principle of**
free assembly and association,
interference with   843–844
free speech, interference with   844–845
legal obligations, imposition of   853

doubtful penalisation, principle against –
contd
legal process, statutory interference
with   853–858
– *and see* **legal policy**
life or health, interference with   780, 831–
836
litigation, right of parties to
compromise, and   857
nature of   1–2, 517–518, 526, 527, 784,
825, 1062
physical restraint of the person   784, 836–
840
– *and see* ***habeas corpus*;
prisoners, rights of**
privacy, statutory interference with   852
– *and see* **domestic sanctuary,
principle of**
property, interference with   829
– *and see* **taxing Acts**
public interest and   790
religious freedom, interference with   842–
843
– *and see* **religion**
reputation or status, detriment to   851–852,
965
retrospectivity, presumption against,
and   317–319, 827
– *and see* **retrospectivity**
savings, interpretation of, and   726
status or reputation, statutory
interference with   851–852
voting rights, interference with – *see*
elections
drafter, legislative
amendments and   40, 640
commentary by, on Act drafted   712
intention of   475–477
interpretation, value of views of, in   33
mistakes by   415
role of   475–477
use of term   10n
– *and see* **Parliamentary
Counsel**
drafting error
commencement, as to   325–326
definition, as to   566
genus, depiction of   1234
law, mistake of – *see* **mistake**
legal doctrine flouted   875–877, 1148n
missed consequentials – *see*
amendment of Act
nature of   877
omission   924–925
presumption against   413–416
strained construction and   882, 1131
– *and see* **strained construction**
tautology – *see* **surplusage;
tautology**

drafting error – *contd*
transitional provisions, as to – *see*
transitional provisions
– *and see* **ambiguity**
(grammatical); deeming;
disorganised composition;
drafting technique;
homonyms; mandatory
and directory
requirements; obscurity,
semantic; rectifying
construction
drafting, legislative
Acts in pari materia, of – *see in*
pari materia, **Acts**
archival – *see* **incorporation by**
reference
competence presumed   413–416, 1217
complexity of   135
compression of language – *see*
ellipsis
computer, by   232
criticism of   409–416, 452–455, 614–615,
700–701, 804–805,
840, 1250
delegated legislation, of   410, 413
encompassing the unforeseen   481
ex abundanti cautela   1258
government control of   412
judges, by   464
numbers, expressing   1216
plain language – *see* **plain language**
movement
precision drafting – *see* **precision**
drafting
private bills, of   410
reform of – *see* **statute law**
'shorthand' in   447
style of   413–416, 866, 892
words used correctly in,
presumption that   1186
– *and see* **drafter, legislative;**
drafting error; drafting
technique; meaningless
terms; Parliamentary
Counsel Office; user of
legislation
drafting technique – *see* **amendment**
to Act; asifism; belt-and-braces
phrase; broad terms;
codification; comminution;
consolidation Act; copyout;
disorganised composition;
drafting error; drafting,
legislative; enactment;
examples; functional
construction; heading;
implication; incorporation by
reference; Jamaica Schedule;

drafting technique – *contd*
Keeling Schedule; order, court;
plain language movement;
precision drafting; purpose
clause; saving; Schedule;
section; weightless drafting
accidental fit   482–483
amendment, method of   146
– *and see* **amendment to Act**
commencement provisions – *see*
commencement of Act
common sense, reliance on – *see*
commonsense construction
rule
'elegant variation'   1160
European Union   1461–1473
'general principle' approach   487–488
'individual', use of word   577
lay persons, when intended to read
text   35–36
overlapping technique – *see*
belt-and-braces phrase
shorthand, drafter's   447
sweeping-up provisions   1014
transitional provisions   325
– *and see* **transitional provisions**
Drake J   989
Driedger, E A   8, 23, 473, 546, 587, 899,
1233
– *and see* **Bibliography (pp 1475**
to 1507)
Du Parcq, Lord   69, 70, 436, 437
due process   851, 853, 1055
– *and see* **decision-making rules;**
legal proceedings; process
Dunn LJ   669, 1185
Duomatic **principle**   60
DU Parcq, Lord   1102n
duplication of statutory remedies,
powers etc   393
Durack, P   740
duress   1046, 1105, 1134–1135, 1136
duty – *see* **court; good**
administration, duty of;
legislation; moral duty;
statutory duty
Dwarris, F   7, 463, 1250n
– *and see* **Bibliography (pp 1475**
to 1507)
Dworkin, Gerald – *see* **Bibliography**
(pp 1475 to 1507)
Dworkin, Ronald   14, 132, 514, 523n, 770,
771, 772, 778, 782
– *and see* **Bibliography (pp 1475**
to 1507)
Dyson J   602, S56
Eady J   1329
Eardley-Wilmot, J E – *see*
Bibliography (pp 1475 to 1507)

All references are to page numbers

Earl Warren CJ   858
ecclesiastical court   117, 154, 163
  – and see ecclesiastical law
ecclesiastical law   154, 157, 197–198, 775,
                                        1041
  – and see ecclesiastical court
Dunn LJ   669, 1185
EC Treaty (Treaty of Rome) defined   1274
Edmund-Davies, Lord   170n, 412n, 525,
                            599n, 872, 1126
education, convention right to – see
    European Convention on
    Human Rights
Edwards, J L G   74n
  – and see Bibliography (pp 1475
    to 1507)
Edwards, Susan   133n
  – and see Bibliography (pp 1475
    to 1507)
EEA agreement   1396
EEA state   1396
Eire   354
ejusdem generis principle
    description of   1231–1234
    examples of   671n, 1229, 1231–1245
    exclusion, express, of   1242–1243
    exclusion, implied, of   1244–1245
    general words followed by narrower
        term   1242–1243
    genus   1234–1237
    nature of   1231–1245
    single term   1237–1239
    terms followed by wider residuary
        words   1239–1241
    terms surrounding wider word 1241–1242
Eldon, Lord   435, 478, 1011
elections   54, 68n, 859, 957, 1046–1047
elegant variation   1160, 1161
Eliot, T S   967
Ellenborough, Lord   229, 736n, 832
Ellesmere, Lord   33, 170n, 412n, 599n
ellipsis   x, 450, 488, 491, 493, 1176, 1231
Elwyn-Jones, Lord   284
emails   905n
embracery   199
emergency powers   250
employment   1146–1147
  – and see agency; vicarious
    liability
Employment Appeal Tribunal   104, 147
enabling Act – see Act of Parliament
enacting formula   216n, 224, 225, 226, 713,
                          718, 719, 741, 744–
                                        745
enacting history – see legislative
    history
enactment
    citation of   1391
    classification of   396–401

enactment – contd
    common law rule, replacement of,
        by   609
    constitutional   49
    curtailing legislative power,
        purporting to   405
    declaration of incompatibility and –
        see incompatibility,
        declaration of, under Human
        Rights Act 1998
    effectiveness of, challenge to 404–409
    international law, contrary to   409
    interpretative   27
    meaning of   396–401
    mischief of – see mischief
    multi-lingual   24
    modifying a judicial decision   401
    natural law, contrary to   407–408
    nature of   396–401, 718
    operation of, dual aspect to   393
    opposing constructions of – see
        opposing constructions
    purpose of – see purposive
        construction
    substantive and procedural
        contrasted   400
      – and see limitation of actions
    territorial extent of – see territorial
        extent of Act
    validity of, challenge to   404–409
    unit of inquiry, as   391, 394–396
      – and see comminution;
        delegated legislation; legal
        thrust of enactment;
        legislation
enforcement agencies
    adjudicating with appellate
        jurisdiction   142–154
    adjudicating with original
        jurisdiction   138–142
    administrative and executive   85–92, 166–
                        167, 479, 702–706,
                        974–977, 1058, 1145
    amendment, legislative, statutory
        duty to propose   978–979
    authorising   92–93
    bailiffs   166–167
    charging orders   166
    delegation by   167
    enforcement procedures, scope of   97
    'enforcement', meaning of   28n
    entrapment and   95
    failure by   87
    interpreters as   27–28
    investigating   93–95
    judicial review of discretion
        exercised by   90
    legislative power of – see court
    local authorities as   88

All references are to page numbers

enforcement agencies – *contd*
membership, types of   104
procedure to be used by   28
processing of enactments, dynamic,
    by   167–178
prosecuting   95–96
   – *and see* **prosecution of
    offences**
remedies available to   114–118
sheriff's officers   166
supervisory   93–95
transfer and distribution of
    legislative functions   86
types of   27–28
   – *and see* **court; correctness,
    presumption of;
    discretion; enforcement
    notice; evasion of Act;
    legislative history; police;
    processing of enactments,
    dynamic; statutory power;
    tax avoidance; taxing
    Acts; trespass**
enforcement notice   51, 56, 88–91, 270, 789
enforcement procedure   28, 97
enforcement procedures   28, 138
England   346, 1396
   – *and see* **Berwlck upon Tweed;
    Monmouthshire**
Engle, George – *see* **Bibliography
   (pp 1475 to 1507)**
entrapment   95
equitable construction   169, 170, 441, 463–
    465, 587, 1065–1066,
    1137
equity of a statute – *see* **equitable
   construction**
equity, rules of
Acts framed with view to   1068
equitable construction contrasted   1065–
    1066
follow the law   500
implied application of   61, 1064–1069
law fused with   198n, 761
need for specialist application   1067
nobile officium – *see* **nobile
   officium**
regulatory statutes and   1066
remedies for infringement of Act   61, 74,
    1067
   – *and see* **confidentiality;
    estoppel; injunction;
    laches**
Erle CJ   1112
   – *and see* **Bibliography (pp 1475
    to 1507)**
error – *see* **drafting error; mistake**
Ert, Gibb van – *see* **Bibliography
   (pp 1475 to 1507)**

Esher, Viscount (Brett LJ)   75, 79, 722
Eskridge, William N Jr   7, 893n, 1458,
    1459, 1460
   – *and see* **Bibliography (pp 1475
    to 1507)**
estoppel
cause of action   1116
discretion and   1094
equitable   1067
executive   92, 616, 633–640
general   106, 1067
in pais   1094
issue   788–789
per rem judicatam (res judicata)   106, 788–
    789
**EU Treaty (Maastricht Treaty),
   defined**   1274
eugma   525n
**European Charter of Fundamental
   Rights**   1315
**European Commission of Human
   Rights**   1320
European Community – *see*
   European Union
European Community law
acte clair   1306
agreements, pre-EC Treaty   1275–1276
arrest warrant   1286–1287
Barber principle and   1279–1280
Community instrument, reference to   1391
composition of   1274
direct effect of   1287–1290
directives   1288–1289
double jeopardy, presumption
    against, in   1286
drafting technique   1284n
effectiveness of, principle of   1277
human rights and   1276, 1285
ignorance of   43
incompatibility of UK law with   1293–
    1300
interpretation of   8, 465, 1283–1287,
    1299–1300
legal certainty, principle of, in   1277–1279
legitimate expectation, principle of,
    in   1278–1279
member states laws   1275, 1309
natural justice, concepts of, in   1285–1286
principles of   1275–1276
proof of   1283
proportionality, principle of, in   1280–1282
   – *and see* **proportionality**
public policy, in   785
purposive construction in   966–968
   – *and see* **purposive
    construction**
regulations, direct effect of, in   1289
retrospectivity, presumption against
    in   1279–1280

All references are to page numbers

European Community law – *contd*
solidarity, principle of, in   1277
status of   1273, 1282, 1293–1300
strict construction in   1286
subsidiarity, principle of, in   1282
transposition of – *see* **transposition**
  of European Community law
Treaty provisions, direct effect of,
  in   1287–1290
UK law, effect of, on   1293–1300
– *and see* **Developmental**
  method of statutory
  interpretation; foreign;
  judicial notice;
  predictability of law

European Convention on Human
  Rights
Art 1 (respect for human rights)   1318
Art 2 (right to life)   xi, 836, 1319, 1347,
              1348, 1441–1442
Art 3 (torture)   836, 1348, 1443
– *and see* **Soering** principle
Art 4 (slavery and forced labour)   840,
              1350, 1443
Art 5 (liberty and security)   840, 858,
              1350, 1442–1443
Art 6 (fair trial)   121, 845, 858, 1062n,
              1316, 1353, 1444
Art 7 (no punishment without law)   318–
              319, 322, 1445
Art 8 (private and family life)   120, 842,
              852, 1314, 1445
Art 9 (thought, conscience and
  religion)   843, 1445
Art 10 (expression)   845, 852, 1434, 1445
Art 11 (assembly and association)   844,
              1434, 1446
Art 12 (marriage)   842, 1316, 1446
Art 13 (right to an effective remedy)   1318
Art 14 (discrimination)   1446
Art 15 (derogation)   1377
Art 16 (political activity of aliens)   1318,
            1347, 1367, 1446
Art 17 (abuse of rights)   1318, 1446
Art 18 (restrictions on rights)   1318, 1447
changing standards   1317
derogation from   1433–1436
description of   819–822
European Community law, in – *see*
  European Community Law
expulsion from state of which a
  citizen   859
extent of   1321
First Protocol, Art 1 (protection of
  property)   851, 1357, 1447
First Protocol, Art 2 (education)   842, 1447
First Protocol, Art 3 (free elections)   859,
              1447
government policy principle   1355

European Convention on Human Rights –
  contd
illegality and   1320
'incorporation' into English law   1311,
              1319
inquests   1348
interpretation of   1321, 1322
judgment and discretion   128
legal policy on, pre-1998 Act   1038
legal proceedings under – *see*
  Human Rights Act 1998
legal status of – *see* **Human Rights**
  Act 1998
origins of   1319
'overridden by parties' agreement or
  waiver   62, 1315, 1320, 1353
proportionality   1312
reservation to   1434–1435, 1449–1450
statutory interpretation and – *see*
  delegated legislation; Human
  Rights Act 1998; intention,
  legislative; statutes; strained
  construction; reading down
uniform interpretation   1321
waiver of rights under   62
who is bound by   1319
who is protected by   1319
– *and see* **doubtful penalisation,**
  principle against; human
  rights; Human Rights
  Act 1998; margin of
  appreciation; public
  international law

European Court of Human Rights   1316

European Court of Justice
advocates-general of   1301
Court of First Instance of   1302–1303
'creative jurisprudence' of   1284–1285,
              1301–1302
interpretation by   1283–1287
judges of   1301
jurisdiction of   1302–1303
nature of   1274, 1300–1302
precedent and   177
remedies available from   1308–1309
strict construction by   1286, 1310
Treaty rulings   612–613, 1309–1310
weighing and balancing
  interpretative factors, by   1280n,
              1285–1286

European Union
composition of   6
law of – *see* **European Community**
  law
legislation of, drafting guidelines as
  to   1461–1473
European Union, enlargement of   1315
Evans LJ   850, 993, 1005

All references are to page numbers

Evans, Jim 652n
  – *and see* **Bibliography (pp 1475
    to 1507)**
Evans-Lombe J 470, 1298
evasion of Act
  adjournment of hearing, by 279, 1013
  avoidance, distinguished from 1014–1017
  court, by 1013
  deferring liability, by 1024–1025
  express provision against 1010–1011
  fraud on an Act 1010–1014
  indirect 1023–1024
  injunction, use of, to prevent 1025–1026
  integrity of Act and 1028–1029
  legal proceedings, hindering – *see*
    legal proceedings
  presumption against 1009–1014
  repetitious acts, by 1025–1026
  tax avoidance – *see* **tax avoidance**
  – *and see Ramsay* **principle**
Eve J 59
Eveleigh LJ 460, 492, 993, 1254
Everett, C W – *see* **Bibliography (pp
  1475 to 1507)**
Evershed, Lord 43, 606n, 961, 994, 1004,
    1184
  – *and see* **Bibliography (pp 1475
    to 1507)**
every word to be given meaning –
  see **construction as a whole**
evidence
  Act, of 184, 228, 233, 234–235
  – *and see* **judicial notice**
  admissibility of 125, 525, 1026, 1223–
    1224
  affidavit 158, 806
  burden of proof – *see* **burden of
    proof**
  certifying of facts by Minister – *see*
    Minister of the Crown
  child, of 461, 901
  compellable 813, 857
  cross-examination 777
  Crown privilege – *see* **public
    interest immunity**
  de bene esse, admission 596, 693
  depositions 52
  discovery 525
  – *and see* **discovery**
  DNA 1361
  estoppel – *see* **estoppel**
  European Community instrument,
    admissibility as 1283
  exceptions rule 1090–1094
  expert 1088, 1223–1224
  – *and see* **judicial notice**
  fresh 150, 1088
  hearsay 1086n
  implied application of rules of 1086–1097

evidence – *contd*
  judge, by 103, 428
  Official Journal of the European
    Communities, admissibility as 1283
  parliamentary proceedings, of 181, 234–
    235
  parole evidence rule 647
  personal Act, of 185
  preamble or recital, statement in 731–733,
    735
  presumption of fact in lieu of 1086, 1145
  privilege 59–60
  publication of 121
  public interest immunity – *see*
    public interest immunity
  Queen's 99
  report, statement in 1148
  rules of, implied importation of 1086–
    1097
  silence, right to – *see* **procedure,
    criminal**
  standard of proof – *see* **standard of
    proof**
  statutory instrument, of 274
  technical terms, of 1205–1206, 1223–1224
  torture, of 1349
  without prejudice rule 1097
  witnesses 29, 813, 857, 1106
  words, of meaning of 1223–1224
  – *and see* **advocate;
    enforcement agencies;
    European Community
    law; fact; judicial notice;
    jury; retrospectivity;
    technical terms**
Ewing, K D – *see* **Bibliography (pp
  1475 to 1507)**
ex abundanti cautela 211, 565, 725, 1014,
    1165, 1250, 1258
ex post facto **law** – *see* **retrospectivity**
ex visceribus actus **construction** – *see*
  construction as a whole
examples
  added by amendment 740
  delegated legislation, in 741
  primary legislation, in 739–741
  reliance on 739–741
  value of 17
  – *and see* **technical terms**
exception – *see* **Act of Parliament;
  evidence; proviso**
exclusionary rule, the
  chronological development of 652–666
  Commonwealth, in 673–682
  – *and see* **Australia; Canada;
    Ghana; New Zealand**
  consolidation Acts and 606
  control of its procedure by court
    and 680–682

All references are to page numbers

---

exclusionary rule, the – *contd*
  parole evidence rule and   647
  reasons for   625, 645–652
  relaxation of – *see* ***Pepper v Hart*,**
    rule in
  statement of rule   644
  – *and see* **amendment to Bill;**
    Bill, parliamentary;
    comity
execution   166
executive – *see* **executive power;**
  separation of powers, doctrine
  of
executive agencies – *see* **enforcement**
  agencies
executive estoppel – *see* **estoppel**
executive instrument   43, 270, 272, 324
  – *and see* **enforcement notice;**
    ignorantia juris neminem
    excusat; **order**
executive power, abuse of
  abuse of   87
  Parliamentary powers, separation   S9
exercise of judgment
  application of enactment, in relation
    to   124–126
  breach of statutory duty, in relation
    to   67–68, 80–82
  discretion, confused with   127–129
  fact and degree, questions of – *see*
    fact
  guidel;ines as to   129–130
  nature of   124–127, 629–630, 1167–1168,
         1170
  reopening of judgment   114
  review of   117
  – *and see* **broad terms;**
    differential readings;
    discretion
existence   1192–1193
Expiring Laws Continuance Acts   186
explanatory material on Bill,
  interpretative use of   641–644, 1456
explanatory memorandum – *see* **Bill,**
  parliamentary
explanatory notes – *see* **delegated**
  legislation
expressio unius **principle**
  Crown immunity and   210
  definitions and   988
  designation words and   1252–1254
  examples of   65, 337, 1250–1259
  exception, categories of, and   1256–1257
  extending words and   1255–1256
  judicial notice and – *see* **judicial**
    notice
  nature of   76, 1250–1259
  savings and – *see* **saving**
  specific procedures and   1254–1255

expressum facit cessare tacitum   89, 490,
         525, 1225, 1249, 1250,
         1251
  – *and see* **expressio unius principle**
extent – *see* **territorial extent of Act**
exterritoriality   369–370
extradition   100, 136, 188, 209, 361n, 374,
         876, 898, 945, 1000,
         1286–1287, 1350,
         1444
extra-statutory concession   15, 191, 277,
         299–300, 635, 703,
         1021
extra-statutory discretion   51
extra-statutory payment   251
extra-statutory payments, crown, by   251
extra-territoriality   363, 370, 371–378, 374,
         376, 378, 382
extrinsic material – *see* **legislative**
  history
exturpi causa non oritur actio – *see*
  illegality
fact
  ascertainment of   587
  evidence of – *see* **evidence**
  fact and degree, questions of   428–429,
         1262–1270
  factual outline, the – *see* **factual**
    outline, the
  generalising   424–426
  ignorance of – *see* **ignorance**
  judicial notice of – *see* **judicial**
    notice
  matrix of   587, 591
  mistake of – *see* **mistake**
  presentation of   426–427
  proof of   427
    – *and see* **evidence**
  relevant and irrelevant   391, 423–428
  unforeseen   482–483
  – *and see* **fact and law; factual**
    outline, the
fact and law   122, 393, 1221–1222
  – *and see* **fact; factual outline, the**
factors, interpretative – *see*
  interpretative factors
factual outline, the
  function of   391, 416–421
  judicial use of   416–421
  mistake of fact and – *see* **mistake**
  nature of   391, 416–421
  statutory   416–421, 425–426
  – *and see* **fact**
Fagan, J – *see* **Bibliography (pp**
  1475 to 1507)
fairness – *see* **legal policy; natural**
  justice

All references are to page numbers

Falconer of Thoroton, Lord 3
  – *and see* Bibliography (pp 1475
    to 1507)
family law
  'clean break' principle 787–788
family rights, interference with – *see*
    doubtful penalisation, principle
    against; European Convention
    on Human Rights
Farwell LJ 650, 657, 699n, 1198, 1257
fasciculus – *see* format of Act
Ferguson, William – *see*
    Bibliography (pp 1475 to 1507)
feudal tenures 359
fiction – *see* absurdity; artificial
    person; asifism; deeming
Field J 843, 970
figures – *see* numbers
finance – *see* Bill, parliamentary;
    Commons, House of; Crown;
    disobeying Act; jurisdiction;
    money; taxing Acts
Financial Memorandum 641
Financial Services Authority 157
financial year 1396
Finch CJ 407
Finlay, Judge John 923
Finlay, Lord 976
Fitzgibbon LJ 657
Fleta 652
  – *and see* Bibliography (pp 1475
    to 1507)
foetus 105, 500, 509, 577–578, 600, 834n,
    957–958, 1370
footnotes – *see* format of Act
Forbes J 42, 294, 526, 528, 811, 830
foreign
  aspects regarding application of Act
    – *see* application of Act
  context, english word used in – *see*
    words
  conviction 1084
  courts 1100
  jurists – *see* jurists
  law 393–394, 1100
    – *and see* European Community
      law; judicial notice
  matters 976, 1212–1213, 1215–1216
  money – *see* money
  nationals 988
  passport 1045–1046
foreseeability 80
forfeiture rule 1142
formalities – *see* technicalities
format of Act 719–720, 749–750
forms 52, 54, 1123
Fortescue J 1112
Fortescue, John – *see* Bibliography
    (pp 1475 to 1507)

'forthwith', meaning of 558
Foskett J S22
Fowler, H W – *see* Bibliography (pp
    1475 to 1507)
Fox LJ 78n, 320, 951, 1030, 1074
Frankfurter J 666
  – *and see* Bibliography (pp 1475
    to 1507)
Fraser of Tullybelton, Lord 521, 740, 829,
    985, 997, 1114, 1150,
    1189
fraud – *see* evasion of Act; illegality
freedom – *see* doubtful penalisation,
    principle against; legal
    policy;speech, freedom of
free-standing Act, doctrine of 289, 293,
    384n, 1165, 1166
free-standing term 346, 352, 1039, 1200,
    1211
French J S27, S45
Friedmann, W 773
  – *and see* Bibliography (pp 1475
    to 1507)
Fry LJ 1211
functional construction
  amendable descriptive components
    of Act 713–714, 727–741
  delegated legislation and 265
  operative components of Act 713–714,
    718–726
  rule 466, 713–717
  unamendable descriptive
    components of Act 713–714, 741–
    758
  – *and see* Act of Parliament;
      chapter number; enacting
      formula; examples; format
      of Act; heading;
      incorporation by
      reference; long title;
      preamble; proviso;
      punctuation; purpose
      clause; purview; recital;
      repugnancy; saving;
      Schedule; section; short
      title; sidenote
functus officio 1062, 1305
fungible property 1067
futility – *see* absurdity
G v G, principle in 144
Gaffney approach 175–177
Gane, C P – *see* Bibliography (pp
    1475 to 1507)
garbled text – *see* rectifying
    construction
Gardiner, Lord – *see* Bibliography
    (pp 1475 to 1507)
Gaveston, Piers 832
Geddes, R S 8

All references are to page numbers

---

gender 579, 909, 1046–1047, 1047, 1202,
1212, 1327, 1328,
1332, 1387–1388,
1410
general notice 271, 273
generalia specialia derogant 1164
generalia specialibus non derogant 304,
306, 307, 1164
Geny, Francois – *see* Bibliography
(pp 1475 to 1507)
Ghana 170, 349, 680
Ghosh, I J 588n, 607n
– *and see* Bibliography (pp 1475
to 1507)
Gibbs CJ 300n
Gibraltar 330
Gibson (Peter) LJ 80, 448n, 603, 809, 971,
1183
Gibson, J – *see* Bibliography (pp
1475 to 1507)
Gifford, D J – *see* Bibliography (pp
1475 to 1507)
Gillick test 1150n
Gladstone, W E 314
Glanvill 30
Gleeson, Hon Murray S3
Glidewell LJ 750, 868, 1013n, 1054, 1118,
1188
Global method of statutory
interpretation – *see* statutory
interpretation
gloss, judicial – *see* judicial gloss
Gloster J 897, 1167
Goddard, Lord CJ 11, 32, 332n, 488, 1121,
1187
Goff of Chieveley, Lord 103n, 707, 821,
899–900
Goffmann, Erving – *see*
Bibliography (pp 1475 to 1507)
'golden rule' 12–13, 514, 545, 870
good administration, duty of 91
Goodall, Judge Anthony Charles 1213
Goodall, Kay ix, 1n, 634n, 826n, 1381
– *and see* Bibliography (pp 1475
to 1507)
Goode, Roy 32
– *and see* Bibliography (pp 1475
to 1507)
Goodhart, A L 660
– *and see* Bibliography (pp 1475
to 1507)
Gordon, Richard – *see* Bibliography
(pp 1475 to 1507)
Goudie, James – *see* Bibliography
(pp 1475 to 1507)
Gough, W J – *see* Bibliography (pp
1475 to 1507)
Goulding J 586, 1208

government 475, 514, 962–963, 1061
– *and see* Crown; enforcement
agencies; government
departments; Minister of the
Crown; Prime Minister
government department
Act, in charge of 610
enforcement agency, as 85–86
guidelines issued by 90, 702–706
official statements by 703
government 'in right of the' 348–350
government policy principle 858n, 1355
Governor-General 1396
Gowers, Ernest 557, 1189, 1219
– *and see* Bibliography (pp 1475
to 1507)
Graham J 1182
Graham, R N 1457–1459
– *and see* Bibliography (pp 1475
to 1507)
grammatical meaning 11, 15, 24, 25, 103,
123, 441, 443–444,
446, 447, 451, 453,
454, 455, 456, 466,
490, 523, 529, 531,
533, 548, 586, 754,
864, 878, 952, 966,
1177
– *and see* ambiguity
(grammatical); legal
meaning; ordinary meaning;
plain meaning rule
Gray, J C – *see* Bibliography (pp
1475 to 1507)
'Great Britain', meaning of 346–348
greater includes less 39, 555–557
Greenberg, Daniel 7n, 191n, 411n, 1284n
– *and see* Bibliography (pp 1475
to 1507)
Greene, Lord 89, 407, 1018, 1053, 1199
Greenwood, Christopher – *see*
Bibliography (pp 1475 to 1507)
Greschner, D 518
– *and see* Bibliography (pp 1475
to 1507)
Grey, T – *see* Bibliography (pp 1475
to 1507)
Griffith, J A G – *see* Bibliography
(pp 1475 to 1507)
Griffiths, Lord 89, 125, 129n, 508, 601,
627, 630, 636, 665,
670, 1002, 1013, 1185
Grove J 412, 413, 477, 657, 970, 1015,
1132
guardian ad litem 1103, 1137, 1140
Guide to Legislative Procedures 181, 616,
643n, 706n

All references are to page numbers

guidelines, statutory   129, 704
  – *and see* broad terms; court;
    discretion; government
    departments; legislative
    history
guides to legislative intention – *see*
    interpretative criteria
Gulmann, Adv Gen   **1286n**
Gummow, Justice W M C   1459–1460
  – *and see* Bibliography (pp 1475
    to 1507)
Gunasekara, Gehan N – *see*
    Bibliography (pp 1475 to 1507)
Gurney, B   879
Gutteridge, H C   29
habeas corpus   136, 166, 197, 343, 564, 837,
                    838, 839, 994, 995,
                    1002
Hadley, E A   63n
  – *and see* Bibliography (pp 1475
    to 1507)
Hailsham of St Marylebone, Lord   177,
                322, 786, 803, 1210
  – *and see* Bibliography (pp 1475
    to 1507)
Hailsham, Viscount   961, 1208
hairsplitting   26, 866
Haldane, Viscount   646, 658, 867, 1048,
                    1058
Hale CJ   809, 843n
Hale J   543
Hale, Matthew – *see* Bibliography
    (pp 1475 to 1507)
Halkerston, Peter – *see* Bibliography
    (pp 1475 to 1507)
Halsbury, Earl of   33, 57, 118, 379, 418,
                419, 471, 477, 478,
                614n, 645, 656, 657,
                694n, 696, 986, 1194
Halsbury's Laws of England   549, 699,
                    702–703
Hanbury, H G – *see* Bibliography
    (pp 1475 to 1507)
Hannen P   361n, 1098
Hansard – *see* legislative history
Hanworth, Lord   1217, 1263
Hardcastle, H – *see* Bibliography
    (pp 1475 to 1507)
Hardcastle, R   S34
hardship – *see* duress
Hardwicke, Lord   331
Hargrave, Francis – *see*
    Bibliography (pp 1475 to 1507)
Harman J   169, 715n, 736n, 745, 754, 842,
                901n, 962, 1214
Harman LJ   415, 755, 888, 994, 1121
Harries, Jill – *see* Bibliography (pp
    1475 to 1507)

Harris, D J – *see* Bibliography (pp
    1475 to 1507)
Harris, J W – *see* Bibliography (pp
    1475 to 1507)
Harrison, Nicolas – *see* Bibliography
    (pp 1475 to 1507)
Harrison, W Graham – *see*
    Bibliography (pp 1475 to 1507)
Hart, H L A   171n, 507n, 514, 515n, 893
  – *and see* Bibliography (pp 1475
    to 1507)
Hartley, T C   1302n
  – *and see* Bibliography (pp 1475
    to 1507)
hate incident   94
Hatherley, Lord   655, 902n, 903
Hatsell, J – *see* Bibliography (pp
    1475 to 1507)
Hatton, Christopher   7
  – *and see* Bibliography (pp 1475
    to 1507)
Havery, Judge Richard   1346
Hawkins, W   63n
  – *and see* Bibliography (pp 1475
    to 1507)
heading
  alteration of   215–216
    – *and see* printing corrections
  delegated legislation, in   716
  interpretation by reference to   715, 745–
                    746, 1454–1456
  nature of   745–746
    – *and see* functional
      construction rule
health, danger to – *see* doubtful
    penalisation, principle against;
    legal policy
hear both sides – *see* audi alterum
    partem principle
Heathcote-Amory, David – *see*
    Bibliography (pp 1475 to 1507)
Hebrides, the   356
hendiadys   1197
Hengham CJ   33
Henry LJ   118, 127, 143, 246, 626, 745n,
                1000n, 1140, 1218
Henry VIII clause   245–246, 294n
Heptarchy, the   353
Her Majesty's dominions   327, 348–350
Her Majesty's independent
    dominions   327, 350
Her Majesty's Revenue and Customs   1396
Her Majesty's Stationery Office –
    see HMSO
Herman, Shael   800, 965n
  – *and see* Bibliography (pp 1475
    to 1507)
Herschell, Lord   75, 605, 608, 609, 889n,
                    1163

All references are to page numbers

Heuston, R F V – *see* Bibliography
  (pp 1475 to 1507)
Hewart, Lord   196, 465, 763, 1138, 1139
Heydon J   S12
Heydon's Case, resolution in   471, 1009–
     1010, 1034
High Court   102, 111–114, 138–140
  – *and see* court
high seas
  jurisdiction over   356
  meaning of   350–351, 385–387
hijacking   376, 1211
hi-jacking   376
Hilbery J   491
Himsworth, C   S3
Hine, R L   752n
  – *and see* Bibliography (pp 1475
    to 1507)
Hirst LJ   1079
history, legislative – *see* legislative
  history
HMSO   226–227
  – *and see* Queen's Printer;
    Stationery Office Limited,
    The
Hobbes, Thomas   182, 894
  – *and see* Bibliography (pp 1475
    to 1507)
Hobhouse of Woodborough, Lord   199,
    494, 681n
Hodgson J   854n, 927, 1011, 1157
Hodson, Lord   993
Hoffmann, Lord   12n, 82, 86n, 117, 127,
    442, 499n, 562, 576,
    590, 602, 632, 633,
    639, 646, 704, 732,
    770, 799, 822, 900,
    904, 949, 957, 1081,
    1090, 1147, 1159,
    1170, 1195, 1223n,
    1288, 1291, 1324,
    1326, S33
Hogan, B – *see* Bibliography (pp
  1475 to 1507)
Holmes J   36, 132, 394n, 801, 830, 986,
    1156
  – *and see* Bibliography (pp 1475
    to 1507)
Holroyd J   749
Holt CJ   913
Home Office   87
home, sanctity of – *see* domestic
  sanctuary, principle of
homonym   1217–1219
  – *and see* words
Hong Kong   25
Honoré, T   805n
  – *and see* Bibliography (pp 1475
    to 1507)

Hooper J   1140
Hope of Craighead, Lord   45, 148, 192,
    265, 347, 515, 637,
    638, 671, 805n, 876,
    1033, 1139, 1316,
    1318, 1335, 1345
Horabin, I S – *see* Bibliography (pp
  1475 to 1507)
house – *see* domestic sanctuary,
  principle of
Howard J   991
  – *and see* Bibliography (pp 1475
    to 1507)
Hudon, Edward G – *see*
  Bibliography (pp 1475 to 1507)
human rights   2, 518–519, 790, 1050, 1276
  – *and see* doubtful penalisation,
    principle against; European
    Community law; European
    Convention on Human
    Rights; Human Rights
    Act 1998
Human Rights Act 1998
  amendment of   1320
  commencement   1311
  common law and   822
  compatibility, ministers' statements
    of   1334, 1439, S67
  compatible construction rule under   2, 509,
    885–886, 1322, 1426–
    1427
  Convention jurisprudence, duty to
    take account of   1321
  'Convention rights', meaning of   1317, –
    1425–1426
  damages under   1346
  declaration of incompatibility – *see*
    incompatibility, declaration
    of, under Human Rights Act
    199
  drafting of   1312, 1322
  effect on legislation   6, 1312, 1322
  general   ix
  incompatibility, declaration of – *see*
    incompatibility, declaration
    of, under Human Rights
    Act 1998
  incompatible acts and omissions of
    public authorities   1338
  interpretation of   1313, 1439–1440
  public authority, liability of   1338, 1428–
    1432
  remedial orders to rectify
    incompatibility   1335, 1433, 1448–
    1449
  Scotland, procedures in, under – *see*
    Scotland
  text of   1425–1451
  treatment of in this book   1312, 1315

All references are to page numbers

Hume, David (Baron Hume)   10, 1136n
 – *and see* **Bibliography (pp 1475
   to 1507)**
Hunt, Brian – *see* **Bibliography (pp
   1475 to 1507)**
Hunt, Murray   1
 – *and see* **Bibliography (pp 1475
   to 1507)**
Hutchison LJ   1034
Hutton, Lord   417, 509, 552, 609, 615, 743n
Hutton, Noël   738, 753
 – *and see* **Bibliography (pp 1475
   to 1507)**
hypothetical point – *see* **deeming;
   legal proceedings**
*id certum est quod certum reddi
   potest*   982
ignorance
 adviser, of   42
 – *and see* **advocate**
 English law of, by foreigner   42
 fact, of   40, 59
 law, of   40–44
 – *and* see *ignorantia juris
     neminem excusat*; **mistake**
*ignorantia eorum quae quis scire
   tenetur non excusat*   41
ignorantia juris neminem excusat   **40, 41**
 – *and see* **legislation; limitation of
   actions; mistake; mistake of
   law**
ignorantia facti excusat   41
Ilbert, Courtenay   33
 – *and see* **Bibliography (pp 1475
   to 1507)**
illegality
 *allegans suam turpitudinem non est
     audiendus*   1105–1111
 contracts or covenants and   61, 1069–1070,
                                              1107
 court's duty to notice   1110
 defences, effect on   1108–1109
 domicile, and   1111
 European Community law and   1111
 European Convention on Human
     Rights and   1320
 fraud   201, 793
 impracticability and   977–978
 in bonam partem (in good faith)
     construction   792–795
 locus poenitentiae and   1111
 reliance on   1105–1111
 residence, and   1111
 scope of   1105–1111
 severance   61, 1110
 third party rights and   1108–1109
 – *and see* **decision-making
     rules; evasion of Act; legal
     policy;** *nullus commodum*

illegality – *contd*
 third party rights and – *contd*
   – *and see* decision-making *rules;
       evasion of Act; legal policy; nullus
       commodum* – *contd*
       *capere potest de injuria sua
       propria; severance; tax
       avoidance*
immigration Appeals Tribunal   142
Immigration Acts, The   1396
immorality   501, 976
 – *and see* **legal policy; moral duty**
immunities – *see* **privileges and
   immunities**
impecuniosity   78–79, 126–127
implication
 ancillary powers, of   497–498
 broad terms – *see* **broad terms**
 courts, implied powers of – *see*
   inherent judicial powers
 Crown immunity, as to   210
 – *and see* **Crown immunity,
   doctrine of**
 definitions and   569
 delegated legislation and – *see*
   delegated legislation
 description only partly met, where –
   see **description, statutory**
 duties, as to   37
 European Convention on Human
     Rights   1319
 – *and see* **European Convention
   on Human Rights**
 express words exclude   1249–1250
 – *and see* *expressio unius*
   principle
 'if any', of   1269–1270
 imprecise language and   496
 legitimacy of   491–499
 limitation on express words, of   498–499
 literal construction and   463
 logic, in – *see* **logic, use of in
   intepretation**
 mandatory and directory
   requirements, as to – *see*
   **mandatory and directory
   requirements**
 maxims, application of – *see*
   maxims, legal
 nature of   487–490
 'necessary'   210, 493–494
 oblique reference, by   1259–1262
 'obvious'   495
 persons lacking capacity, exclusion
   of – *see* **incompetents**
 powers, and – *see* **statutory power**
 'proper'   113, 495–496
 related law, affecting   499–501
 right, implied extinguishment of   499

All references are to page numbers

implication – *contd*
rules of law, implied application of
   – *see* **implied ancillary rules**
statutory description, partially met,
   and   1262–1270
use of   50, 373
   – *and see* **amendment to Act;**
      application of Act;
      ejusdem generis **principle;**
      expressio unius **principle;**
      expressum facit cessare
      tacitum; **processing of**
      enactments, dynamic;
      statutory power;
      territorial extent of Act
implied ancillary maxims – *see*
   maxims, legal
implied ancillary powers   497–498
implied ancillary rules – *see*
   ancillary rules of law
impossibility 404–405, 973–974, 1129–1133
   – *and see impotentia excusat legem*
impotence – *see impotentia excusat*
   legem
impotentia excusat legem   1128
impracticability – *see* **absurdity**
impression, matters of   130, 586, 1030
   – *and see* **differential readings**
in bonam partem **construction** – *see*
   illegality
in pari materia, Acts 6, 184, 189, 588, 603,
                  604, 605, 708, 709,
                  710, 738, 759, 764,
                  765, 795, 889, 919,
               951, 954, 1165, 1167,
                         1200
   – *and see* **collective title;**
      construction as one;
      incorporation by reference;
      legal regimes; legislative
      history
in personam, proceedings – *see* **legal**
   proceedings
in rem, proceedings – *see* **legal**
   proceedings
inarticulate major premise – *see*
   judge
incapacity – *see* **incompetents**
incompatibility, declaration of,
   under Human Rights Act 1998
Crown, joinder of, in proceedings   1333,
                          1427–1428
delegated legislation, in respect of   1333,
                            1428
primary legislation, in respect of   1330,
                            1428
rectifying of legislation   1335, 1433
   – *and see* **Human Rights**
      Act 1998

Income Tax Acts   1396
incompatibility, declaration of,
   under Human Rights Act 1998
   effect of   1333
primary legislation, in respect of   1331
incompetents
bodily interference with   834
court, role of, in respect of   105
criminal enactments, application to   193,
                 1042, 1077–1078
housing of   125, 1012–1013
limitation period for   988
open court principle and   120
'person', reference to   578
property of, interference with   847
   – *and see* **children; death;**
      discrimination, legislation
      against; foetus; *impotentia*
      excusat legem; **mental**
      disability; procedure,
      criminal
inconsistency – *see* **repugnancy**
inconvenience – *see* **absurdity**
incorporation by reference
archival drafting   140, 151, 161, 162, 199,
                    209n, 759–761
construction as one   759, 762–764
general   758
nature of   758–765
   – *and see* **Clauses Act; collective**
      title; common law;
      functional construction;
      High Court; *in pari*
      materia, **acts; Keeling**
      Schedule; practice
indemnity Act – *see* **Act of**
   Parliament
India   247n, 333n, 343n, 693–694
'individual', meaning of   577, 1275
inducing words – *see* **Schedule**
infants – *see* **children**
information
power to publish   90
required to be true   37
information technology, implications
   of   377
informed interpretation
ambiguity and   587
common law and   589
consolidation Acts and   604–607
   – *and see* **consolidation Act**
context   588–590, 919
contextual material, submitted to
   court de bene esse   596
doubt and   25, 26
explanatory material on Bill and 641–644
facts and   587
Law Commission's views on   590–591

All references are to page numbers

---

informed interpretation – *contd*
legal knowledge required   593, 716, 804–
                                                805
    need for   122
    predictability of law and   590–591
    prolonging proceedings and   590–591
    rule   585–588
    treaties and   682–691
    – *and see* **legislative history**
inherent judicial powers
    alteration of unperfected judgment   112
    alteration of perfected judgment   S10
    codification of   203
    effectiveness of court orders,
        ensuring   113, 787, 1002–1003
    jurisdiction, statutory   51, 203
    nature of   111–114, 123, 1045
    procedure, as to   102, 111–114, 596, 598,
                              644, 680–682, 691–
                                                692
    – *and see* **jurisdiction**
injunction
    Crown immunity – *see* **Crown
        immunity, doctrine of**
    form of   115
    mandatory and directory
        requirements   56
    – *and see* **mandatory and
        directory requirements**
    power to grant   73, 114–116, 128, 163,
                              811, 1025–1026, 1067
    types of   114–116
    – *and see* **equity, rules of;
        judicial review**
injustice – *see* **justice**
inner London borough   1397
intention, ascertainment of   1104
intention, legislative
    accidental fit to unforeseen
        circumstances   482–483
    contrary intention, apparent   978
    delegated legislation, as to – *see*
        delegated legislation
    determination by judiciary   123, 337, 367,
                                                377
    drafter and   475–477
    duplex approach to   477–479
    enforcement powers, statutory, and   88
    European Community law, effect
        on   1299–1300
    fictitious, whether   472–474, 477–481
    'freezing' of   170
    function of the concept   472
    guides to – *see* **interpretative
        criteria**
    Human Rights Act 1998, effect of,
        and – *see* **Human Rights
        Act 1998**
    implied – *see* **implication**

intention, legislative – *contd*
    incomplete   481
    mandatory and directory
        requirements, in – *see*
        **mandatory and directory
        requirements**
    motive, distinguished from   484–486
    non-existent, where   366, 480–481
    paramount criterion, as   18, 86, 438, 469–
                                                472
    preamble as guide to   731–733
    purpose or object, distinguished
        from   483–784
    repeal and – *see* **repeal**
    retrospectivity and   317
    – *and see* **retrospectivity**
    sections, organisation of, as guide to   720–
                                                721
    tacit legislation and – *see* **tacit
        legislation**
    textual amendment and   289–292
    – *and see* **legal policy;
        legislative history;
        predictability of law;
        processing of enactments,
        dynamic**
interest   1256, 1259
interest reipublicae ut sit finis litium
    – *see* **protracted legal
        proceedings, interest of state to
        avoid**
interim relief   1297, 1353
'internal waters', meaning of 334, 341, 351
**International Convention for the
    Protection of Performers,
    producers of Phonograms, and
    Broadcasting
    Organisations (1961)**   70
**International Covenant on Civil and
    Political Rights (1966)**   322n, 683,
                                                1354
international law – *see* **private
    international law; public
    international law**
international organisations – *see*
    privileges and immunities
interpret, meaning of   23–24
Interpretation Act 1978
    contrary intention and   575, 583
    definitions in   576–583, 1200, 1387, 1394–
                                                1403
    – *and see* **definitions, statutory**
    free-standing terms and   1199–1200
    general   575–583, S8
    'person', definition of   1399
    – *and see* **artificial person**
    post, service by – *see* **service**
    provisions to which applicable   576, 1404–
                                                1405

All references are to page numbers

Interpretation Act 1978 – *contd*
  subordinate legislation, construction
    of   1388
  text of   1387–1408
  time, treatment of   1388
  white paper on   1409–1417
interpretation, rules of – *see* **rules**
interpretation, statutory – *see*
  statutory interpretation
interpretative conventions – *see*
  presumptions of construction
interpretative criteria
  checklist of   1383–1385
  common law, part of   513–514
  excluded by implication   1262
  legal policy, changes in, and 537–539
  nature of   24, 511–515
  operation of   512–513
  statutory   514
  types of   514–515
  – *and see* **interpretative factors;**
    legal policy; statutory
    interpretation
interpretative factors
  'bundles' of   524
  change in weight of   537–539
  consistent result from, effect of 521–523
  grammatical ambiguity – *see*
    ambiguity (grammatical)
  nature of   511–515, 519–523
  number of, in a case   525–526
  positive and negative   520–521
  priority between   526–527
  same interpretative criterion, drawn
    from   525
  semantic obscurity – *see* **obscurity,**
    semantic
  strained construction – *see* **strained**
    construction
  weighing and balancing of 523–528, 852,
          866–867, 873, 905–
                    906
  weight indicated by enactment,
    where   528–529
  – *and see* **interpretative**
    criteria; strict and liberal
    construction
interpretative presumptions – *see*
  presumptions of construction
interpretative principles – *see* **legal**
  policy; doubtful penalisation,
  principle against
interpreter of enactment
  types of   26–36
  – *and see* **Judges**
interstitial articulation
  advantages of   509
  effect of   171

interstitial articulation – *contd*
  examples of   171, 490, 507–508, 530,
              534–537, 1005
  meaning of   504, 1176–1177
  – *and see* **advocate;**
    codification; judicial gloss;
    sub-rules
investigating agencies – *see*
  enforcement agencies
Ireland
  'British Islands', as part of   342
  general   796
  name of   354
  treated as 'home' country, on
    occasion   355
  United Kingdom, as part of   354
  – *and see* **Eire; Irish Free State;**
    Northern Ireland
Irish Free State   342, 354
irregularity, procedural   50, 51, 1111
  – *and see* **decision-making rules**
Irvine of Lairg, Lord   955n, 1051, 1052,
                   1331
  – *and see* **Bibliography (pp 1475 to**
    1507)
Jackson (Robert H) J   626
  – *and see* **Bibliography (pp 1475**
    to 1507)
Jackson, Bernard S   **217**
Jacob J   622
Jacobs (F G) Adv Gen   1281n
Jamaica Schedule   196–197
James LJ   1005
James V-C   784, 1133n
Jamieson, N J   472
  – *and see* **Bibliography (pp 1475**
    to 1507)
jargon – *see* **legal terms; technical**
  terms
Jauncey of Tullichettle, Lord 81, 209, 902
Jekyll MR   785
Jenkins LJ   1259
Jenkins, David – *see* **Bibliography**
  (pp 1475 to 1507)
Jessel MR   484, 783, 866
John, Rowena – *see* **Bibliography**
  (pp 1475 to 1507)
joint tenants   579, 1207
Jones, Timothy H – *see* **Bibliography**
  (pp 1475 to 1507)
Jowitt, Earl   465
  – *and see* **Bibliography (pp 1475**
    to 1507)
Joyce J   772
judge
  antagonism to legislation, former 814–816
  appointment of   2–5
  bias by – *see* ***nemo debet esse judex***
    in propria causa

All references are to page numbers

judge – *contd*
checklist of interpretive criteria   1383
comprehension of meaning of
  enactment, difficulty of   451–453
de facto   1356
dicta, inadequate   10, 11
drafting, inadequate, response to   409–413
  – *and see* **disorganised
    composition**
early legislation, as drafter of   652–653
ellipsis, recognition of   493
  – *and see* **ellipsis**
function of   393–394, 548
inarticulate major premise
  underlying decisions   132
independence of   152–153
interpretative factors, reluctant
  acknowledgement of   527–528, 544–
    547
interpreter of legislation, as   102, 108,
    122–133, 588–589,
    697–701
interstitial articulation by   506–507, 548
law, knowledge of, presumed   42, 133,
    1221–1223
legislative language, knowledge of
  presumed   1221–1223
legislator, as   11, 168–170, 785–786
  – and *see* **court**
lis, concerned to decide   29, 392, 430
misbehaviour by   118–119
mistake of law by   135, 728–729
  – *and see* **mistake**
Parliament, respect for   963–965
  – *and see* **comity**
philologist, as   1221
precision drafting, recognition of   411
pre-trial powers of   984
private knowledge of   428
prosecutors, criticism of   99
puisne   140
recusal by   394, 1139
statutory interpretation, function
  exclusive to   699
  – *and see* **statutory
    interpretation**
text writers, views on – *see* **jurists**
uniform terminology for
  interpretation, and   589–590
well-informed, need to be   137–138, 591,
    593, 641, 691
witness, as   103
  – *and see* **assessor; court;
    death; delegated
    legislation; differential
    readings; discretion;
    drafting, legislative;
    evidence; judicial notice;
    judicial power of the state;**

judge – *contd*
  witness, as – *contd*
  – *and see* **assessor; court; death;
    delegated legislation; differential
    readings; discretion; drafting,
    legislative; evidence; judicial
    notice; judicial power of the
    state;** – *contd*
    legal policy; legislative
    history; magistrates;
    political factors
Judge, Lord LCJ   S11
judge in own cause – *see* **nemo debet
    esse judex in propria causa**
Judge, Igor (President)   170
judgment
exercise of – *see* **exercise of
    judgment**
form of   62, 117
reopening of   114
secret   118
summary   26
  – *and see* – **appeal**
judicial act   1120
  – *and see* **act in law**
Judicial Appointments Board   2–5
judicial assistant   394, 595
**Judicial Committee of the Privy
    Council**   154, 333
  – *and see* **Privy Council**
judicial gloss   480–481, 491, 506, 548
  – *and see* **interstitial articulation**
judicial notice
Act, of   136, 184, 196, 233, 1387
Bill, of   43, 196
common law, of   136
custom, of   136
delegated legislation, of   135
dictionary, reference to   1222–1223
discretion as to taking   134
doctrine of   133–138
European Community law, of   136, 1283
European Court of Justice, decisions
  of   135, 613
expertise, non-legal, of   138
fact, of   28–29, 136–138, 428
judge's private knowledge   428
law, of   28–29, 133–136, 599–600
legislative history, of   610
meaning of words, of   1202, 1221–1223
personal Act, not judicially noticed
  – and – *see* **personal Act**
public international law, of   823
scope of   134
technical terms, of   1202
treaty, of   823
  – *and see* **Act of State; evidence**

All references are to page numbers

judicial power of the state   9, 101, 103, 104,
                                    152, 392, 434
– *and see* **Crown**
judicial review
  agencies subject to   90, 91
  – *and see* **enforcement agencies**
  alternative remedies, need to pursue   159–
                                          161
  Anisminic clause   109–110
  anticipatory   111
  application for   155
  breach of statutory duty, for   67, 71
  byelaws, of   270
  categories of case   161
  certiorari – *see* **quashing order**
    (*certiorari*)
  challenges in other proceedings   164
  commencement order, of failure to
    make   284–286
  Court of Appeal and   158
  Crown immunity – *see* **Crown**
    immunity, doctrine of
  damages   163–164
  decisions of enforcement agencies   90, 91
  declaration   163
  – *and see* **declaration**
  delegated legislation, of   166, 247, 253,
                                          260
  discretion, as to exercise of   1054–1055,
                                          1059
  evidence in   158
  good administration, duty of   91
  habeas corpus and   166, 838–839
  – *and see* ***habeas corpus***
  Hansard, citing   670–671
  High Court decision, of   108
  injunction, grant of   163
  – *and see* **injunction**
  last resort, remedy of   154
  leave for   155, 163
  locus standi   158–159, 539, 776–777
  mandatory order (mandamus)   56, 110,
                                          154, 161–162
  national security and   104
  nature of   90–91, 95, 154–166, 1051
  Ostler clause   109
  prerogative instrument, of   240
  prerogative order   111, 162–163
  principles governing – *see*
    decision-making rules
  private Act, and   156
  prohibiting order (prohibition)   117, 154,
                                          162–163
  prosecutions   100
  public law remedy – *see* **public law**
  quashing order (*certiorari*)   109, 110, 162
  quo warranto   154, 165–166
  religion and   157
  remedies available for   161–166

judicial review – *contd*
  severance   258–259
  – *and see* **severance**
  standing   158, 539, 776–777
  supervisory rather than appellate   158
  Supreme Court and   158
  time factors   159, 872
  university disputes   110
  – *and see* **appeal;** *Carltona*
    principle; contempt of
    court; contempt of statute;
    doubtful penalisation,
    principle against;
    enforcement notice;
    jurisdiction; prisoners,
    rights of; reference, works
    of
Judicial Studies Board   130
Junius, Letters of   800n
jurisdiction
  absence of   50, 116
  Admiralty   330, 357, 368, 913
  agreement, whether conferrable by   105–
                                          106, 143
  appellate – *see* **appeal**
  civil and criminal contrasted   1049, 1354
  contracting out   62
  court, of, interference with
    contractual right   S7
  court's determination as to its   111–114
  criminal – *see* **procedure, criminal**
  doubt as to   50, 105–106
  duplication of   811
  European Convention on Human
    Rights and   1318
  excess of   50–51, 107
  failure to exercise   106–107, 112
  implied   105–106, 559
  inherent – *see* **inherent judicial**
    powers
  mandatory and directory
    requirements   50–51
  – *and see* **mandatory and**
    directory requirements
  nature of   104–107, 559
  non-court, of   105–106
  ouster clause   S9
  ouster of   108–111
  resource implications   107
  states, disputes between   106–109
  submission to   105, 375
  – *and see* **appropriate forum**
    test; Brussels Convention
    on Jurisdiction and the
    Enforcement of Judgments
    in Civil and Commercial
    Matters; commencement
    of Act; court;
    decision-making rules;

All references are to page numbers

jurisdiction – *contd*
  submission to – *contd*
    – *and see* **appropriate forum test;
      Brussels Convention on
      Jurisdiction and the Enforcement
      of Judgments in Civil and
      Commercial Matters;
      commencement of Act; court;
      decision-making rules;** – *contd*
      **estoppel; exterritoriality;
      magistrates;** *Scherer*
      **principle; territorial
      extent of Act; territorial
      waters**

jurists
  authority of, early   30–31
  cited by judges   31–32
  deceased, need to be?   32–33
  errors in textbooks   31, 32
  foreign   34
  interpreters as   28–34
  judges and barristers as authorities   28, 32
  living, authority of   32–33
  opinions of   712

jury
  commonsense construction rule, and   558
  function of   393–394
  grand   489
  interpretation by   558
  judge's instructions to   781
  mistake of law by   118
  public authority, not   1379
  public interest and   791–792
  question left to   52
  trial by   554, 781, 854, 926, 992, 1083,
                                                      1356
    – *and see* **procedure, criminal**

justice
  access to   255, 854
  law should serve   795–799
  natural – *see* **natural justice**
  should be done   142–144, 1138
  should be seen to be done   1138–1139
    – *and see* **European Convention
      on Human Rights, Human
      Rights Act 1998; open
      court, the**
    – *and see* **court;
      decision-making rules;
      legal policy; legal
      proceedings; Parliament;
      retrospectivity**

Justinian   30, 170, 817
  – *and see* **Bibliography (pp 1475 to
    1507)**

Kafka, Franz   252

Kay LJ   242, 815

Keeling Schedule   643
  – *and see* **incorporation by
    reference**

Keenan, D J – *see* **Bibliography (pp
  1475 to 1507)**

Keene LJ   1372

Keir, D L – *see* **Bibliography (pp
  1475 to 1507)**

Keith of Avonholm, Lord   421, 955

Keith of Kinkel, Lord   51n, 127

Kelly CB   30

Kennedy LJ   1358

Kenny, C S   926n
  – *and see* **Bibliography (pp 1475
    to 1507)**

Kent, Harold   412, 589
  – *and see* **Bibliography (pp 1475
    to 1507)**

Kenyon CJ   653

Kerr LJ   977, 1011

Kersell, J E – *see* **Bibliography (pp
  1475 to 1507)**

Kersley, R H – *see* **Bibliography (pp
  1475 to 1507)**

Khan, A N – *see* **Bibliography (pp
  1475 to 1507)**

Kiefel J   S45

Kilgour, D G   654n, 666n, 681
  – *and see* **Bibliography (pp 1475
    to 1507)**

Kilner Brown J   1027

Kindersley V-C   1223

Kipling, Rudyard   883n
  – *and see* **Bibliography (pp 1475
    to 1507)**

Kirby M   S43

Kirby P   675, 676
  – *and see* **Bibliography (pp 1475
    to 1507)**

Knox J   493, 568, 950

Labouchère, H   482

Lacey, Nicola – *see* **Bibliography (pp
  1475 to 1507)**

laches   1067

lacuna – *see* **rectifying construction**

land
  definition of   581, 1398
  meaning of   1030, 1258
  occupier's liability   1073
  rights over   846–849, 1030
    – *and see* **leasehold
      enfranchisement;
      property; trespass**

Landon, P A – *see* **Bibliography (pp
  1475 to 1507)**

Lands Clauses Acts   1397

Lands Tribunal   106, 142, 146

Landsdowne, Lord   225n

All references are to page numbers

Lane, Lord   135, 554, 730, 787, 805, 835,
                          845, 962, 990, 1003,
                          1030, 1142, 1256,
                          1269
Langdale, Lord   434, 699
Langton, Stephen   412
Lanham, David – *see* Bibliography
     (pp 1475 to 1507)
Latey J   152
Latham J   1253
Latin, use of   1101–1103, 1117, 1203
law
  anticipated change of   695
  casual change of   782, 812–816
  certainty, need for – *see*
       predictability of law
  church – *see* **ecclesiastical law**
  churning – *see* **law-churning**
  consistency in, need for – *see* **legal**
       policy
  corpus juris (body of law)   197
  ecclesiastical – *see* **ecclesiastical**
       law
  equality before   330–331
  expertise, is an   129
  foreign – *see* **foreign**
  ignorance of – *see* *ignorantia juris*
       neminem excusat
  integrity of, need to preserve   782, 993–
                                               995
  international – *see* **private**
       international law; public
       international law
  judicial disregard of   313–314
  judicial notice of – *see* **judicial**
       notice
  liberty removed not granted by   782–783,
                          821–822, 844–845,
                                               846
  nature of 6, 36–37, 40, 191–194, 197–198,
                          206–207, 363, 395
  point of   148
  predictability of – *see* **predictability**
       of law
  protection by   372–373
  public – *see* **public law**
  reports – *see* **precedent, doctrine of**
  rule of   140n, 193, 1135
  soft   706
     – *and see* **Act of Parliament;**
          common law; delegated
          legislation; equity;
          European Community
          law; fact and law; implied
          ancillary rules; justice;
          law-churning; Law
          Commission; law
          merchant; legal policy;
          legal proceedings;

law – *contd*
  soft – *contd*
     – *and see* **Act of Parliament; common**
          law; delegated legislation; equity;
          European Community law; fact
          and law; implied ancillary rules;
          justice; law-churning; Law
          Commission; law merchant; legal
          policy; legal proceedings; – *contd*
          legislation; Lords, house
          of; maxims, legal;
          mistake; natural law;
          statute law
law-churning   135n, 928
Law Commission
  breach of statutory duty, views on   70
  changing social values and
       interpretation, views on   904
  components of Act, interpretation by
       reference to, views on   715–726
  consolidation Acts and   606
  contempt of statute, views on   66
  delegated legislation, interpretation
       of, views on   716
  disobeying Act, views on   66
  history of   32n
  legislative history, views on 612, 650, 692
  'mischief', views on   922–923
  reports of, reference to   32, 614–615, 661
     – *see* **legislative history**
  statutory interpretation, views on   519,
                                590–591, 592
  territorial waters, views on   334, 335n
  users of legislation, views on   804
Law Commission: – *see* **codification**
law management – *see* **central**
     function of practitioner
law merchant   136, 609n, 1070
Law Officers – *see* **Attorney General**
law reports
  neutral citation   856–857
  precedent and   854–855
     – *and see* **precedent, doctrine of**
  procedures regarding   119
  restrictions on   120
     – *and see* **open court, the**
Law Society, supervisory function of   92
Lawrence J   841
Laws LJ   53, 90, 95, 97, 101, 390, 708, 757
     – *and see* **Bibliography (pp 1475**
          to 1507)
Lawson, F H – *see* **Bibliography (pp**
     1475 to 1507)
Lawton LJ   173, 550, 586, 662, 949, 1085,
                          1148, 1157, 1207
Le Sueur, A P   836n
     – *and see* **Bibliography (pp 1475**
          to 1507)
Learned Hand J   588

All references are to page numbers

---

leasehold enfranchisement   848, 1023n
Lee J   676
legal adviser – *see* **advocate**
legal aid   457, 704, 911, 925, 975, 1023
legal certainty – *see* **predictability of law**
legal concepts   1040
legal meaning
   bilingual systems   25
   deductive reasoning, use of – *see*
     logic, use of in interpretation
   doubt as to – *see* **differential**
     readings; doubt as to legal
     meaning
   grammatical meaning and,
     contrasted   441–443
   interpreter's duty to arrive at   24–25, 592,
     699
   legislative history and   24
   multilingual systems   25
   nature of   24–26, 123, 175–177, 394, 430,
     441–443, 592, 1197
   paradoxical   1192
   partial meaning point   x
   time point   x
   wide and narrow construction – *see*
     strict and liberal
     construction
     – *and see* **opposing**
      constructions; plain
      meaning rule; processing
      of enactments, dynamic
legal policy
   adopted by reference to Acts   765, 769,
     775–776, 781–782,
     816
   arbitration, regarding   812
   avoidance of duplication   1116
   categories of   779–782
   cause of action, as to   422
   changes in   499, 537–539, 776–777, 785–
     786
   common law and   771, 775
   conflicts within   779, 790–792
     – *and see* **interpretative factors**
   constituent elements of   773–778
   court required to observe   1100
   court, citizen's access to   108, 112
   disputes, settlement of   807
   duplication of offences, avoidance
     of   810
   duplication of remedies, avoidance
     of   810
   equality before the law   330–331, 782, 853
   European Convention on Human
     Rights, and – *see* **European**
     Convention on Human
     Rights
   evasion of Act – *see* **evasion of Act**

legal policy – *contd*
   fairness, principle of   374, 770, 795–799
   finality   582, 787–788
   freedom, restraints on   784–785, 836–840,
     965
   imported by Acts   1038
   impracticability, need to avoid   977
   inconvenience – *see* **absurdity**
   international law – *see* **private**
     international law; public
     international law
   international relations   817–824
   interpretative criteria and   537–539
   jury, constitutional right as   854
   jury, exclusion of trial by   854
   law should be certain and
     predictable   799–807
   law should be consistent   782, 808–812
   law should be effective   1277
   law should be just   177, 795–799
     – *and see* **justice**
   law should be knowable   194
   law should not be changed casually   812–
     816
     – *and see* **law**
   law should serve the public interest   211–
     212, 319–320, 786–
     795, 1046
   legal principles and   765, 769–786
   legal proceedings – *see* **legal**
     proceedings
   legal process, rights of   854
   liberty of the person, safeguarding
     of   52, 836–840
     – *and see* **doubtful penalisation,**
      principle against; *habeas*
      corpus; **prisoners, rights of**
   life and health, preservation of   537–539,
     780, 831–836, 1134,
     1257
     – *and see* **doubtful penalisation,**
      principle agains
   morality and   773–778, 780
     – *and see* **immorality; moral**
      duty
   municipal law should conform to
     international law   817–824
     – *and see* **public international**
      law
   nature of   168, 765, 769–786
   overlapping legal regimes,
     minimisation of   809–810
   penalisation, doubtful – *see*
     doubtful penalisation,
     principle against
   preserving the peace – *see* **peace,**
     Queen's

All references are to page numbers

legal policy – *contd*
property rights, and   42, 52–53, 58, 537–
539, 785, 828–829,
846–851
public and private interests, conflict
between, and   790–792
public policy, and   62, 765, 769, 772
reasonableness, and   770
rights removed not conferred – *see*
law
security of the state, regarding   104, 379,
779, 1046, 1135
statutory interpretation and   778
tax avoidance schemes and   1019
– *and see* **tax avoidance**
waiver of statutory right   62
– *and see* **application of Act;
costs; counter-mischief;
court; European
Convention on Human
Rights; European
Community law;
extra-erritoriality; human
rights; illegality; implied
ancillary rules; intention,
legislative; jurisdiction;
justice; law; maxims,
legal; legislative steer;
natural law; open court,
the; predictability of law;
principles of construction;
religion; retrospectivity**

legal proceedings
academic or hypothetical point   143, 164,
1306
adjournment of   113, 279, 997
anomalies regarding   997
avoidance of protracted   787–788
change of law, effect on   320
civil and criminal distinguished   93–94
conduct, right to   854–855
costs – *see* **costs**
defences – *see* **defences;
procedure, criminal**
defendant, absence of   1081
delay, minimizing   320, 590–591, 983–985
due process – *see* **process**
evidence in – *see* **evidence**
facilitate, need to   320, 975–977, 1026–
1027
forum non conveniens, doctrine of   374
in personam   687–688, 1065
in rem   687–688, 997, 1027, 1065
inconvenience to   983–985
jury, trial by – *see* **jury**
lengthening of, need to avoid   590–591,
983–985, 984
– *and see* **protracted legal
proceedings, avoiding**

legal proceedings – *contd*
letter before action   1002
litigant in person   113
open court, principle of – *see* **open
court, the**
parties, duties of   509
pleading – *see* **pleading**
pointless   320, 1001–1002
– *and see* **protracted legal
proceedings, avoiding**
publicity of – *see* **open court, the**
reporting, restrictions on – *see* **open
court, the**
rules of court – *see* **court**
satellite litigation, – *see* protracted
legal proceedings, avoiding
seat of justice, access to – *see*
justice
service of process – *see* **service**
technicality, need to minimize – *see*
technicalities
– *and see* **advocate; court;
doubtful penalisation,
principle against; equity;
justice; legal aid; legal
policy; limitation of
actions; predictability of
law; procedure, civil;
procedure, criminal**

legal scholars – *see* **jurists**

legal terms
contextual interpretation of   1200
conveyancing   190
creation, judicial, of   1213
free-standing   28, 1199–1200
interpretation of   1199–1203
– *and see* **technical terms**
multi-jurisdictional enactments, in   1202–
1203
status, as to   1201–1202
terms of art   1200–1201
uncertain meaning of   1202

legal thrust of enactment   15, 391, 392,
396, 416, 417, 419,
421–423, 425, 428,
433, 516, 941, 1174,
1175, 1267

– *and see* **comminution;
enactment; factual outline,
the; precision drafting;
selective comminution**

**legality, principle of (constitutional
rights)**   2, 190, 773, 822–823, 843–844,
1048n, 1324

Leggatt LJ   1013n

All references are to page numbers

legislation – *see* **Act of Parliament; delegated legislation; intention, legislative; legal regimes; legislator; statute; statute law; tacit legislation**
ancient   695
duty to obey – see **disobeying Act;** *ignorantia juris neminem excusat*
extra-territorial – *see* **extra-territoriality**
modifying a judicial decision   401
understanding of   40–44, 801, 1184–1185
   – *and see* **user of legislation**

legislation by reference – *see* **incorporation by reference**

Legislative and Regulatory Reform Act 2006   91

legislative drafting – *see* **drafting, legislative**

legislative history
   amendment to Bill and   640–641
   basic rule   610–612
   commentaries on Act   712
   committee reports   614–616, 694, 696–697, 711–712, 924, 936–937
   consolidation Acts and   604–607
   costs and   612, 624
   delegated legislation and   266, 598
   enacting history   588–590, 609–702
   guidelines   704
   Hansard   616–640, 1245, 1332
   – *and see* **exclusionary rule, the;** *Pepper v Hart*, **rule in**
   inherent power of court to consider   123, 692
   inspection of, by court   691–692
   legislative intention, as guide to   697–698
   literal meaning and   700–701
   mischief, to ascertain   696–697
   nature of   598, 610–612
   official statements on meaning of Act   702–706
   parliamentary history – *see* **exclusionary rule, the;** *Pepper v Hart*, **rule in**
   persuasive nature of   698–701
   post-enacting history   588–590, 702–712
   pre-enacting history   588–590, 599–604, 1208–1209
   private judicial use of   691
   specific reference to in enactment   612–614
   treaty – *see* **treaty**
   weight given to   610, 612, 892–893
   white papers and   643, 692n
   – *and see* **amendment to Bill; Bill, parliamentary;**

legislative history – *contd*
   white papers and – *contd*
   – *and see* **amendment to Bill; Bill, parliamentary;** – *contd* **comity;** *contemporanea expositio*; **informed interpretation; judicial notice; Law Commission; legal meaning; predictability of law; tax avoidance; taxing Acts**

legislative intention – *see* **intention, legislative**

legislative sentence   398
   – *and see* **drafting, legislative; enactment**

legislative steer   782

legislator
   early – *see* **statute**
   executive as – *see* **Minister of the Crown**
   intention of – *see* **intention, legislative**
   interpreter, as   26–27
   judge as – *see* **court**
   mistake by – *see* **mistake**
   nature of   26–27
   purpose of – *see* **purposive construction**
   – *and see* **Parliament**

legitimate expectation – *see* **decision-making rules**

LEGOL   473n, 1174

Leigh, Ian – *see* **Bibliography (pp 1475 to 1507)**

Leng, Roger – *see* **Bibliography (pp 1475 to 1507)**

Lenz, Adv Gen   1284n

Lester of Herne Hill, Lord – *see* **Bibliography (pp 1475 to 1507)**

Leung, Matthew – *see* **Bibliography (pp 1475 to 1507)**

Lewis, B N – *see* **Bibliography (pp 1475 to 1507)**

Lewis, G – *see* **Bibliography (pp 1475 to 1507)**

Lewison J   S12

lex non cogit ad impossibilia – *see* **impossibility**

liabilities, statutory transfer of   827

liberal construction – *see* **strict and liberal construction**

liberty of the person – *see* **legal policy; doubtful penalisation, principle against**

liberty removed not granted   782–783, 821–822, 844–845, 859

All references are to page numbers

---

licensing – *see* **enforcement agencies;**
   local authority
Lightman J   32, 128, 508, 704, 891, 1156,
                    1241, 1379, 1455
limitation of actions
   anomalies   988, 993
   Crown and – *see* **Crown**
   equity, and   500
   exterritoriality, and   370
   historical   996
   ignorance of law, and   44
   judicial treatment of   130
   pleading of – *see* **pleading**
   procedural and substantive rules,
      distinction between   392, 948–949
   reasons for   800–801, 932, 996
   rectification and   173
   retrospectivity and   321
   specialties and   39
      – *and see* **specialty**
   statutory right and   601
Lincoln (Anthony) J   500
Lindley MR   371, 697, 1236
Lindsay J   46, 452
linguistic canons – *see* **canons of**
   construction, linguistic
literal construction
   anomaly and   997–998
   arguments for and against   42, 461–463,
                        803, 864–869, 1002–
                                          1003
   context and   840
   enacting history and   700–701
   integrity of Act, preserving, and   1029
   Law Commission's criticism of   461–462
   legal certainty and   803
   maxims and   1101
   nature of   432, 455–456, 458–461, 533
   ouster clauses, watering down of   108
   public interest and   791
      – *and see* **canons of**
         construction, linguistic;
         factual outline; 'literal
         rule'; predictability of law
'literal rule'   12, 13, 457, 458, 459, 460,
                        545, 547–459, 653,
                        864–869, 1177, 1178,
                                          1179
   – *and see* **literal construction**
litigation – *see* **doubtful penalisation,**
   principle against; legal
   proceedings
Littledale J   412, 994
Littleton (Thomas) J   26n, 30, 1186
Llewellyn, Karl   815
   – *and see* **Bibliography (pp 1475**
      to 1507)
Lloyd J   31, 311, 681, 810
Lloyd of Berwick, Lord   153, 601

local Act   92, 123, 183, 185, 203, 245, 743,
                    793, 1229, 1242,
                    1247 – *see* **private Act**
local authority
   administration of enactment by   87, 97,
                                     366, 1002
   audit of   76
   charges, power to make   88, 1048
   councillors etc   934, 953, 1001, 1139–1140
   delay by   1149
   European Convention on Human
      Rights and   1319
   legal proceedings by   74, 815
   licensing by   92
   local Acts, and – *see* **local Act**
   Local Commissioner for
      Administration   1140
   local planning authority   87
   meetings of   54
   officer of   1107
   'person aggrieved', as   173
   policy decision by   83
   powers of   87–88, 400, 497–498, 1047–
                                          1048
   taxation by   1047–1048
   territory of   351
      – *and see* **adoptive Act;**
         byelaws; enforcement
         agencies; provisional
         order; public authority
local land charges register   1397
location, deemed   327, 387, 389–390
Lock, G F – *see* **Bibliography (pp**
   1475 to 1507)
Locke, John   39, 773, 800, 801
   – *and see* **Bibliography (pp 1475**
      to 1507)
logic, use of in interpretation
   ambiguous middle term   1175–1177
   conceptualism – *see* **conceptualism**
   contradiction, principle of   1177–1179
   deductive reasoning   1171–1179
   hypothetical syllogism   1174–1175
   implication   1173
   inarticulate major premise – *see*
      judge
   inductive and deductive reasoning   1172–
                                          1173
   interpretation, use in   126, 986–987
   syllogism   1172–1175
   symbolic   1174
      – *and see* **LEGOL**
London borough   1397
London, Greater   6n, 292
long title
   drafting deficiencies, remedying, by
      reference to   730
   ejusdem generis principle and   1234
   extent of Act and   336–337

long title – *contd*
function of   727–731
interpretative use of   379, 701, 727–731,
    1098, 1099
    mischief, identifying, by   935, 941
    mistakes in   730–731
    parliamentary procedure and   717, 728
    purpose, legislative, and   960–961
Lopes LJ   1251
Lord Chancellor   3, 140, 217, 219, 222,
    231, 1045, 1397
Lord Chancellor's Department   229n
Lords, House of
    abolition of, proposals for   405
    Appellate Committee, of   151–153
    appellate functions of   148–153
    commune forum, as   333
    law, duty to oversee   151–152
    legislative procedure   213–216
    – *and see* **Act of Parliament**
    legislature, as part of   40, 475
    precedent and   168, 174–175
    – *and see* **precedent, doctrine of**
    resolutions of   248–249
    revising chamber as   x
    – *and see* **Act of Parliament;**
       Lord Chancellor;
       Northern Ireland;
       Parliament; precedent,
       doctrine of; Scotland
Loreburn, Lord   412, 787
Lowry, Lord   163n 203, 524, 566, 620, 753,
    958, 1042, 1053, 1054,
    1065
Lücke, Horst Klaus   8n, 546
    – *and see* **Bibliography (pp 1475**
       to 1507)
Lush J   724
Lushington, Dr   372, 558, 874, 1007, 1182
Lusky Louis   893n
    – *and see* **Bibliography (pp 1475**
       to 1507)
Luxmoore LJ   659
Lyndhurst, Lord   30
Lynskey J   907
MacCormick, D N   8n, 131, 430, 437, 538n,
    770, 808, 1178
    – *and see* **Bibliography (pp 1475**
       to 1507)
MacDermott, Lord   442, 1220
Mackay of Clashfern, Lord   617, 624
Mackinnon LJ   452
    – *and see* **Bibliography (pp 1475**
       to 1507)
Macmillan, Lord   79, 377, 414n, 956, 1198
Macnaghten, Lord   331, 545, 784, 796, 804,
    1223
Macpherson J   210

magistrates' court
    appeals from   145
    appeals to   145
    commonsense construction rule, and   558
    definition of   1397
    jurisdiction, civil   75, 92, 141, 1259
    jurisdiction, criminal   141, 315, 998n
    lay magistrates   92, 141, 558
    procedure before   279, 884, 997, 1060,
    1202
    supervisory functions of   92
    warrant   811, 1075
    – *and see* **contempt of court;**
       court; death; evidence;
       inherent judicial powers;
       legal proceedings;
       procedure, criminal
Magna Carta   180, 189n, 412, 836, 837n,
    847, 853, 912, 916,
    1014, 1351
Maine, Henry J S   817, 895
    – *and see* **Bibliography (pp 1475**
       to 1507)
maintenance   199, 777–778
Maitland, F W   11, 104n, 204, 234n, 894n,
    1165
    – *and see* **Bibliography (pp 1475**
       to 1507)
mala in se   39, 1049
mala prohibita   39, 1049
    – *and see* **strict liability**
maladministration   135n, 681, 1140
    – *and see* **enforcement agencies**
malice   80, 93, 417, 895, 1092
Mallory, J R – *see* **Bibliography (pp**
    1475 to 1507)
Man, Isle of   342, 346, 347, 351–352, 484
Mance LJ   1289, S15, S23
Mancini J   1301
    – *and see* **Bibliography (pp 1475**
       to 1507)
mandatory and directory
    requirements   23, 40, 44–57, 63, 65,
    66, 110, 114, 118, 248,
    253, 256, 285, 397,
    400, 460, 569n, 956,
    1055n, 1132, 1133n,
    1469, 1471
mandatory order (mandamus) – *see*
    injunction; judicial review
Mann LJ   109, 110, 120, 413, 435, 614, 736,
    779, 905, 1095, 1168
Mann, F A   690n
    – *and see* **Bibliography (pp 1475**
       to 1507)
Mansfield, Lord   365, 463, 604, 708, 780,
    800, 845, 1011, 1108

All references are to page numbers

Marcello, D A   477n
 – *and see* **Bibliography (pp 1475 to 1507)**
Marcellus   1209
margin of appreciation   1281, 1282, 1314, 1318, 1326, 1327, 1361, 1369
marginal note – *see* sidenote to section
Mark, R   922n
 – *and see* **Bibliography (pp 1475 to 1507)**
market   1037
Markesinis, Basil – *see* **Bibliography (pp 1475 to 1507)**
Markson, H E   805
 – *and see* **Bibliography (pp 1475 to 1507)**
Marleasing principle   1298–1299, 1323
Marmor, A   13
marriage   911, 1099, 1132, 1215–1216
Martin, Andrew – *see* **Bibliography (pp 1475 to 1507)**
Martin, B   1187, 1221
masculine and feminine – *see* gender
Mason CJ   360n, 651, 676
 – *and see* **Bibliography (pp 1475 to 1507)**
massage parlours, licensing of   92, 185
Maugham, Viscount   956
Maule J   1212
 maxims, legal   1103
 nature of   1101–1103
Maxwell, D – *see* **Bibliography (pp 1475 to 1507)**
Maxwell, Peter   7
 – *and see* **Bibliography (pp 1475 to 1507)**
May LJ   43, 142, 603, 942, 1102
May, Thomas Erskine – *see* **Bibliography (pp 1475 to 1507)**
McCardie J   1235, 1237, 1243, 1244
McCowan LJ   602, 1013
McCullough J   433, 1006
McGlynn, C   133
 – *and see* **Bibliography (pp 1475 to 1507)**
McKenzie friend   112, S12
McLeod, Ian   13n, 122n, 132, 637, 638n, 1092n, 1223n
 – *and see* **Bibliography (pp 1475 to 1507)**
McNair, A D – *see* **Bibliography (pp 1475 to 1507)**
McNeill LJ   1227
McWhirter, Norris   65
meaning – *see* archaisms; composite expressions; grammatical meaning; homonyms; judicial

meaning – – *contd*
 notice; legal meaning; legal terms; meaningless terms; *noscitur a sociis* principle; ordinary meaning; technical terms; updating construction; words
meaningless terms   453–455, 1219, 1220–1221
Measure, interpretation of   1391
mechanical etc apparatus – *see* description, statutory
medical treatment   833–834, 921–922
Megarry V-C   32, 234, 246n, 753, 754, 783, 950, 1002, 1028, 1189, 1246, 1257
 – *and see* **Bibliography (pp 1475 to 1507)**
Megaw LJ   802
Mellinkoff, D   171n, 185n, 751, 757
 – *and see* **Bibliography (pp 1475 to 1507)**
Mellish LJ   61, 1065
Mellone, S H   1174
 – *and see* **Bibliography (pp 1475 to 1507)**
mens rea – *see* criminal law
mental disability   52, 77, 125, 867, 884, 887
 – *and see* incompetents
Miers, D R   7, 549
 – *and see* **Bibliography (pp 1475 to 1507)**
Mill, J S   1224
Millett, Lord   446, 494, 633, 710, 809, 969, 1124, 1323, S61
Milmo J   555
Milner, JB – *see* **Bibliography (pp 1475 to 1507)**
Milton, John   952
 – *and see* **Bibliography (pp 1475 to 1507)**
Minister of the Crown
 administration of enactment by   85–86
  – *and see* enforcement agencies
 certifying of facts by   824
 delegation by   88–89, 273
  – *and see* decision-making rules
 delegation to   241, 251–252
  – *and see* delegated legislation
 knowledge, imputation of   87, 88–89
 policy decision by   82
 powers under Legislative and Regulatory Reform Act 2006   91
 remedies against   207–208
 submissions to court by   86
 transfer of functions of   85–86
  – *and see* Attorney General; *Carltona* principle; Crown; discretion;

All references are to page numbers

Minister of the Crown – *contd*
  transfer of functions of – *contd*
    – *and see* Attorney General; *Carltona*
      principle; Crown; discretion; –
      contd
      enforcement agencies;
      government; legislative
      history; legislator;
      Lord Chancellor; Ministry
      of Justice; prerogative,
      Royal; Prime Minister;
      Secretary of State
Ministry of Justice   252
minor – *see* age; children; wardship
mischief
  ambit of   77–78, 929
  ascertaining the   621, 696–697, 931–933
  casus male inclusus and   887–889
  changes in   895–897
  changes in law, and   897
  common law mischiefs, examples of   920
  counter-mischief – *see*
    counter-mischief
  drafting error, as   924–925
  enactment, of   929–933
  Heydon's Case, resolution in   697, 918–
    922
  identifying   929, 933, 935–937
  in pari materia Acts and   708–710
  interpretation by reference to   883, 937–
    939, 1000–1001, 1245
  legal   916–917, 923–926
  lesser includes greater   557
  meaning of   916–918
  multiple ordinary meanings and   1188
  objections to the term   922–923
  party-political   927–929, 940–941
  phasing out of   934
  preamble as guide to   731–933
  presumptions as to   80, 915
  remedy for   78–79, 933–734, 940–942
  social   78–79, 772, 901–904, 916, 922–923
  statutory   923–926
  treaty, giving domestic legislative
    effect to, and   935
  unknown   936–937
  – *and see* 'mischief rule';
    Pepper v Hart, rule in;
    purposive construction;
    updating construction
'mischief rule'   12–13, 545, 943
misdemeanour, statutory   63, 64, 199, 922
  – *and see* contempt of statute
misdescription   1024
misfeasance in public office – *see*
  public office
misrepresentation   43, 446, 622, 793
  – *and see* tort

mistake
  Act, in   228
  defence, as   41–42
  drafting in   415
  enactment procedure in   232–236
  fact, as to   41, 421, 883
  law, as to – *see* **mistake of law;** *per*
    incuriam **decisions**
  mitigation as   40
  rectifying mistake of law – *see*
    rectifying construction
  statutory interpretation, in   293n, 303–304,
    1156
  – *and see* **communis error facit**
    ***jus;* drafting error;**
    judges; jurisdiction;
    mistake of law; precedent,
    doctrine of; printing
    corrections; rectifying
    construction; Royal
    assent; slip rule
mistake of law
  Acts, in   228
  compensation for   41
  drafter, by   27, 1270
  fact, when mistake as to constitutes
    mistake of law   421
  general   41–42
  guidelines, in   129
  ignorantia juris neminem excusat –
    see **ignorantia juris neminem**
    excusat
  judge, by   108, 135
  Parliament, by   604, 694–695, 709–710
  slip rule   110
  – *and see* **mistake;** *Padfield*
    approach; *per incuriam*
    decisions; rectifying
    construction
modus et conventio vincunt legem   57
Mogridge, C – *see* Bibliography (pp
  1475 to 1507)
Moncrieff, Lord   337
money
  bill – *see* **money Bill**
  foreign   378
  public   84–85, 126, 190–191, 1130
  references to   245, 378, 909
  resource implications relative to
    decision making   107, 126–127
  – *and see* **Bill, parliamentary;**
    Commons, house of;
    Crown; debt, statutory;
    Parliament; Parliament
    Acts 1911 and 1949; Royal
    assent; tax avoidance;
    taxing Acts
money Bill   191n, 223, 224, 251n, 567
Monmouthshire   352–353

All references are to page numbers

'month', definition of   1397

Moorcock, the, doctrine of – *see* business

moot point   143

moral duty   39, 407–408, 780–781, 939
   – *and see* immorality; legal policy

More, Thomas   35
   – *and see* Bibliography (pp 1475 to 1507)

Morgan J   S24

Morgan, Jonathan – *see* Bibliography (pp 1475 to 1507)

Morle, André – *see* Bibliography (pp 1475 to 1507)

Morris of Borth-y-Gest, Lord   178, 233, 475, 732, 873, 1056

Morris, Geoffrey   ix

Morris, J H C – *see* Bibliography (pp 1475 to 1507)

Morritt V-C   775, 1372, 1379

Morton of Henryton, Lord   573, 709n, 791n

Moses L J   634, 635, 693, 799

Moses LJ – *see* Bibliography (pp 1475 to 1507)

Moulton, Lord   658

multilingual systems – *see* legal meaning

Mummery LJ   105n, 128, 135n, 431, 615, 797, 848, 1105, 1139, 1142n, 1314, S13

Munday, Roderick   579n, 638, 643n, 857n, 1103
   – *and see* Bibliography (pp 1475 to 1507)

Munro, C R – *see* Bibliography (pp 1475 to 1507)

Murphy, Jim   91

Murphy, W I – *see* Bibliography (pp 1475 to 1507)

Murray, D F – *see* Bibliography (pp 1475 to 1507)

Mustill, Lord   113, 125, 143, 322, 681, 778, 869, 1058, 1059, 1143

name, company   37

National Debt Commissioners   1397

natural justice
   contrary legislative intention and   1060–1062
   criminal law and   1081
   European Community law, in – *see* European Community law
   fairness   211–212, 374, 430–431, 460, 797–798, 977, 1055–1059, 1111–1115, 1352, 1353, 1355, 1357
   legitimate expectation and   1056–1057

natural justice – *contd*
   mandatory and directory requirements – *see* mandatory and directory requirements
   nature of   148, 1058
   reasons, duty to give   1062–1064
   representations, opportunity to make   1058–1059
   requirements of   316
   transparency   1059
   – *and see audi alteram partem*; decision-making rules; justice; nemo debet esse judex in propria causa; notice; retrospectivity

natural law   233, 407–408, 773, 1137, 1141

ne exeat regno – *see* prerogative, Royal

necessitas non habet legem – *see* necessity

necessity – – *see* duress; impossibility; *impotentia excusat legem*

negative resolution procedure – *see* delegated legislation

negligence
   breach of statutory duty   71, 82–84
   contributory   114
   European Convention on Human Rights and   1349
   not impliedly authorised by statute   68
   nuisance and   1076
   tort of   419, 537–538, 579, 775, 833–834
   vicarious liability for   1074
   – *and see* natural justice; nuisance; tort

Neill LJ   50n, 201, 563, 1086

Neill of Bladen, Lord – *see* Bibliography (pp 1475 to 1507)

nemo debet bis vexari – *see* B

nemo debet esse judex in propria causa   1056, 1136

neologism   1181, 1211, 1213

Neuberger of Abbotsbury, Lord   190, 524, 595, 695, 747n, 1311, 1339, S37

New Zealand
   extra-territorial legislation and   327
   Hansard, use of, in   679–680
   international legislation, common approach to, and   333
   Law Commission   679
   liberal construction requirement, in   519
   Maori land   1206
   Statute of Westminster and   339
   tax avoidance and   1018n
   Westminster Parliament and   327, 338, 348n

Newey, Judge John   815

All references are to page numbers

Newman, Cardinal 26
Nicholl MR 718
Nicholls of Birkenhead, Lord 75, 95n, 144,
192, 333n, 470, 494,
506, 592, 875, 946n,
1059, 1089, 1200,
1264, 1312, 1317,
1322, 1325, 1326,
1332, 1339, 1340,
1362, 1366
nobile officium 877, 878
Nolan, Lord 130, 446, 775, 844, 1139
non liquet **principle** 24, 448, 453
– *and see* **meaningless terms**
non obstante, **device of** 238
non-existence – *see* **existence**
non-justitiable matters 107, 360, 364
Norman, Ken – *see* **Bibliography (pp**
1475 to 1507)
Normand, Lord 430, 589n
North J 1001
Northern Ireland
application of legislation 1393
extent of Act to 336–338
– *and see* **territorial extent of**
Act
Northern Ireland Court of Criminal
Appeal 322
'Northern Ireland legislation',
definition of 1397
Northern Ireland Statutory
Publications Office 232n
territory of 354, 355
terrorism and 820
noscitur a sociis **principle** 525, 1225–1231,
1234, 1259, 1262
– *and see* *ejusdem generis*
principle; rank principle
notes on clauses 641–642, 642, 643, 663,
699
notice, statutory
appeal, of 56
construction of 55
fax, by 1149
form of 54
fraudulent 793
internet, by 1149
invalid 871
mandatory or directory, whether 50, 54,
55
need for 59, 422, 957, 1113, 1255, 1261
quit, to 1072
service of 38, 55n, 570, 582–583, 1113,
1149
waiver of 59–60, 1068–1069
withdrawal of 55, 1068–1089
– *and see* ***audi alteram partem***
principle; enforcement
notice; general notice

Nottingham, Lord 653
Nourse LJ 172, 793, 971, 1113, 1159, 1192,
1227
Nugee, E 1158
nuisance
byelaws for suppression of 269
common 1201
history of 1075–1076
ingredients of 1075–1076
power to take proceedings for 815
statutory 163, 1002
varieties of 1075–1076
whether authorised by statute 68, 82–83,
200–201, 1075–1076
whether committed where statutory
power exercised 498, 1075–1076
– *and see* **negligence; tort**
nullus commodum capere potest de
injuria sua propria 1141
number 579–581, 1387–1388
– *and see* **fractions; singular and**
plural
O'Boyle, M – *see* **Bibliography (pp**
1475 to 1507)
objective test
duress 1134–1135
justice, and 123
provocation and 504, 578
statutory duty, as to 65–66, 68, 80
obscurity, semantic
'corrected version' 451–455, 551, 954
interpretative factors and 531–532, 954
nature of 451–455, 954
remedying 451–455, 531–532
– *and see* **disorganised**
composition; plain
meaning rule; rectifying
construction
Odgers, Charles 7, 647n, 902n, 1233
– *and see* **Bibliography (pp 1475**
to 1507)
offence
duplicated 583, 810, 1391
extra-territoriality and 374
– *and see* **extra-territoriality**
ingredients of 202
location of 374
meaning 1119
prosecution of – *see* **prosecution of**
offences
– *and see* **contempt of court;**
contempt of statute;
criminal law; criminal
procedure
office – *see* **public office**
Office of Fair Trading 87, 92
Office of Public Sector Information
(OPSI) 227

All references are to page numbers

Official Journal of the European
   Communities 1283
Official Solicitor, the 799
officer of Revenue and Customs 1398
oil rig, law prevailing on 386
Oliver of Aylmerton, Lord 670, 986n, 1455
Ombudsman
   general 80
   Parliamentary 157n
   Pensions 106, 142
omission of words – see rectifying
   construction
omission to act 327, 387–389, 895, 1193
omne majus continet in se minus –
   see greater includes less
omnia praesumuntur rite et
   solemniter esse acta – see
   correctness, presumption of
onus of proof – see burden of proof
open court, principle of the
   hearings in camera 119–120
   nature of 103, 118, 1115, 1357
   reporting restrictions and 119–120, 306,
         528, 845, 867–868,
         936
   – and see anonymity
opposing constructions
   ambiguity and 448–450
   – and see ambiguity
      (grammatical)
   examples of 467, 841, 998, 1007–1008
   form of 429–438
   inquisitorial proceedings, in 436
   significance of 123, 429–438, 695, 871,
         1176
   – and see interpretative factors
Order in Council 85, 194, 237–240, 250,
         266, 286, 344
Order of Council 251
order, search for 1, 6
order, administrative or legislative 89,
         267–268, 278, 1051
   – and see commencement order;
     costs; court; delegated
     legislation; enforcement
     agencies; executive
     instrument; Order in
     Council; Order of Council;
     provisional order;
     revocation, power of; special
     procedure order; ultra vires,
     doctrine of
order, court
   consent 116
   inherent powers of court regarding 112,
         1002–1003
   invalid, duty to obey until set aside 102,
         115–116

order, court – contd
   jurisdiction, made without 50
   – and see jurisdiction
   quashing of 116, 787
   statutory power to make 104
   ultra vires 91
ordinance 271, 272, 359, 802, 1228
ordnance map 1398
ordinary meaning
   constructive meaning and 1193
   educated usage, in 1184–1185
   foreign context, ordinary English
     meaning presumed 1193
   multiple ordinary meanings 1186–1188
   nature of 443–444, 1181–1193
   no ordinary meaning 1188
   non-legal expertise, used to
     determine 1183
   officially laid down 1183
   prima facie to be given 177–178, 870
   substance rather than form
     presumed, in 1191–1192
   technical meaning and 1198–1199, 1206–
         1209
   – and see plain meaning rule;
     technical terms; uniform
     statutes
ordination of women 293n
Orkneys, the 347, 356
Ormrod LJ 810, 904, 929, 964, 984, 1007,
         1200
Ostler clause – see judicial review
Otton LJ 331n
ouster clause – see jurisdiction
outer London borough 1397
overlapping meaning 1160, 1189, 1194–
         1195, 1197
   – and see belt-and-braces phrase;
     words
overruling 172–177
– and see precedent, doctrine of
pacta privata juri publico derogare
   non possunt 60, 61
Padfield approach 53, 89, 90, 260
   – and see delegated legislation;
     discretion
Page, Alan C 7
   – and see Bibliography (pp 1475
     to 1507)
pairs of words – see words
Pakistan x
palm tree justice 471, 513, 551
Pannick, David 594, 595
   – and see Bibliography (pp 1475
     to 1507)
paragraphing – see format of Act
pardon
   Bill for 213
   power to grant 238n

All references are to page numbers

parens patriae doctrine – *see* **Crown**
Park J 523
Parke, B 514, 653, 875, 879, 1105, 1182
Parker CB 847n
Parker LJ 835, 998, 1158, 1159
Parker, Graham 7
  – *and see* **Bibliography (pp 1475**
   to 1507)
Parker, Lord 404, 824, 865, 908, 938, 953,
                  992, 1026, 1145, 1186,
                  1222, 1244, 1267
Parliament – *see* **Act of Parliament;**
  Bill, parliamentary; Clerk of
  the Parliaments; delegated
  legislation; evidence; intention,
  legislative; legislative history;
  legislator; Lords, House of;
  mistake; Parliament Acts 1911
  and 1949; printing corrections;
  Royal assent; tacit legislation;
  territorial extent of Act
  absurd result, does not intend 969–971
  body purporting to assume function
    of 180
  does nothing in vain 1000, 1157
  ellipsis, recognition of 493–
                  494 *see* **ellipsis**
  government as emanation of 475
  journals of 181, 234–235
  judges and 1325
  judicial function of 152
  jurisdiction of – *see* **territorial**
    extent of Act
  justly, presumed to act 795–799, 963–965,
                     1104
  – *and see* **justice**
  law and custom of 743
  law, knowledge of, presumed to
    have 547
  legality, principle of 822–823
  legislative intention 471
  members of 40
  mistake as to existing law, by 709–710
  'Muslim Parliament', so-called 180n
  ouster clauses and parliamentary
    sovereignty S9
  powers of, curbs on 405
  powers of, and powers of the
    executive S9
  privilege of 182, 666–673, 1049
  – *and see* **contempt of**
    Parliament
  procedure of, control over 181, 714–715
  proceedings in 644–645
  – *and see* **exclusionary rule, the;**
    Pepper v Hart, **rule in**
  prorogation of 222
  public expenditure, authority for 1047–
                      1049

Parliament – *contd*
  Roll – *see* **Parliament Roll**
  session 719
  sovereignty of 197, 233, 236, 316, 406–
                  407, 409, S9
  style of 354
  taxing powers of 1047–1049
  – *and see* **Commons, house of; tax**
    avoidance; taxing Acts
Parliament Acts 1911 and 1949
  Acts that have been passed under 225, 246
  money Bills and 224–225
  other Bills, and 224–225
  remodelling of legislative procedure
    by 242
  validity of 235
Parliament Roll 227, 234, 751–752, 757
Parliamentary agent 184
Parliamentary Bar 184
Parliamentary Counsel 40, 66, 250, 264,
                  476, 738
Parliamentary Counsel Office 415, 476,
                  724
Parliamentary election 1398
Parliamentary proceedings,
  privileged 182, 666–673, 678n
  – *and see* **contempt of Parliament;**
    Parliament
Parmoor, Lord 55, 239
Parris, H W – *see* **Bibliography (pp**
  1475 to 1507)
Parts, division of Act into 749–750
  – *and see* **Australia; format of Act**
patents 333, 411, 548, 570
Patten J S12
Patterson J 669
Patteson J 994n, 1129
PAYE income 1398
PAYE regulations 1398
peace, Queen's 93, 96, 791–792
Pearce, D C 8
  – *and see* **Bibliography (pp 1475**
   to 1507)
Pearce, Lord 131, 1036
Pearson, Lord 403
penal Act – *see* **doubtful**
  penalisation, principle against;
  retrospectivity; uniform
  statutes
Pennycuik J 983
Penzance, Lord 47, 723, 1215
Pepper v Hart, **facts and law in** 627–632
Pepper v Hart, **rule in**
  advocate, duty of 623–627
  clarity of sponsor's statement, need
    for 616
  constitutional law and 618
  control of its procedure by court
    and 680–682

All references are to page numbers

Pepper v Hart, **rule in** – *contd*
costs and 624
criminal statutes, application to 633
de bene esse admission 596
earlier decision, overruling 616, 627
enactments to which applicable 618–621
facts and law in *Pepper v Hart*, 444
inadmissibility of ministerial
    statement on Act, under 705
judicial application of 620–621
judicial practice prior to 654–666
  – *and see* **exclusionary rule, the**
legislative history, and 616–640
mischief aimed at by enactment 621
objections to 672
  – *and see* **exclusionary rule, the**
parliamentary materials 616, 617
penal statutes, application to 633
promoter's statements 616, 622–623
resolution of House of Commons
  and 617
sponsor's statements 616, 622–623
statement of rule 616
when applicable 616, 617–618
  – *and see* **amendment to Bill;**
    contempt of Parliament
perfection, alteration of order before
  or after 112, S9
per incuriam **decision**
commonsense construction rule,
    failure to apply, and 554
departure from 173–174, 504n
examples of 106, 173–174, 583n, 730,
    1329
nature of 173–174, 554
  – *and see* **comity**
'person' 576–579, 1399
substance form or part of 576
  – *and see* **Interpretation Act 1978**
personal Act 136, 183, 184, 185, 743, 1163,
    1374, 1440
  – *and see* **private Act**
perverting the course of justice S26
Phillimore LJ 715, 748, 1224, 1454, 1455
Phillimore, Robert 818
  – *and see* **Bibliography (pp 1475**
    to 1507)
Phillips of Worth Matravers MR,
  Lord 32, 508, 817, 1103, 1145, 1194,
    1278, 1319, S46
Phillips, G G – *see* **Bibliography (pp**
  1475 to 1507)
Pigot's case, rule in 236
Pill LJ 137n, 183, 294n, 360, 415, 974n,
    1113
Pitt, William (Lord Chatham) 1124

place 388, 1267–1268
  – *and see* **application of Act;**
    location, deemed; omission to
    act
plain English – *see* **plain language**
  movement
plain language movement 36
plain meaning rule
codifying Acts and 609
  – *and see* **codification**
consolidation Acts and 605
  – *and see* **consolidation Act**
meaning of 548–551
where meaning not 'plain' 551
  – *and see* **interpretative**
    criteria; interpretative
    factors
pleading
demurrer 426
implied application of rules of 114
matters required to be pleaded 58, 393
punctuation in 752
Plowden, E 206
Plowman J 517
Plucknett, T F T 7, 8, 513, 652, 653n, 972n,
    1010
  – *and see* **Bibliography (pp 1475**
    to 1507)
plural – *see* **singular and plural**
police
acting in execution of duty 1126–1127
'acting in execution of' an Act 95
area 1398
arrest powers 152
authority 1398
chief constables, duties of 98
constable, office of 93, 199, 425, 1075,
    1263
discipline 1095, 1268
duty to enforce law 98, 844, 934, 974
  – *and see* **legal policy;**
    prosecution of offences
entry, powers of 199, 201
investigation by 93, 783, 837, 1117, 1358
obstruction of 1133
prosecution and – *see* **Crown**
  Prosecution Service;
  prosecution of offences
stop and search 1360
  – *and see* ***de minimis non curat***
    ***lex*; evidence; good**
    administration, duty of
politic uncertainty 52, 684, 1323
political factors
commencement of Act, affecting 283–284
drafting style, affected by 763
enactment, behind 484
evasion of Act, in relation to 1015–1016

<hr>

All references are to page numbers

political factors – *contd*
exercise of statutory power, behind 1268–1269
party ideology 922, 1219
politic uncertainty – *see* **politic uncertainty**
purpose clause 734
– *and see* **purpose clause**
Sunday observance 895
unnecessary legislation, behind 916n, 927–928
– *and see* **mischief**
Pollock CB 78, 516, 655, 1187, 1221
Pollock MR 58
Pollock, Frederick 32
– *and see* **Bibliography (pp 1475 to 1507)**
polygamy 929, 1098
Pope, Alexander 131
– *and see* **Bibliography (pp 1475 to 1507)**
Popplewell J 305, 527, 644, 668n, 669
Porter, Lord 435, 729, 941, 1229
– *and see* **Bibliography (pp 1475 to 1507)**
post, service by – *see* **service**
Potter LJ 1161
Potter, Platt – *see* **Bibliography (pp 1475 to 1507)**
Potts J 131
Powell J 653
power – *see* **executive power, abuse of; statutory power**
practice
archival drafting and 199, 759–761
changes in 34
codification of 608
contemporanea expositio – *see* **contemporanea expositio**
directions 112n
interpretation, effect on 51, 321
origin of 34
preservation of 199, 913
Royal assent, concerning – *see* **Royal assent**
saving for – *see* **saving**
– *and see* **statutory power**
practitioner, central function of – *see* **central function of practitioner**
Prashar, Lady (Usha) 3
– *and see* **Bibliography (pp 1475 to 1507)**
Pratt CJ 846
preamble
interpretative use of 356, 731–733, 961, 1099
mischief, determining, by 935
nature of 339, 731–733
private Acts, in 731–733

preamble – *contd*
purpose, legislative, and 356, 961
repeal of 731–733
statutory instrument 254
use of 731–733
– *and see* **evidence; private Act; purpose clause; recital**
precedent, doctrine of
common law and 177
Court of Appeal and 174
erroneous decisions and 503–504
European Court of Justice and 177
factual outline, the – *see* **factual outline, the**
law reports, and 854–855
Lords, House of, and 168, 174–175, 504
nature of 168–178, 427, 502–504, 514, 808–809
obiter dictum 168
obsolete precedent 172
over-generalising facts 424
overruling – *see* **overruling**
Pepper v Hart, rule in, implications for 627
per incuriam decision – *see* ***per incuriam* decisions**
previous transactions, effect on 175–176
ratio decidendi 168
reasons, failure to give 169
– *and see* **reasons, duty to give**
references to European Court of Justice and 1305–1306
– *and see* **interstitial articulation; legal thrust of enactment; processing of enactments, dynamic; sub-rules**
precision drafting
comminution and 401–404
implied repeal, presumption against, and 305
nature of 409–413, 709, 1234
provisos and 723–725
punctuation and 752
sanctions for breach of Act, statement of 75
selective comminution and 402–403
predictability of law
declaration of incompatibility, and – *see* **Human Rights Act 1998**
European Community law principle of 801–803, 1277–1278
– *and see* **European Community law**
European Convention on Human Rights and 1322
knowability – *see* **promulgation of Act**
literal construction and 869

All references are to page numbers

predictability of law – *contd*
principle of   590–591, 799–807
sentencing and   803–804
– *and see* **differential readings;**
legal policy; legislative
history; retrospectivity
preposition   755, 756, 1189
prerogative instrument
interpretation of   240, 818
nature of   237–240
territorial extent of   343–344
– *and see* **Act of State; Order in**
Council; Order of
Council; prerogative,
Royal
prerogative order – *see* **judicial**
review
prerogative, Royal
Channel Islands and – *see* **Channel**
Islands
chartered corporation – *see*
artificial person
choosing Minister to administer an
Act   85–86
comity of nations, and – *see* **comity**
curbing of   548
habeas corpus, and – *see* **habeas**
corpus
judicial review and   238, 240
nature of   237–240
ne exeat regno, writ of   1125
orders etc under – *see* **habeas**
corpus; judicial review;
Order in Council; Order of
Council; prerogative
instruments
parens patriae, doctrine of – *see*
wardship
Royal charter – *see* **Royal charter**
statutory curtailment of   204, 239
territorial waters, as to – *see*
territorial waters
territory of the state, as to   334, 356
third power   238
– *and see* **act of state; Crown**
prescription   203, 1037
pressure groups   975, 1135–1136
– *and see* **criminal law**
presumptions of construction
absurdity, against – *see* **absurdity**
consequences of a construction,
consideration of – *see*
consequential construction
evasion, against – *see* **evasion of**
Act; tax avoidance
implications and – *see* **implication**
literal construction, favouring – *see*
literal construction

presumptions of construction – *contd*
maxims, favouring application of –
see **maxims, legal**
mischief, as to – *see* **mischief;**
'mischief rule'
nature of   863
'no-scheme' rule   442
Parliament knows existing law, that   547
Pointe Gourde rule   442
purposive construction, favouring –
see **purposive construction**
rectification of error, favouring –
see **rectifying construction**
remedy for mischief, favouring –
see **mischief; 'mischief rule'**
rules of law, favouring application
of – *see* **implied ancillary**
rules
text as primary guide, favouring –
see **literal construction**
updating construction, favouring –
see **updating construction**
– *and see* **correctness,**
presumption of;
interpretative criteria;
ultra vires, **doctrine of**
Prime Minister   85
– *and see* **government; Minister of**
the Crown
principle of legality – *see* **legality,**
principle of
principles of construction   514, 543–544
– *and see* **interpretative criteria;**
legal policy
Pringle, Karen – *see* **Bibliography**
(pp 1475 to 1507)
printing correction 216, 224, 225, 226, 715,
                         716, 727, 741, 753,
                                        1455
prison rules – *see* **prisoners, rights of**
prisoners, rights of
citizenship rights   858–859
clear authority needed to imprison   837
courts, access to   854
hunger strikes   833
legitimate expectation of   1057
licence, release on   868
Parole Board   1061
Prison Rules   255, 1005–1006, 1050
remission, loss of   1005–1006
– *and see* **contempt of court;**
European Convention on
Human Rights; *habeas*
corpus
privacy – *see* **domestic sanctuary,**
principle of; doubtful
penalisation, principle against;
European Convention on
Human Rights

All references are to page numbers

private Act
construction of 1072
contract law and – *see* **contract**
Crown immunity and – *see* **Crown immunity, doctrine of**
desuetude and 313
drafting of 410, 910–911
interpretation of 910–911
judicial notice of – *see* **judicial notice**
judicial review and – *see* **judicial review**
local Act – *see* **local Act**
nature of 183–191
personal Act – *see* **personal Act**
procedure 184–185
promoter of 184
property law and 1072
publication of 184
recital in, as evidence 735
savings in 1163, 1165
– *and see* **savings**
validity of 233
– *and see* **Act of Parliament; special procedure order**

private international law
application of Act 367
contract and, interpretative implications 1097–1100
legislative intention and 1097–1100
presumption, general, enactment imports 1097–1100
statutory regulation of 1097–1100
taxing acts and application of 381
– *and see* **extra-territoriality**

private prosecutions – *see* **prosecution of offences**

privileges and immunities
diplomatic 368–369
general 360, 367–368
international organisations 369–370
professional privilege 436
public interest immunity – *see* **public interest immunity**
removal of 244
sovereign immunity 368–369, 1034–1035
– *and see* **act of state; application of Act**
state immunity 368–369, 1034–1035
– *and see* **act of state; application of Act**
visiting forces 370
waiver of 370–371
– *and see* **contempt of Parliament; exception; exterritoriality; judges; Parliament**

Privy Council
full name of 250

Privy Council – *contd*
Judicial Committee of 154, 504
legislative powers of 250
– *and see* **Order in Council; Order of Council**

probate action 436

procedural due process – *see* **decision-making rules**

procedure, civil 51, 58, 320–322, 42–4232, 807, 984, 1030–1031, 1084
– *and see* **decision-making rules; inherent judicial powers; irregularity, procedural; legal proceedings; pleading; retrospectivity**

procedure, criminal – *see* **criminal procedure**

procedure, statutory
mandatory and directory 50–51
– *and see* **mandatory and directory requirements**
waiver of 58

proceedings, legal – *see* **legal proceedings**

process
abuse of 53, 100, 161, 163, 787–788, 1357
due 853
– *and see* **decision-making rules**
immunity from – *see* **exterritoriality; privileges and immunities; sovereign immunity**
service of 167, 1191–1192
– *and see* **irregularity, procedural**

processing of enactments, dynamic
broad terms – *see* **broad terms**
courts, by 392, 479, 893
– *and see* **interstitial articulation**
enforcement agencies, by 167–178, 893
factual outline, the – *see* **factual outline**
implication, finding and declaring – *see* **implication**
nature of 392–393, 502–504
processed terms, use of – *see* ***Barras* principle**
reversal by legislation 319, 344, 401, 499, 815, 842, 895, 932, 941, 1110
sub-rules – *see* **sub-rules**
tacit parliamentary approval of – *see* **tacit legislation**

All references are to page numbers

processing of enactments, dynamic – *contd*
  updating meaning of Act by – *see*
    updating construction
    – *and see* **judicial gloss; legal**
      thrust of an enactment;
      precedent, doctrine of;
      technical terms
processing of enactments, static   502
proclamation – *see* **Crown**
professional misconduct   1055, 1088
prohibition (prohibiting order) – *see*
  judicial review
promulgation of Act
  entry on Rolls – *see* **Roll**
  late   230n
  legal certainty and   801
  methods of   228–229
  promulgation list   229
  publication by Stationery Office   184, 228
  revised editions   230–231
  settling of text   225–230
  validity, effect on   228–230
  – *and see* **Act of Parliament**
proof – *see* **burden of proof;**
  standard of proof
property
  alienability of   847
  law of, implied application of   1072
  nature of   58
  private Acts and property law   1072–1073
  rights of, safeguarding – *see* **legal**
    policy
  waiver of statutory rights to   57
  – *and see* **land**
proportionality
  European Community law, in   1054–1055,
          1280–1282
  UK law, in   1054–1055, 1312
  – *and see* **decision-making**
    rules; European
    Community law;
    European Convention on
    Human Rights
prosecution of offences
  body corporate, by   99
  charge, choice of   99
  Code for Crown Prosecutors   99
  commencement of prosecution   101
  Crown, in name of   96
  discretion and   97
  facilitating   1026–1027
  history of   96, 1083
  immunity from, offered   99
  overzealous   100
  policy regarding   98–100, 202, 682–683
  private prosecutions   96, 100–101, 927
  prosecutive power of the state   96, 98, 99
  stale offences   99

prosecution of offences – *contd*
  time limits   99, 202, 1013, 1086
  – *and see* **Attorney General;**
    criminal procedure;
    Crown; Crown
    Prosecution Service;
    Director of Public
    Prosecutions; Director of
    Revenue and Customs
    Prosecutions; enforcement
    agencies; judicial review;
    nolle prosequi; **offence;**
    peace, Queen's; police;
    process
protracted legal proceedings,
  avoiding   582, 787–788
  – *and see* **estoppel**
provisional order   185n, 224, 245, 268
proviso
  burden of proof and   723–725
  disorganised composition and   723–725
  drafting errors in   1148n
  interpretation of   723–725
  nature of   399, 723–725
  precision drafting and   723–725
  saving compared   723–725
  – *and see* **evidence; private Act**
public authority – *see* **artificial**
  person; discretion; local
  authority
  acts and omissions of, incompatible
    with Human Rights Act 1998
    – *see* **Human Rights**
    Act 1998
  claim against   163
  – and see Human Rights
    Act 1998
  Crown   206–212
  – *and see* **Crown**
  decisions by, rules governing taking
    of   1050–1064, 1268
  fairly, must act   211
  financial considerations – *see*
    disobeying Act
  Human Rights Act 1998 and
    decisions of – *see* **Human**
    Rights Act 1998
  neglect of duty by   38
  negligence by   84
  pressure groups, and   1135–1136
  property of   828–829
  'public body', whether   898, 1243
  public law, and – *see* **public law**
  statutory duty, mode of discharge by   37,
          50–51, 211
  – *and see* **statutory duty**
Public Bill Office   745
public document   1222
public document, construction of   1222

All references are to page numbers

public good construction – *see* **statutory interpretation**

public interest – *see* **legal policy; public interest immunity**

public interest immunity   259, 525, 538, 786, 791, 1094–1097, 1268

public international law

application of Act and   378–384

crimes under   376, 1000

disputes between states   107

domestic incorporation of, by judicial decision   817

extra-territoriality recognised by   378–384

national law conforms to, presumption that   362–363, 370, 817–824

nature of   817–824

piracy jure gentium   376, 1000

territorial waters and   356–358

  – *and see* **adoption; comity; extra-territoriality; high seas; treaty**

public law

nature of   68–71, 82, 155, 789, 1050–1051

private law compared with   155–157

public and private interests, conflict between, and   790–792

rise of   68–70

  – *and see* **breach of statutory duty, tort of; decision-making rules; judicial review**

public mischief   1007, 1085

public nuisance – *see* **nuisance**

public office

appointment to, presumed valid   1145

meaning of   166

misfeasance in   72

usurpation of   166

public order – *see* **peace, Queen's**

public park   185

public policy

comity of nations and – *see* **comity**

conflicting considerations   790–792

contracting out, and – *see* **statutory right**

estoppel and   788–789

European Union, in – *see* **European Union**

legal professional privilege and   788–789

nature of   499n, 501, 772, 785–788, 1151

protracted legal proceedings, avoidance of   787–788

retrospectivity and – *see* **retrospectivity**

  – *and see* **illegality, legal policy;** *nullus commodum capere potest de injuria sua*

public policy – *contd*

retrospectivity and – *contd*

  – *and see* **illegality, legal policy;** *nullus commodum capere potest de injuria sua* – *contd* propria; privileges and immunities; restraint of trade

public procession   185, 1232

publication of Act – *see* **promulgation of Act**

Pufendorf, S von   170, 445, 456, 459, 1182, 1203

  – *and see* **Bibliography (pp 1475 to 1507)**

Pugh, Idwal   86

  – *and see* **Bibliography (pp 1475 to 1507)**

punctuation

alteration of   215–216

comma   738, 876

delegated legislation, interpretation of, by reference to   716

error in   751–758, 878, 1219n

interpretation by reference to   714, 716, 751–758, 1249

legislation, in   185, 751–758

private Acts, in   185

public Acts, in   185n

textual amendment and   292

use of, in legislation, misapprehension over   751–758

  – *and see* **precision drafting; updating construction**

Purchas LJ   899, 1050

purpose clause

drafters' dislike of   734–735

European Community law, in   1286–1287

nature of   734–735, 959–963

rare in UK legislation   734–735

use in interpretation   734–735, 959–963

  – *and see* **preamble; recital**

purposive construction

alteration of purpose and   951

deeming provisions and   949–751

European Community law and UK law, compared   966–968, 1284

examples of   381, 687

government policy and   962–963

identifying purpose   800, 946

judicial acceptance of purpose   960–962

literal construction contrasted   945

multiple ordinary meanings and   1187

nature of   944–951

non-purposive-and-literal construction   951–952, 954–955

operative provisions and   959

presumption in favour of   943–944

All references are to page numbers

---

purposive construction – *contd*
  purposive-and-literal construction 944–945, 951–955
  purposive-and-strained construction 944, 955–959
  retrospectivity and 319
  statutory statement of purpose – *see* **purpose clause**
  taxing Acts – *see* **taxing Acts**
  treaties 687, 689–690, 961
  unknown or doubtful purpose 963
  – *and see* **teleological interpretation**
purview – *see* **enacting formula**
quashing order (*certiorari*) – *see* **judicial review**
Queen's peace – *see* **peace, Queen's**
Queen's printer 226–227, 231, 266, 267, 274, 879, 1283
Quekett, A S – *see* **Bibliography (pp 1475 to 1507)**
qui facit per alium facit per se – *see* **agency**
quilibet potest renuntiare juri pro se introducto 57, 371, 375
quo warranto – *see* **judicial review**
Radcliffe, Lord 602, 606, 869–870, 914
  – *and see* **Bibliography (pp 1475 to 1507)**
Radin, Max 473, 480
  – *and see* **Bibliography (pp 1475 to 1507)**
Radzinowicz, L – *see* **Bibliography (pp 1475 to 1507)**
Ramsay **principle** 538, 1018–1023
Ramsey, Lynn E 1291n
  – *and see* **Bibliography (pp 1475 to 1507)**
rank principle 988, 1225, 1226, 1234, 1240, 1245–1247
rating 548
rating of property 548, 798, 799, 804, 914, 950, 954, 1115, 1205
ratio decidendi – *see* **factual outline, the; precedent, doctrine of**
Rawlings, R W – *see* **Bibliography (pp 1475 to 1507)**
reader of legislation – *see* **user of legislation**
'reading down' 1324
  – *and see* **strained construction**
Reading, Marquis of 867
'real doubt' S4
real and personal – *see* **legal proceedings**
reasonableness 38, 43, 132–133, 269–270, 424–425, 770, 791–792, 956n
reasons, duty to give – *see* **B**

recital 253, 254, 267, 727, 731, 733, 735, 847, 850, 959, 960, 1471, 1472
  – *and see* **preamble; purpose clause**
recklessness, test for 420–421
record 647
  – *and see* **court**
rectifying construction
  casus male inclusus 887–889
  – *and see* **broad terms**
  casus omissus 169–170, 811, 885–887, 1329
  conflicting texts 889
  examples of 325, 574
  garbled text 878–881
  meaning, error of 881–885
  nature of 875–889
  punctuation error – *see* **punctuation**
  subordinate legislation, of 887
  – *and see* **incompatibility, declaration of, under Human Rights Act 1998; meaning; mistake; nobile officium; obscurity, semantic; repugnancy; slip rule**
recusal 394, 1139
reddendo singula singulis **principle** 1247–1249
redundancy – *see* **surplusage**
reference, works of 134, 1222, 1224
  – *and see* **dictionary reference to; judicial notice**
referential legislation – *see* **incorporation by reference**
reform – *see* **Law Commission; statute law; Statute Law Revision Act**
Reform Act 1832 244–245
registered medical practitioner 1398
registered midwife 1398
registered nurse 1398
Regnal year – *see* **Crown**
regularity, presumption of – *see* **correctness, presumption of**
Reid, Lord 169, 411, 433, 457, 502, 520, 538, 549, 644, 650, 660, 661, 694, 696, 699n, 714, 716, 746, 747, 753, 790, 797, 816, 851n, 872, 873, 940, 966, 972, 973, 981, 1001, 1037, 1049, 1052, 1079, 1094n, 1096, 1112, 1131, 1166, 1220, 1222, 1223, 1454
relator action 73, 74

> **All references are to page numbers**

religion   780–781, 842–843
  – *and see* **Christianity;**
    discrimination, legislation
    against; doubtful
    penalisation, principle
    against; European
    Convention on Human
    Rights; Jews; moral duty
Renton report   487, 643n, 735n, 739, 1166n
repeal
  advance, in   302
  amendment and   288
  commencement of Act, before   282–283
  delegated legislation and – *see*
    delegated legislation
  'double' repeal, practice of   302–304
  effect of   197, 301–302
  express   293, 300–301
  implied   300–301, 304–305, 991
  in same session   300, 302
  nature of   194, 300–302
  proviso, and   723–725
  re-enactment, and   310–312, 1391
  reference to repealed enactment   310–311
  referential definitions, and   572
  repeal of   1390
  repealed enactment considered as
    legislative history   604
  – *and see* **legislative history**
  'revoke', use of term   301
  savings on – *see* **saving**
  Schedule – *see* **Schedule**
  transitional provisions, and – *see*
    transitional provisions
  twice over   302–304
  – and see *Attorney General v*
    Lamplough, **rule in;**
    generalia specialibus non
    derogant; generalibus
    specialia derogant;
    strained construction
repugnancy
  of different Acts   889
  strained construction, requiring   466, 741
  – *and see* **strained construction**
  within same Act   465–466, 559, 1163
  – *and see* **construction as a**
    whole; duplication of
    statutory remedies, powers
    etc; *genenalia specialibus*
    non derogant; generalibus
    specialia derogant; **logic,**
    use of in interpretation;
    rectifying construction
reputation, detriment to – *see*
  doubtful penalisation, principle
  against
res ipsa loquitur   1077, 1103
res judicata – *see* **estoppel**

res magis valeat quam pereat rule   558, 559,
                   849
restitution   1074, 1107
restitution in integrum   1074
retrospectivity
  amending enactment, of   320
  declaratory enactment, of   187
  doubt, causes of   325–326
  European Community law,
    presumption against in   1279–1280
  events over a period   322–324
  evidential provisions   322
  nature of   315–320
  penalty, increase of   322
  pending actions, and   320
  presumption against   177, 315–320, 323,
        807–808, 1279–1280
  procedural provisions, and   320–322
  public interest and – *see* **legal**
    policy
  – *and see* **delegated legislation;**
    European Convention on
    Human Rights; legal
    proceedings; taxing Acts
Revenue and Customs Prosecutions,
  director of   97
Revenue and Customs,
  commissioners for   96, 352n
review – *see* **appeal; judicial review**
revocation, power of   90
Ribeiro PJ   S10, S41
Richardson J   611
Richardson, H G – *see* **Bibliography**
  (pp 1475 to 1507)
right, implied extinguishment of   499
right, statutory – *see* **statutory right**
rights, human – *see* **human rights**
Rix LJ   848
Robertson, E (Lord Lochee) – *see*
  Bibliography (pp 1475 to 1507)
Robertson, Lord   1047
Robinson, R G F   562n
  – *and see* **Bibliography (pp 1475**
  to 1507)
Robson, Glenna – *see* **Bibliography**
  (pp 1475 to 1507)
Roch LJ   136, 574, 1057, 1300
Rockall, Isle of   355, 356
Rodger of Earlsferry, Lord   497, 550, 1010,
        1166, 1339, S8, S15,
                S65
Roll
  Chancery   227, 234
  inspection of   228, 234
  nature of   227
  Parliament – *see* **Parliament Roll**
  Statute   1010–1011

All references are to page numbers

Roman law 6, 12, 13, 21, 28–30, 41, 197, 347, 463, 876–877, 1106, 1116, 1291, 1298

Romer LJ 108, 871, 1233

Romilly MR 757, 769

Rose LJ 104n, 170, 326, 547, 555, 621, 700, 729n, 818, 928

Roskill, Lord 69, 76n, 161n, 304, 305, 411, 532, 533, 539, 602, 620, 761n, 777, 812, 816, 899, 985, 1160, 1195, 1252

Ross, David 591

Ross, Ursula – *see* **Bibliography (pp 1475 to 1507)**

Rougier J 1089

Rousseau, J J 39

Rowe, Henry 476
　– *and see* **Bibliography (pp 1475 to 1507)**

Rowlatt J 488, 496n, 849

Roxburgh J 588

Royal assent
　absence or illness of Monarch, during 222
　commission, by 220–222
　communication of, to Parliament 220–222
　date of 226
　demise of Crown and 223
　error as to 235
　formula 185, 221
　in person 220–222
　letters patent signifying 217–218
　money Bill 224
　notification, by 220–222
　Parliament Acts 1911 and 1949 224–225
　procedure, two-stage 216–217, 714
　refusal of 218
　regency, during 223
　signification of 217–220
　text of Act and 226
　　– *and see* **chapter number; Clerk of the Parliaments; Parliament Acts 1911 and 1949**

Royal charter 239

Royal Commission on Criminal Procedure 1981 99

Royal prerogative – *see* **prerogative, Royal**

Rozenberg, Joshua – *see* **Bibliography (pp 1475 to 1507)**

Ruggle, George 752

rule of law – *see* **law**

rules
　delegated legislation, type of 268
　interpretation of 413

rules of construction
　basic rule 544–548
　common law 543–544
　common sense, use of – *see* **commonsense construction rule**
　contrary intention 547
　functional construction rule – *see* **functional construction**
　informed interpretation rule – *see* **informed interpretation**
　nature of 543–544
　plain meaning rule – *see* **plain meaning rule**
　pluralistic 547
　principles of construction and, contrasted 543–544
　regard to nature of an enactment 548
　rule where meaning not 'plain' 551
　statutory 129, 543–544
　　– *and see* **interpretative criteria;** *res magis valeat quam pereat* **rule**

rules of court – *see* **court**

Russell of Killowen, Lord 965, 997, 1144

Rutherforth, Thomas – *see* **Bibliography (pp 1475 to 1507)**

Sachs LJ 1208

Safire, William – *see* **Bibliography (pp 1475 to 1507)**

Saint German, Christopher – *see* **Bibliography (pp 1475 to 1507)**

Sainty, J C – *see* **Bibliography (pp 1475 to 1507)**

Sales J S38

Salmon, Lord 131, 790, 1007n, 1095

salus populi suprema lex 773, 1046

same words, construction of – *see* **words; homonyms**

Sampford, Charles 6n
　– *and see* **Bibliography (pp 1475 to 1507)**

sanctions for contravention – *see* **contempt of statute; disobeying Act; offence; statutory duty; tort**

Sanders, Andrew – *see* **Bibliography (pp 1475 to 1507)**

Sankey, Lord 659, 678n, 910

Sardinia Sulcis, **The, rule in** 172

Savill LJ 586, 1265

saving
　commencement of substituted provisions and 310
　common law and 309
　Crown, for 207
　general 725–726, 1389–1390
　interpretation of 725–726, 1163, 1165
　nature of 725–726

All references are to page numbers

saving – *contd*
practice, for 220
private and personal Acts, in 1163
proviso and, compared 725
repeal of enactment, effect on 188, 303,
307–310
revocation of delegated legislation,
on 308
special 308
– *and see* **privileges and**
immunities; proviso
Sayles, G – *see* **Bibliography (pp**
1475 to 1507)
Scalia J 651n
Scarman, Lord 35n, 246, 366n, 403, 467,
492, 523, 534, 538,
558, 588, 639, 649,
651, 663, 686, 716,
773, 774, 792, 823,
834, 841, 843, 845,
925, 933, 962, 965,
1038, 1057, 1087,
1119, 1127, 1156,
1228, 1244, 1255
Schedule
byelaws, to 269
format of 721–723
forms in 1123
inducing words of 721–723
interpretation of 721–723
notes to 721–723
repeal 302–304, 721–723
statutory instruments and 295
use of 721–723
– *and see* **functional**
construction; Jamaica
Schedule; Keeling
Schedule
scheme 271
Scherer **principle** 148–149, 461n
– *and see* **also jurisdiction**
Schiemann LJ 176, 875, 950, 1121
Scilly, Isles of 346, 347
Scotland
Act, extending to, presumption of 336–
338
desuetude of Acts in 313n
English law, treatment in 1038, 1202–
1203
devolution and 6
Human Rights Act 1998 procedures
in – *see* **Human Rights**
Act 1998
law of 331–332, 347, 387, 984, 1038,
1125, 1136n
nobile officium – *see* ***nobile***
officium
pleading in 434n

Scotland – *contd*
presumption of uniform application
of enactment in 331–332
pre-Union law, act altering 333
private prosecution in 927
punctuation, treatment of, in 753–754
sheriff principal 1398
territory of 355–356
Union with Scotland Act 1706 236, 250n,
333, 347
– *and see* **devolution; Lords,**
house of; Scottish
Parliament; technical
terms; territorial extent of
Act
Scott LJ 902, 1238, S15
Scott Baker J 621, 1167, S64
Scott of Foscote, Lord 117n, 127n, 360n,
363, 366n, 562, 1108,
S41, S52, S58
Scott v Scott, rule in – *see* **open**
court, principle of the
Scott, C P 1184
Scottish Parliament 242, 1392, 1396
– *and see* **Scotland**
Scrivener, Anthony 1102
– *and see* **Bibliography (pp 1475**
to 1507)
Scrutton LJ 134, 137, 453, 519, 714, 738,
848, 962, 1029, 1071,
1110
– *and see* **Bibliography (pp 1475**
to 1507)
seabed 334, 335
– *and see* **territorial waters**
seas, beyond the 1214
'seas, beyond the' 1214
Secretary of State 86, 252, 1398
– *and see* **Minister of the Crown**
section
enacting formula and 718, 719–721
name – *see* **section name (sidenote,**
heading or title)
organisation of, as guide to
legislative intention 719–721
paragraphs in 719–721
sidenote to – *see* **section name**
(sidenote, heading or title)
statement of purpose of 719–721
subsections 719–721
– *and see* **functional**
construction
section name (sidenote, heading or
title)
alteration of 715, 747–749
delegated legislation, interpretation
of, by reference to 716
formerly sidenote 747–749

All references are to page numbers

section name (sidenote, heading or title) –
  contd
  interpretation by reference to   715, 747–
              749, 1014, 1454–1458
  nature of   747–749
  – *and see* **functional**
        construction
security of state – *see* **legal policy**
Sedgwick, T   464
Sedley LJ   10n, 82, 125n, 156, 470, 551,
              600, 698, 699, 784,
              828n, 1033, 1159,
              1060n, 1316, 1292n,
              S24
  – *and see* **Bibliography (pp 1475**
        to 1507)
Selborne, Earl of   306
Selden, John   229
  – *and see* **Bibliography (pp 1475**
        to 1507)
selective comminution
  examples of   367, 403, 416, 432, 532,
              534–537, 701, 882,
              1126
  implied words   x
  meaning of   401–404
  – *and see* **comminution**
self help   35
self-incrimination – *see* **procedure,**
    criminal
Sellers LJ   74, 848
semantic obscurity – *see* **obscurity,**
    semantic
Senior Courts – *see* **court**
Sentencing Guidelines Council   704
separation of powers, doctrine of 104, 121,
              1326, 1354
Serious Fraud Office   94
service
  notice, of – *see* **notice**
  post, by   570, 582–583, 1388
  process, of – *see* **process**
  waiver of procedural rules of   58
severance
  contract, in   61
  delegated legislation, in   254–255, 258–
              259
  illegality and   1110
  where matter only partly within
        statutory description   1270
sewerage undertaker   1398
sex discrimination – *see*
    discrimination, legislation
    against
sex shops, licensing of   92, 185, 187
sexual offences prevention order 393n
sexual orientation   914, 1328
  – *and see* **transsexuality**
Shadwell V-C   335n

Shakespeare, William – *see*
    Bibliography (pp 1475 to 1507)
Sharma, Sujata – *see* **Bibliography**
    (pp 1475 to 1507)
'shall'   46n
Shaw LJ   496, 554, 984, S53
Shaw of Dunfermline, Lord   746n, 753,
              1103
Shaw, Terence – *see* **Bibliography**
    (pp 1475 to 1507)
Shawcross and Beaumont – *see*
    Bibliography (pp 1475 to 1507)
Shearman J   983
Shee, Sjt   137
Sheen J   665, 906, 988
Sheldon J   318
Shepherd, Nigel – *see* **Bibliography**
    (pp 1475 to 1507)
sheriff   166, 167, 229, 878, 904, 1195, 1399,
              1437, 1438
sheriff's officer – *see* **enforcement**
    agencies
Shetlands, the   347, 356
ship, law prevailing on   385–386
short title
  informal   736
  interpretation by reference to 714–715,
              738, 935
  mischief, determining, by   935
  misleading   353
  nature of   735–739
  punctuation in   738
  wording of   735–739
  – *and see* **collective title;**
        functional construction;
        Royal assent
sidenote to section – *see* **section**
    name (sidenote, heading or
    title)
signature   219, 223, 236, 388, 603, 905n,
              992, 1040
Silber J   100, 305, 582
silence, right of – *see* **procedure,**
    criminal
Simon Brown LJ – *see* **Brown**
    (Simon) LJ
Simon of Glaisdale, Lord   372, 476, 478,
              587, 645, 660, 662,
              669, 696, 700n, 726,
              731, 961, 976, 986,
              1118, 1173, 1198,
              1220
Simon, Viscount 588, 870, 898, 1018, 1038,
              1235
Simonds, Viscount 51, 108, 379, 452, 458,
              588, 668, 669, 819,
              1144
Singer J   781, 841, 847n

All references are to page numbers

singular and plural   579–581, 1387–1388
  – *and see* **number**
skeleton argument   593–596 , 855n
Slade LJ   290, 630, 731, 748, 776, 948
slang   1181, 1209–1213
slavery   365, 372, 382, 840, 1124, 1350,
                                        1443
slip rule   110, 146, 839
Slynn of Hadley, Lord   260n, 904
Smith (Peter) J   1313
Smith, A T H – *see* **Bibliography (pp
  1475 to 1507)**
Smith, J C   420, 517, 1080
Smith, John – *see* **Bibliography (pp
  1475 to 1507)**
Smith, K J M   1036
  – *and see* **Bibliography (pp 1475
    to 1507)**
social attitude, change in   S12
social security appeal tribunal   142
social security appeal tribunals   142
Soering principle   1349
solicitor
  acting as   774n
  agent, as   363, 1148–1149
  body corporate as   577
  duty of   48
  foreign   363
  negligence of   788n
  practising certificate   92, 794
  professional indemnity insurance   1067
    – *and see* **advocate; central
      function of practitioner;
      costs; legal proceedings;
      subject, the**
Somervell of Harrow, Lord   589n
sovereign immunity – *see* **privileges
  and immunities**
special procedure order   268
specialty   39, 647, 1237n
  – *and see* **limitation of actions**
speech, freedom of
  broadcasting and   820
  conditional nature of   197
  defamation and   821
  press censorship   312
    – *and see* **discrimination,
      legislation against;
      doubtful penalisation,
      principle against;
      European Convention on
      Human Rights**
Spencer, J R   284n, 404, 451, 920
  – *and see* **Bibliography (pp 1475
    to 1507)**
Spigelman CJ   S27
Spiliada principle   333n
St Germain, C   653

Stair, Viscount   877, 1008
  – *and see* **Bibliography (pp 1475
    to 1507)**
Stamp LJ   1227
standard of performance   48
standard of proof
  civil   1088–1091
  common law applies where Act
    silent   1088–1091
  criminal   830, 977, 985–986, 1088–1091
  enactment detrimental to rights, and   830
  interlocutory proceedings, in   1088–1091
  unusual   1088–1091
    – *and see* **burden of proof;
      evidence**
Stanley Burnton J   138, 335, 544, 972
stare decisis – *see* **precedent,
  doctrine of; processing of
  enactments, dynamic; sub-rules**
state
  act of – *see* **act of state**
  emanation of – *see* **European
    Community law**
  immunity – *see* **privileges and
    immunities**
  judicial power of – *see* **judicial
    power of the state**
  security of – *see* **legal policy**
    – *and see* **Crown; legal policy**
Stationery Office Limited, The   226, 666
  – *and see* **HMSO**
statute book
  defects in   923–926
  drafting of   409–413, 804–806
  free-standing Act, doctrine of   1165
  modern growth of   815
  nature of   483
  publication of   230–232
  'statute book of the session'   742
  Statute Law Database   232
  tacit legislation   996
  'tidying' of   188, 509, 897
  undermining of, by recourse to
    Hansard   652, 657
  unified system   309
statute law
  nature of   5, 182
  reform of   12
Statute Law Committee   231
Statute Law Revision Act   188, 725–726
Statute Law Society   1166n
statutes
  ancient   184, 189, 232
  deficiencies of   9–10
  glossing of   33, 170
    – *and see* **judicial gloss**
  early   182, 652–653, 719, 916–918, 1216
  legal meaning of, duty to determine   24–
                                      25, 403

All references are to page numbers

statutes – *contd*
'modern'   184, 189, 232
nature of   182–183
obsolete, repeal of   509
prerogative and   239
primacy of   201
statute book – *see* **statute book**
Statutes in Force   231
Statutes of the Realm   226
Statutes Revised   231
subordinate legislation modifying   182
uniform – *see* **uniform statutes**
   – *and see* **Act of Parliament;**
       Human Rights Act 1998;
       judicial gloss; user of
       legislation
Statutes in Force – *see* **Statutes**
Statutes of the Realm – *see* **Statutes**
Statutes Revised – *see* **Statutes**
statutory analogy   499–501
   – *and see* **implication**
statutory benefit – *see* **statutory**
   right
statutory debt – *see* **debt, statutory**
statutory declaration   980, 1399
statutory definitions – *see*
   definitions, statutory
statutory description – *see*
   description, statutory
statutory discretion – *see* **discretion**
statutory duty
absolute   37, 59
act of God and   1104–1105
after performance of, matters arising   56
ambit of   37, 591, 1130
amendment, legislative, to propose   978–
       979
breach of, civil sanctions for – *see*
   breach of statutory duty, tort
   of; tort; *volenti non fit injuria*
breach of, consent, and   1150–1151
breach of, criminal sanctions for –
   see **contempt of statute;**
   criminal law
breach of, technical   56
common law duty, corresponding,
   and   75
compliance, mode of   37–38
continuity of   1388–1389
contracting out of, when not
   permitted   60–62
contracting out of, when permitted   57–60
discretion, must not be reduced to   126
doubtful – *see* **doubtful**
   penalisation, principle
   against
duplication of duties or remedies   810,
       1000
duty *sub modo*   37, 57, 59, 60

statutory duty – *contd*
enforcement of   57
'gateway' duty   810
hardship, as defence for
   non-performance of   39
impecuniosity, defence of   126–127
implied   49
manner of performance required   37–38,
       49
necessity, as defence for
   non-performance of   39
over-performance of   39
performance from time to time   581–582
prohibitory and mandatory   63, 65
resource implications – *see* **money**
tort, application of, to   1073
types of   37
volenti principle – *see* *volenti non*
     fit injuria
   – *and see* **discretion; disobeying**
       Act; judicial review;
       mandatory and directory
       requirements; moral duty;
       reasonableness; statutory
       power; statutory right
statutory exposition   122, 188n, 293
   – *and see* **declaratory enactment**
statutory inspectorates   93
statutory instrument – *see* **delegated**
   legislation
Statutory Instruments Issue List
   ('Daily list')   267, 274
statutory interpretation
affordability, relevance of   107
basic rule   ix, 2, 13, 176, 544–548
changed view of legal meaning   151
consequential provisions   295–297
construction summons   114
corpus juris, within   193
court, exclusive function of – *see*
   Judge
delegated legislation, by reference
   to   242n, 706–708, 710
delegated legislation, of   257–258, 263–
       266, 716
   – *and see* delegated legislation
Developmental method of (EU)   1283–
       1287, 1323
dynamic   1457
equitable construction – *see*
   equitable construction
Global method of (common law
   system)   5, 9, 13
Hansard, use of – *see* **exclusionary**
   rule, the; *Pepper v Hart*, **rule**
   in
history of   8, 11
importance of   6–9, 13–14, 151
in pari materia Acts, use of, in   708–710

All references are to page numbers

---

statutory interpretation – *contd*

intuition, use of	470
judicial rulings on	114, 151
lay person, by	1222–1223
legal policy and	778
legality, principle of	822–823
long title and	727–731
method of	191–192

– *and see* interpretative criteria;
    interpretative factors

mistake in – *see* **judges; mistake of
    law**

NESSSI Method	1
old Acts, drafting style in, and	866
Originalism	1457
over-subtlety in, to be avoided	806–807, 866
paragraphing and	720, 749
pejorative connotation of	170–171
perverse	461
pluralism of	13
public good construction	319
public interest	791–792
'reading down'	1324
reform of	12
Schedule, notes to, and	721–723
statute, nature of, and	191–192
statutory regulation of	171

sub-rules and – *see* **sub-rules**

taxpayers, inconvenience to	981–982

teological – *see* **teological
    interpretation**

treaties, use of	682–691
two-stage approach to	591–592
uniform terminology for	589–590
viscera, use of	470

    – *and see* **amendment to Bill;
    Bill, parliamentary;
    canons of construction,
    linguistic; Book, this;
    Code, the;
    counter-intuitive readings;
    definitions, statutory;
    'golden rule';
    hairsplitting;
    Interpretation Act 1978;
    interpreter of enactment;
    Law Commission;
    legislative history; literal
    construction; 'literal rule';
    'mischief rule'; opposing
    constructions; prerogative
    instrument; presumptions
    of construction; principles
    of construction; purposive
    construction; rules of
    construction; strained
    construction; uniform**

statutory interpretation – *contd*
  viscera, use of – *contd*

    – *and see* **amendment to Bill; Bill,
    parliamentary; canons of
    construction, linguistic; Book,
    this; Code, the; counter-intuitive
    readings; definitions, statutory;
    'golden rule'; hairsplitting;
    Interpretation Act 1978;
    interpreter of enactment; Law
    Commission; legislative history;
    literal construction; 'literal rule';
    'mischief rule'; opposing
    constructions; prerogative
    instrument; presumptions of
    construction; principles of
    construction; purposive
    construction; rules of
    construction; strained
    construction; uniform** – *contd*
    **statutes; Vienna
    Convention on Law of
    Treaties**

statutory mischief – *see* **mischief**

statutory misdemeanour – *see*
  contempt of statute

statutory power

administration of	91

ancillary powers – *see* ***Attorney
    General v Great Eastern
    Railway*, rule in; implication;
    local authority**

anticipatory exercise of	1389
concurrent	499
conditional	257, 868

    – *and see* **description, statutory**

consult, duty to – *see*
    **decision-making rules;
    delegated legislation**

continuity of	1388–1389

duplication – *see* **duplication of
    statutory powers, remedies
    etc**

duty to exercise	51, 253
exercise of, from time to time	581–582
implied narrowing of	152, 492–493, 498–499
invalid exercise of	165–166

nuisance and – *see* **nuisance**

practice and	34

quo warranto – *see* **judicial review**

reversal of exercise of	90
search, to	496
tort law, application of, to	1073

    – *and see* **discretion;
    implication; local
    authority; mandatory and
    directory requirements;
    statutory right; *ultra vires*,**

All references are to page numbers

statutory power – *contd*
  tort law, application of, to – *contd*
    – *and see* discretion; implication; local
      authority; mandatory and
      directory requirements; statutory
      right; *ultra vires,* – *contd*
      doctrine of; *vigilantibus*
      non dormientibus leges
      subveniunt
statutory procedure – *see* procedure,
  statutory
Statutory Publications Office (SPO)   231
statutory right
  conditional   53–54
    – *and see* description, statutory
  contracting out of   60–62
  death, survival on   847–848
  debt   72
  duplication – *see* duplication of
    statutory powers, remedies
    etc
  limitation period – *see* limitation of
    actions
  other rights, effect on   52
  specialty, as – *see* specialty
  waiver of, when not permitted   60–62,
        1096–1097
  waiver of, when permitted   57–60, 1096–
        1097
  – *and see* illegality; statutory
    power
statutory rules and orders   266
Staughton LJ   70, 318, 436, 820, 827, 853,
    992n, 1141, 1191,
    1248n
Stein, Alex – *see* Bibliography (pp
  1475 to 1507)
Stephen, J F – *see* Bibliography (pp
  1475 to 1507)
Stephenson LJ   507, 816, 954
Sterndale, Lord   722
Stewart, Gordon   747n
  – *and see* Bibliography (pp 1475
  to 1507)
Steyn, Lord   128, 153, 176, 538, 547, 551,
    583, 601, 622, 632,
    633, 637, 638, 642,
    682n, 782, 803, 868,
    943, 945, 967, 970,
    1010, 1013n, 1055,
    1323, 1324, 1331,
    1340, 1361, 1455,
    1456, S5, S9, S36
Stockdale, John Joseph   205
Stocker J   1077
Stone, R T H – *see* Bibliography (pp
  1475 to 1507)
Stone, Samuel – *see* Bibliography
  (pp 1475 to 1507)

Strachey J   694
strained construction
  absurdity and   970, 972–973
  ambiguity and   872
  – *and see* ambiguity
    (grammatical)
  compatible construction rule – *see*
    Human Rights Act 1998
  consequential construction   872
  contradiction, principle of – *see*
    logic, use of in interpretation
  declaration of incompatibility – *see*
    Human Rights Act 1998
  deeming provision and   951–955
  dicta opposing   457–459
  examples of   148, 367, 459–461, 493,
    515–516, 798, 882,
    883–885, 938, 956,
    958, 974–975, 983,
    989–990, 1021, 1131,
    1218, 1329
  inconvenience, avoidance of, and   979
  judicial acceptance of 169, 872, 966, 972–
    975, 1029
  judicial reluctance to admit using 457–458
  nature of   169, 456–458, 490, 515–516,
    1324
  public interest and   791
  reasons justifying 212, 458–463, 480, 482,
    490, 523, 529, 533–
    537, 700, 791, 972–
    973, 1020, 1116, 1177,
    1179, 1218, 1299–
    1300
  universal repealer, the   459–460
  when inapt   319
  – *and see* absurdity;
    consequential
    construction; drafting
    error; equitable
    construction; purposive
    construction; repugnancy
Street, A G – *see* Bibliography (pp
  1475 to 1507)
strict and liberal construction
  consequences, regard to   516–519, 874–
    875
  counter-mischief and   1007–1008
  duty to obey legislation   37–40
  factual error and liberal construction   883
  interpreter, and   34–36
  legal adviser and – *see* advocate
  liberal construction, nature of   516–519
  savings   726
  strict construction, nature of   516, 848–
    849, 1007–1008
  terminology of   519
  updating, where need for – *see*
    updating construction

All references are to page numbers

strict and liberal construction – *contd*
  wide and narrow meaning   431, 516–519
  – *and see* **doubtful penalisation,**
     principle against;
     ignorantia juris neminem
     excusat; **informed**
     interpretation; legislation,
     – *and see* **doubtful**
     penalisation, principle
     against; equitable
     construction; precision
     drafting
strict liability   43, 79, 176, 899, 900, 1026,
             1079, 1104, 1146,
                     1148
  – *and see mala prohibita*; **vicarious**
     liability
Stuart-Smith LJ   72, 587, 615, 619, 620,
                    1201, 1261
sub-delegation – *see* **delegated**
  legislation
subject, the
  duty to obey legislation   36–40
  interpreter   34–44
  legal adviser and – *see* **advocate**
  – *and see* **doubtful penalisation,**
     principle against;
     ignorantia juris neminem
     excusat; **informed**
     interpretation; legislation
subjective test
  differential readings   130–133, 952
  judgment and   127, 133
  justice, and   123
  legislative intent   968
  movement towards   538
  – *and see* **objective test**
subordinate legislation – *see*
  delegated legislation;
  Interpretation Act 1978;
  prerogative, Royal
sub-rules   167, 171–172, 177–178, 417, 418,
              437, 438, 479, 502,
              503, 606, 608, 629,
                    710, 792
  – *and see* **interstitial articulation;**
     processing of enactments,
     dynamic; statutory
     interpretation
subsection   720
subsidiarity   1273, 1282, 1471, 1472
suffragan bishop, appointment of   314
sui generis, **persons who are not** –
  see **incompetents**
suicide   297, 501, 775, 1036, 1089
Sullivan, A M   427n
  – *and see* **Bibliography (pp 1475**
     to 1507)

Sullivan, Ruth   714n
  – *and see* **Bibliography (pp 1475**
     to 1507)
Summers, Robert S   7
  – *and see* **Bibliography (pp 1475**
     to 1507)
summons – *see* **process**
Sumner, Lord   313, 776, 780, 996
Supreme Court   139, 739
  – *and see* **court**
Supreme Court of the United
  Kingdom   152–153, 739
surplusage 305, 315, 461, 539, 1041, 1157–
                   1160, 1233
  – *and see* **construction as a whole;**
     tautology
suspending power – *see* **Crown**
Sutherland, J A   482n
  – *and see* **Bibliography (pp 1475**
     to 1507)
Swinfen-Eady LJ   537
Sykes, C S – *see* **Bibliography (pp**
  1475 to 1507)
Taafe defence   42
tacit legislation   171, 711, 894–895, 996
  limits of   711
  – *and see* **comity; intention,**
     legislative
tacking   224
tailpiece   27
Tapper, C F H – *see* **Bibliography**
  (pp 1475 to 1507)
tautology   146, 147, 1157–1160
  – *and see* **overlapping meaning;**
     surplusage
tax avoidance
  advance clearance and   1022
  anti-avoidance enactments   819, 850–851,
               931, 1017–1023
  Franco scheme   432n, 705
  general   1017–1023
  Inland Revenue rulings on   705
  Ramsay principle – *see Ramsay*
     principle
  tax mitigation and, contrasted   1017–1018,
                  1021–1022
  Westminster principle – *see*
     Westminster **principle**
  – *and see* **evasion of Act; taxing**
     Acts
tax law rewrite Acts   191
taxing Acts
  Crown and   300
  definitions and   567
  double taxation   850
  drafting of   898, 964, 1166, 1199
  enforcement of   97, 99
  extra-territoriality and   363–364, 381
  implication in   298–299, 814, 974–975

All references are to page numbers

---

taxing Acts – *contd*
interpretation of 332, 705–706, 829–830, 937, 965–966, 974–975, 1261
nature of 190–191, 850–851
provisional collection of taxes 190–191, 251
retrospectivity and 323
'Tax Acts, The', definition of 1399
tax law rewrite Act – *see* **tax law rewrite Act**
taxpayers, inconvenience to, and 981–982
uniformity of application of 332
– *and see* **Act of Parliament; Bill, parliamentary; domestic sanctuary, principle of; doubtful penalisation, principle against; enacting formula; evasion of Act; extra-statutory concession; extra-territoriality; illegality; money; Parliament; privileges and immunities; retrospectivity; tax avoidance; uniform statutes**

Taylor of Gosforth, Lord 244, 320, 928

technical contravention S6

technical terms
Act's extent, and 331–332
context in which used 1204, 1205, 1206, 1209
conveyancing 190
different technical meanings 1197–1199
evidence of meaning 1223–1224
examples of meaning 739–741
free-standing 1039
interpretation of 331–332, 11971209
legal terms – *see* **legal terms**
multiple meanings of term 1198–1199
non-legal terms 1203–1206
ordinary and technical meaning 1206–1209
ordinary language, use of 1203–1204
term with both ordinary and technical meaning 1206–1209
– *and see* **box principle; foreign; technicalities**

technicalities 35, 51, 56, 332, 400, 416, 839, 920, 921, 938, 980
– *and see* **irregularity, procedural; pleading; technical terms**

technology, developments in – *see* **updating construction**

teleological interpretation 546, 1284
– *and see* **European Community Law; purposive construction; statutory interpretation**
Templeman, Lord 206, 476, 478, 508, 643, 665, 703, 832, 839, 967, 975, 990, 1020, 1024, 1166, 1188, 1190, 1298n
temporal operation of Act – *see* **time**
temporary Act 183, 186, 311–312, 312, 926, 1412
tenancy in common 1040
tense 892, 1190–1191, 1464
– *and see* **time**
Tenterden, Lord 653, 879, 1182
Terence 802, 965
terminology, legal 61
terms, meaning of (list) 1420
territorial extent of Act
application of Act, contrasted 328
– *and see* **application of Act**
basic rule 327–329
change of territory 329
composition of Act's territory 334–335
extent to Her Majesty's dominions 329–330, 338–340
– *and see* **Australia; Canada; Her Majesty's dominions; Her Majesty's independent dominions; Man, Isle of, new Zealand**
'extent', meaning of, in 329–330
implied 328
implied ancillary rules and 1037
legal policy and 1038
non-residents – *see* **application of Act**
principles governing 194–196, 327–340, 1098–1099
Scotland 363
uniform meaning throughout extent 330–334
– *and see* **uniform statutes**
United Kingdom, presumption extent limited to 328, 335–338
– *and see* **extra-territoriality**
territorial waters
Home Secretary's certificate 358
meaning of 334, 356–358
– *and see* **baseline; high seas; Northern Ireland**
territory, surrender of 238n, 406
terrorism – *see* **criminal law**
text writers, opinions of – *see* **jurists**
text, legislative 5
textual amendment – *see* **amendment to Act**
textual memorandum xi, 643

All references are to page numbers

Thankerton, Lord   105, 785, 786, 850, 1061

Thompson J   693n

Thomson LJ-C   495

Thornton, G C   242n, 314n
– *and see* **Bibliography (pp 1475
    to 1507)**

Thorpe CJ   229

Thorpe LJ   999

three-fold consent, doctrine of – *see*
    Act of Parliament

Thring, Lord   7, 410, 411, 412, 415, 718,
                     732, 734, 747, 749,
                     891, 892, 1249
– *and see* Bibliography (pp 1475 to
    1507)

time
anomalies as to   989
commonsense construction rule and   868–
                                                  869
corresponding date rule   1040
Crown, does not run against   1083
day   196, 273, 278–279, 1119–1121
de minimis principle – *see* **de
    minimis non curat lex**
exclusive day rule   1119–1121
expressions of   868–869
Greenwich Mean Time   581
inclusive day rule   1119–1121
limits   113, 202, 1198–1199
    – *and see* **prosecution of
        offences**
'month', definition of   581
period   431, 1119–1121
summer time   581
temporal operation of Act   196
tense   581, 1190–1191
zones   196
    – *and see* **Act of Parliament;
        age;** *audi alteram partem*
        **principle; commencement
        of Act; Crown; death;
        delegated legislation;
        evasion of Act;
        Interpretation Act 1978;
        judicial review; limitation
        of actions; notice;
        procedure, criminal;
        retrospectivity;
        transitional provisions**

tip-off   425–426

title – *see* **collective title; long title;
    short title**

Tomlins, T E – *see* **Bibliography (pp
    1475 to 1507)**

Toohey J   651, 676

tort
common employment, doctrine of   198

tort – *contd*
contravention of enactment as – *see*
    **breach of statutory duty, tort
    of**
Crown and   387
damages for   176, 1256
detinue, abolition of   198
implied application of law of   1073–1077
statutory   67–85
statutory authorisation of
    commission of   68, 75, 84, 1074–
                                               1075
statutory modification of law of   169, 198,
                                                 889

    – *and see* **confidentiality;
        extra-territoriality;
        interest;
        misrepresentation;
        negligence;** *nuisance; res
        ipsa loquitur; restitutio in
        integrum;* **strict liability;
        territorial waters;
        trespass; vicarious lability;**
        volenti non fit injuria

Tosswill, T M S – *see* **Bibliography
    (pp 1475 to 1507)**

Toulson J   244, 315

trade – *see* **business; restraint of
    trade**

transitional provisions   15, 194, 256, 277,
                             288, 289, 291, 312,
                             314–315, 315, 323,
                             325, 326, 717, 886,
                       934, 940, 1070, 1112,
                             1320, 1336, 1403,
                             1431, 1438, 1441,
                             1448, 1473 –
    and see **retrospectivity**

transparency, open court principle   S11

**transposition of European
    Community law**
copyout technique and   1291
failure of   1292
methods of   1290–1293
residual national law and   1292
UK transposing enactment,
    interpretation of   1291–1292

transsexuality   909n, 1142n, 1327

travaux préparatoires – *see* **legislative
    history; treaty**

'Treasury, The', definition of   1399

treaty
citation of   824
direct enactment of   683
drafting of   684
enactment, giving effect to   518–519
foreign language text of,
    interpretation of enactments
    and   686

All references are to page numbers

treaty – *contd*
implementation of 190, 518–519, 682–691, 818–819, 961
interpretation of 518–519, 682–691
interpretation of enactment, use in 107, 682–691
judicial notice of – *see* **judicial notice**
non-justiciable in municipal court or tribunal 107, 364
reference to 518–519, 961
scheduled to Act 684–685
status of 682–691, 818–819
travaux préparatoires 686–687
uniform statutes – *see* **uniform statutes**
– *and see* **European Court of Justice; European Convention on Human Rights; exterritoriality; extraterritoriality; foreign; legislative history; privileges and immunities; public international law; purposive construction; *ultra vires*, doctrine of; Vienna Convention on Law of Treaties**

trespass
carelessness and 83–84
hunting and 426
implied application of law of 1075
nature of 1126–1127
theft and 484
'tolerated trespass' 1075n

tribunal
appeal from 147
employment 118, 788
expert 117
general 141–142
jurisdiction of 104
reasons, duty to give 1062–1063
– *and see* **appeal; court; decision-making rules; Employment Appeal Tribunal; enforcement agencies; land; non-justitiable matters**

trivia, treatment by law of – *see de minimis non curat lex*

Trollope, Anthony 123
– *and see* **Bibliography (pp 1475 to 1507)**

'trustee of land', definition of 1399
'trust of land', definition of 1399
truth impliedly required 38
Tuckey LJ 555
Tudor Evans J 775, 1230

Turnbull, John H – *see* **Bibliography (pp 1475 to 1507)**
Turner LJ 471, 614n, 1223
Twining, W 549
– *and see* **Bibliography (pp 1475 to 1507)**
typographical error – *see* **rectifying construction**
ubi jus ibi remedium 68
ultra vires, **doctrine of**
'as if enacted in this Act' 257
byelaws, and 260–262
confirmation and 257
delegated legislation, and 254–262, 832
disapply, attempts to 258
examples of *ultra vires* provisions 259–260
nature of 254–262, 1051
orders 91
retrospectivity 324
severance – *see* **severance**
taxation, and 259
validity, presumption of 257–258
– *and see* **ambiguity; decision-making rules; implication; jurisdiction**

unborn – *see* **foetus**
undertaking – *see* **court**
Unger, R M 124
– *and see* **Bibliography (pp 1475 to 1507)**
Ungoed-Thomas J 233
uniform construction 690–691
uniform statutes 333, 824
unincorporated association 576
criminal liability 576
United Kingdom
meaning of 358, 1399
nationals of, defined 380
nature of 6
United Nations Commission on International Trade Law (UNCITRAL) 187
United States
constitution of 316
legislation and common law, relationship of, in 815
legislative history, experience of use of, in 626, 651, 678n
Universal Declaration of Human Rights 852
universal repealer, the – *see* **strained construction**
university disputes 110
unjust enrichment, doctrine of 1072
unlawful act not impliedly authorised by statute 1126–1127
– *and see* **negligence; nuisance**
unnecessary enactment 1003

All references are to page numbers

---

updating construction

definition of 890
employment, as to 900
European Community law 1299
expressio unius principle and 1259
impossibility, supervening 1130
judicial approach, changes in 899–900
law, changes in 897, 1041
limit of 890, 914
medical science, advances in 907
mischief, on change of 895–897, 901–904
Parliament's approach, changes in 900
presumption favouring 889–914
punctuation and 757
responses to Code s 288 1457–1460
social conditions, on change of 897, 901–904, 906
technology, on development in 905–906
words, change of meaning of, and 907–909

– *and see* **legislative history**

Upjohn, Lord 660, 693n, 716
user of legislation 403, 804–806
– *and see* **legislation; subject, the**
Uthwatt, Lord 937
vacant provision 606, 1039
Valéry, Paul 1458n
– *and see* **Bibliography (pp 1475 to 1507)**
validation Act – *see* **Act of Parliament**
van Ert, Gib – *see* **Bibliography (pp 1475 to 1507)**
Van Gerven Adv-Gen 1274n, 1278, 1284n
Vancise, J A 518
Vaughan-Williams J 464
Veale J 1008
vehicle registration mark 1035
vicarious liability 67, 72, 73, 1041, 1074, 1077, 1146–1147
– *and see* **agency; employment**
Vienna Convention on Consular Relations 369
Vienna Convention on Diplomatic Relations 1253
Vienna Convention on Law of Treaties
codifying customary international law 688–690
entry into force of 688
rules of interpretation laid down by 618, 688–690
– *and see* **treaty**
vigilantibus non dormientibus leges subveniunt 1149
Vinelott J 35, 138, 630, 748
Vinogradoff, Paul – *see* **Bibliography (pp 1475 to 1507)**
visitor (academic) 110

Vogenauer, Stefan 8, 546, 633n
– *and see* **Bibliography (pp 1475 to 1507)**
volenti non fit injuria 1101, 1150, 1151, S61
voting rights – *see* **elections**
Wade, H W R – *see* **Bibliography (pp 1475 to 1507)**
Waite LJ 832
waiver – *see* **notice; privileges and immunities; statutory right**
Wales 6n, 25, 346, 347, 359, 725, 731, 735, 744, 1246, 1392, 1399
Walker of Gestingthorpe, Lord 135, 509, 548, 1156, S4, S14, S23
Walker, D M – *see* **Bibliography (pp 1475 to 1507)**
Wall LJ 704, 774, 1062, 1183
Waller LJ 314, 721, 797, 1188, 1367
Walpole, Horace 214
Walton J 56, 1227
war – *see* **act of state**
Warbrick, C – *see* **Bibliography (pp 1475 to 1507)**
Ward LJ 128, 142, 681n, 1102
Ward, Chris – *see* **Bibliography (pp 1475 to 1507)**
wardship 203n, 436, 811, 814, 845, 917, 984, 1044–1046, 1255
– *and see* **Crown**
Warner J 495, 525, 1209
warrant 45, 141, 152, 165, 193, 199, 218, 238n, 271, 333, 460, 497, 534, 535, 783, 811, 838, 846, 876, 934, 1045, 1075, 1082, 1144, 1264, 1286, 1441
– *and see* **Crown; magistrates**
Warrington of Clyffe, Lord 864
Warsaw Convention 1929 32
Waterhouse J 297
waters – *see* **high seas; internal waters; territorial waters**
Watkins LJ 131, 160, 482, 615, 759, 836, 964, 1002
Watson, Lord 75, 494, 605n, 913
Webster J 833, 834, 1076
Wedderburn, Lord 664
Wednesbury principle – *see* **decision-making rules**
weightless drafting 1196–1197
– *and see* **drafting technique**
Wensleydale, Lord (Parke B) 514, 653, 870
West, W A – *see* **Bibliography (pp 1475 to 1507)**
Westbury, Lord 654

All references are to page numbers

Westminster principle   538, 1018
  – and see **tax avoidance**
Whately, R   124
  – and see **Bibliography (pp 1475**
   to 1507)
Wheare, K C *– see* **Bibliography (pp**
   1475 to 1507)
white paper *– see* **legislative history**
Widgery, Lord   553, 558, 645, 661, 685,
     813, 993, 1002, 1003,
     1012, 1141, 1235
Wilberforce, Lord   31, 47, 101, 110, 137,
     190n, 305, 366, 387,
     388, 431, 513, 526,
     587, 605, 613, 637,
     645, 685, 686, 687,
     690, 699, 721, 797,
     849, 850, 897, 902,
     932, 944, 964, 966,
    992, 1019, 1051, 1066,
     1076, 1077, 1092,
     1194, 1207, 1208,
     1222, **1265, 1341**
Wilde J   404
Willes J   233, 408, 493, 494, 646, 653, 654,
     658, 727, 749, 751,
     859
Williams, Glanville   43, 517, 525, 805, 830,
     888n, 938n, 1229
  – and see **Bibliography (pp 1475**
   to 1507)
Williams, Jane M *– see* **Bibliography**
  (pp 1475 to 1507)
Williams, L Norman *– see*
  Bibliography (pp 1475 to 1507)
Willis J   866n
Willis, J W   545
  – and see **Bibliography (pp 1475**
   to 1507)
Wills J   1251
Wilson J   676
Wilson, Alida *– see* **Bibliography (pp**
   1475 to 1507)
Winckel, Anne *– see* **Bibliography**
  (pp 1475 to 1507)
Winn J   1243
Winterton, J *– see* **Bibliography (pp**
   1475 to 1507)
Wisdom, A J T D *– see* **Bibliography**
  (pp 1475 to 1507)
without prejudice rule *– see* **evidence**
women *– see* **discrimination,**
  legislation against; ordination
  of women
Wood J   307, 935
Woolf, Lord   26, 44, 45, 96, 97, 105n, 137,
     155, 156, 157, 163n,
     173, 174n, 261n, 429,
     526, 571, 595, 855,

Woolf, Lord *– contd*
     891, 984, 1051, 1055,
     1087, 1091, 1095,
     1103, 1134, 1135,
     1139, 1151, 1214,
     1312, 1313, 1314,
     1328, 1331, 1334,
     1342, 1346, 1365,
     1366, 1378
  – and see **Bibliography (pp 1475**
   to 1507)
words
  'box principle' and   907–909
  commonly confused   1189
  different words given different
    meanings   1160–1163
  different words given same meaning   411,
     1161
  'elephant words'   1183
  every word to be given meaning   1157–
     1160
  foreign context, application in   1215–1216,
     1229–1230
  meaning, change in   907–909
  modifiers   1194
  nature of   445
  neutral, determining meaning of   1227–
     1228
  no meaning, with   1158–1159
  numbers, drafted in   1216
  order of   1190
  ordinary meaning of *– see* **ordinary**
    meaning
  overlapping meaning of   1160
  pairs of   1195–1197
  purpose of   11
  same words given different
    meanings   1212, 1217
  same words given same meaning   1160,
     1217
  surplus *– see* **surplusage**
  tautologous *– see* **tautology**
  wrong place in Act   881n
  – and see **archaisms; broad terms;**
    chameleon word; construction
    as a whole; doubt as to legal
    meaning; evidence;
    grammatical meaning;
    homonyms; legal meaning;
    meaningless terms; neologisms;
    ordinary meaning; pairs of
    words; singular and plural;
    slang; strained construction;
    technical terms; updating
    construction
Wrenbury, Lord   659
Wright, Lord   32, 659, 696n, 698, 786, 816,
     1235
writing   59, 137, 905, 1399

All references are to page numbers

All references are to page numbers